Institutions and Accounting Practices After the Financial Crisis

Financial globalization, paired with the relaxation of constraints on capital flows between countries before the 2008 crisis, increased merger activities among the world's largest stock exchanges. The financial crisis of 2008 had a severe impact on the development of equity markets, corporate financial stability, and corporate governance, and a multi-step approach is needed to fully appreciate the causes and effects of this event. This book engages the separate strands of literature to advance a more holistic understanding of whether and how the national institutional environments in selected countries around the world has been changed after the crisis.

Institutions and Accounting Practices After the Financial Crisis: International Perspective sets out a framework for the analysis of institutional environments and accounting practices in selected countries around the world during the pre-crisis period, followed by an examination of the impact of the crisis. It scrutinizes the changing roles of debt and equity markets; the shift in accounting practices and capital financing choices due to the economic downturn; and the lessons that can be obtained from the financial crisis, while considering the institutional architecture of international business environments. This ongoing process of integration and globalization increases interdependence between world markets, and allows shocks to propagate across national and continental lines, making the understanding of international markets vitally important to American investors.

Aimed at primarily researchers, academics, and students in the fields of international accounting, management, and finance, *Institutions and Accounting Practices After the Financial Crisis: International Perspective* will additionally be of value to practitioners and policy makers, supplying them with information regarding the changes in accounting practices and risk evaluation due to the crisis.

Victoria Krivogorsky is Professor in the Charles W. Lamden School of Accountancy at San Diego State University, USA.

Routledge Studies in Accounting

The Social Function of Accounts
Reforming Accountancy to Serve Mankind
John Flower

The Role of the Management Accountant
Local Variations and Global Influences
Lukas Goretzki and Erik Strauss

Interventionist Management Accounting Research
Theory Contributions with Societal Impact
Jouni Lyly-Yrjänäinen, Petri Suomala, Teemu Laine, and Falconer Mitchell

Accounting, Innovation and Inter-Organisational Relationships
Martin Carlsson-Wall, Håkan Håkansson, Kalle Kraus, Johnny Lind, and Torkel Strömsten

A History of Corporate Financial Reporting
John Richard Edwards

Public Sector Accounting, Governance and Accountability
Experiences from Australia and New Zealand
Edited by Robyn Pilcher and David Gilchrist

Managerial Accountant's Compass
Research Genesis and Development
Gary R. Oliver

Institutions and Accounting Practices After the Financial Crisis
International Perspective
Edited by Victoria Krivogorsky

For a full list of titles in this series, please visit www.routledge.com/Routledge-Studies-in-Accounting/book-series/SE0715

Institutions and Accounting Practices After the Financial Crisis

International Perspective

Edited by Victoria Krivogorsky

NEW YORK AND LONDON

First published 2019
by Routledge
52 Vanderbilt Avenue, New York, NY 10017

and by Routledge
2 Park Square, Milton Park, Abingdon, Oxon, OX14 4RN

Routledge is an imprint of the Taylor & Francis Group, an informa business

Library of Congress Cataloging-in-Publication Data
Names: Krivogorsky, Victoria, editor.
Title: Institutions and accounting practices after the financial crisis : international perspective / edited by Victoria Krivogorsky.
Description: New York : Routledge, 2019. | Series: Routledge studies in accounting
Identifiers: LCCN 2018050204 | ISBN 9781138204805 (hardback) | ISBN 9781315468655 (ebook)
Subjects: LCSH: Corporations—Accounting. | Accounting—Standards. | Financial statements—Standards.
Classification: LCC HF5686.C7 I537 2019 | DDC 657—dc23
LC record available at https://lccn.loc.gov/2018050204

ISBN: 978-1-138-20480-5 (hbk)
ISBN: 978-1-315-46865-5 (ebk)

Typeset in Sabon
by Apex CoVantage, LLC

To the loving memory of my parents

Contents

Acknowledgments

I would like to thank the Center of International Business, Education and Research at San Diego State University and the Charles W. Lamden School of Accountancy for partial financial support.

My special thanks go to M. Shoaib Shirazi for his tireless work during the last stage of preparing this book for publishing.

Contributors

Henrik Andersson holds MScs in Engineering from Cranfield Institute of Technology (UK) and Linköping Institute of Technology (Sweden) and has worked at Ericsson and Aston Martin Lagonda. He received his PhD from the Stockholm School of Economics in 2003. His dissertation studied real option pricing and commodity price behavior. Henrik teaches corporate valuation and cost accounting and conducts research in the areas of investment analysis and financial risk management.

Samuel Da-Rocha-Lopes is Principal Bank Sector Analyst and representative of the European Banking Authority (EBA–European System of Financial Supervision) in several international fora (e.g. BIS, EC, ESRB, ECB/SSM). He is also Coordinator and Professor of the course "Banking Regulation and Supervision in Practice" at Nova School of Business and Economics (Nova SBE), Portugal, and Visiting Lecturer at Aarhus University, Denmark. He holds a PhD in Finance from ISCTE-IBS (IUL). He is a former economist from the European Central Bank (ECB) and from Banco de Portugal (Central Bank), working in Financial Stability and Supervision, Financial Research, and Risk Management areas, and has over 18 years of work experience in risk management, supervision, and financial stability.

José A. Gonzalo-Angulo is Full Professor of Financial Economics and Accounting at the University of Alcalá (Spain), where he is currently Head of the Department of Economics and Management. Previously, he was Vice President for Economic Affairs and Corporate Relations of the university. In the 2003–2004 term he was President of the European Accounting Association (EAA). During the period 2009–2012, he chaired the Spanish Accounting and Auditing Institute (ICAC) which forms part of the Ministry of Economics and plays the role of accounting standards setter for non-financial companies. He served as an academic member of the Banking Stakeholders Group of the European Banking Authority (EBA) during the years 2014–2016. José earned his PhD from the Autonomous University of Madrid in 1979. His research interests are in the fields of international accounting, auditing, and teaching. Among his books are *Introducción a la Contabilidad Internacional* (Ministerio de Hacienda, 1988, with Jorge Tua); *European Financial Reporting: Spain* (Routledge, 1992, with J.L. Gallizo); *Accounting in Spain* (AECA, 1992, coordinator); *The Convergence Journey: Comparison and Critical Analysis or the Financial Accounting Standards Codification (US GAAP) and International Financial Reporting Standards (IFRS)* (Garceta, 2015, co-director with K. Tenant); and *Contabilidad Internacional. El IASB y la Unión Europea* (Lefebvre, 2016, with A. Garvey).

Niclas Hellman holds a PhD from the Stockholm School of Economics, Sweden (2000). He teaches financial accounting and financial statement analysis and has ongoing research projects investigating financial analysts' evaluations of corporate acquisitions under IFRS accounting and improvements in the efficiency of goodwill impairment tests. Niclas is also a member of the European Financial Reporting Advisory Group (EFRAG) Academic Panel, and he was previously Vice Chairman of the Swedish Accounting Standards Board from 2011 to 2016.

Victoria Krivogorsky is Professor in the Charles W. Lamden School of Accountancy at San Diego State University, USA. She graduated with her PhD in Economics from the Institute of Economics of Academy of Sciences of USSR. Her publications in Russian include one monograph and eight articles. She also received a PhD in Accounting from the University of Wisconsin-Madison. During her affiliation with American academia, she has published more than 30 scholarly articles and has presented her ideas to over 50 national and international conferences. Her research interests include issues of corporate capital structure, decision-making in highly uncertain environments, corporate governance and control, and the effects of governance mechanisms and information environments on accounting. During her career she held visiting teaching and academic positions at numerous renowned universities around the world, including Institute of Economics of the Academy of Sciences, USSR, EASCP-ECP, European School of Management, Paris, France, ESSEC, School of Management, Paris, France, Beijing Polytechnic University, China, Ca'Foscari University, Venice, Italy, and University of California, San Diego, among others. She is teaching Financial Accounting and International Financial Reporting on the graduate and undergraduate levels.

Marcelo Botelho C. Moraes is Assistant Professor of Financial Accounting at the School of Economics, Business Administration and Accounting at Ribeirão Preto at the University of São Paulo (USP), Brazil, and visiting scholar at Sloan School of Management at MIT, USA. He has a PhD in Economics, Organizations and Knowledge Management (2011), MSc in Production Engineering (2007), and BS in Accounting (2003) from the University of São Paulo. His current research focuses on financial accounting, cash holdings, cash flows, and earnings quality.

Paul Munter is Professor of Accounting Practice at the University of Colorado, Boulder, USA. He has published in a variety of academic and professional journals including *Accounting Review*, *Behavioral Research in Accounting*, *Issues in Accounting Education*, *Advances in Accounting*, *Accounting Historians Journal*, *Abacus*, *Journal of Accountancy*, *Managerial Finance*, *International Journal of Management*, *Review of Financial Studies*, *Review of Accounting Studies*, *Journal of Accounting Public Policy*, *European Accounting Review*, *Journal of Banking Regulation*, and *The International Journal of Accounting*, among others, on various aspects of finance, banking, and credit risk management. He has published chapters in *Money, Regulation and Growth: Financing New Growth in Europe* (SUERF, 2014) and in Risk Books publications such as *Europe's New Supervisory Toolkit: Data, Benchmarking and Stress Testing for Banks and Their Regulators* (2015). He has experience teaching in executive education programs through World Bank projects and is a reviewer of several academic journals. He has been a recipient of research and scholarship grants, collaborates as research coordinator with San Diego State University in a network in International Business, Economics and Accounting (iBEACON), and is a researcher of both the UNIDE/ISCTE and CIRSF (Research Centre on Regulation and Supervision of the Financial Sector).

José Luis Ucieda is Associate Professor in Accounting and Finance at the Universidad Autónoma de Madrid, Spain. He has served as Head of the Accounting Department (2009–2012), Vice Dean for International Relationships (2007–2008), Director of International Programs (2008–2010), and Delegate of the Rector for International Programs (2010–2014). He has been a member of working groups at EFRAG (Performance Reporting) and AECA (Environmental Reporting). His research visits include University of Bangor (1995 and 2001), Universidad de Valencia (2001), University of California, Irvine (1996–1997), San Diego State University (2006, 2007, 2014), and he collaborated with the Bank of Spain for several projects in banking regulation (2004–2015). His research is focused on international accounting, carbon accounting, and education. Jose has published research in national and international journals and chapters in books on accounting regulation, and he is Associate Editor of *Spanish Accounting Review* (since 2016), currently in Web of Science.

Part 1

1 The Causes of the 2008 Financial Crisis

The Prospects of IFRS Adoption in the US

Victoria Krivogorsky

Introduction

What was a primary cause(s) of the latest financial crisis? According to Steve Forbes, chairman of Forbes Media, mark-to-market accounting was "the principal reason" that the US financial system seized up in 2008. In particular, he said that "the crisis never would have become so unprecedentedly destructive but for a seemingly arcane accounting principle called mark-to-market, or fair value, accounting."[1] Mr. Forbes' critical assessment of the mark-to-market approach included but was not limited to the following:

- Writing down investments reduces a bank's "regulatory capital," which in turn causes the reduction of lending.
- Reduced lending by banks triggers a chain of events: lack of investment precipitates higher unemployment, which in turn brings about higher loan default rates, which causes the fair value of bank investments to decline even further.
- The accounting rules on fair value aggravate the condition by employing an illiquidity discount to "subprime securities and other suspect assets" even if there has been no direct substantiation of impairment.

His qualified opinion has been supported and repeated numerous times by his colleagues, the *Wall Street Journal*, and members of the US Congress alike. For example, the chief economist at First Trust Advisors, Brian Wesbury, along with Steve Forbes, argues that marking to market impelled many banks toward insolvency and drove them to unload assets at fire-sale prices, which then caused values to fall even further.[2] In his piece "Why Mark-To-Market Accounting Rules Must Die," co-authored with Robert Stain, he advocates for an immediate suspension of FASB 157.[3] Particularly, it was argued that because markets are forward-looking, the existing accounting rules force banks to write off losses before they even happen. In other words, the market overstates current and future losses. The accounting rules force banks to take artificial hits to capital without reference to the actual performance of loans. In this regard, fair value accounting, they believe, undermines the banking system by wiping out capital from the books that in turn starts a chain of negative events. Specifically, it increases the odds of asset fire sales that make markets even less liquid; bad loans multiply, the investment banks fail, and the government proposes bailouts. The latter drives prices down even further, fueling violent downward economic spiral.[4] As a result, the "mark-to-market accounting rules have turned a large problem into a humongous one. A vast majority of mortgages, corporate bonds, and structured debts are still performing. But because the market is frozen, the prices of these assets have fallen below their true value."[5] Persuaded by such arguments, some politicians in the US and Europe have called for the suspension of fair value accounting in favor of historical cost accounting, according to which assets are generally valued at original cost or purchase price.[6] Mark-to-market accounting continues to have its supporters, who are equally unwavering. Among others, there has been an opinion suggesting that accounting simply delivers the news to the market. Professor Lisa Koonce from the University of Texas wrote in *Texas* magazine:

> This is simply a case of blaming the messenger. Fair value accounting is not the cause of the current crisis. Rather, it communicated the effects of such bad decisions as granting subprime loans and writing credit default swaps. The alternative, keeping those loans on the books at their original amounts, is akin to ignoring reality.

Following the same line of logic, the Financial Accounting Standards Board (FASB) investment advisory committee asserted that fair value approach is all the more necessary in today's environment, and that "it is especially critical that fair value information be available to capital providers and other users of financial statements in periods of market turmoil accompanied by liquidity crunches." In this view, if banks did not mark their bonds to market, investors would be very uncertain about asset values and therefore reluctant to help recapitalize troubled institutions.[7]

Another accounting regulation blamed for the financial crisis is the accounting for derivatives. It was publicly stated in literature and press that derivative financial instruments had rendered the current approach to banking regulation obsolete.[8] For example, let's assume that a financial institution holds only one "investment." It is an interest rate swap, with a notional amount of $50 billion. The historical cost of entering into the swap was zero, and its current fair value is $1 billion. Also, assume that the bank has liabilities of $0.5 billion. With a debt/asset ratio of 50%, this bank can be technically considered as well capitalized? However, in a case when interest rates move insignificantly in the wrong direction, a $1 billion asset could transform into a $10 billion liability. Moreover, *the probability of that occurring could be 50% or more.*

As the result, the reliability of the capitalization ratios based on US GAAP and their ability to measure banks financial strength had been questioned, especially after derivatives hit the bank balance sheets in a big way. The supporters of this point of view rejected the existing opinion that policies similar to those of Franklin D. Roosevelt from the time of the significant depression might save the day.[9] FDR had no derivatives problem, they argued, and therefore old logic and conceptual approaches won't work in the new economic environment.

Supporters of all points of view were united in believing that the US Congress should hold hearings related to financial reform. They were all in favor of coming to an understanding that if a regulatory modernization adequately addresses only a single risk, it is destined to fail. Every potential threat to the financial system must be an integral part of the comprehensive legislative response to the economic crisis. Even if financial reporting did play some role in fueling the crisis, changing accounting rules that cover an insignificant percentage of assets that banks mark to market is probably not going to make a big difference. It seems that along with looking into the notion of capital adequacy based on capitalization ratios, it is also essential to restructure banks' business models. For example, as a part of the restructuring project, it had been recommended that the most relevant information about bank financial strength should come from the stress testing of cash balances and future cash in- and outflows. For a bank with no derivatives on its balance sheet, a strong correlation between a static capitalization ratio (based on accounting rules) and the probability of future insolvency is obtainable and might be relevant; but for a bank holding loads of derivatives, that correlation might be spurious.[10]

Regardless of who or what to hold responsible, the periodical press had delivered the "consensus" verdict that the total devotion to the free market fostered the economic recession. Jacob Weisberg's *Slate* column "The End of Libertarianism" sums up this official verdict:

> We have narrowly avoided a global depression and are mercifully pointed toward merely the worst recession in a long while thanks to a global economic meltdown made possible by the libertarian idea. Any competent forensic work has to put the libertarian theory of self-regulating financial markets at the scene of the crime.[11]

Generally speaking, the press made Alan Greenspan, Phil Gramm (former chairman of the Senate Banking Committee), and SEC chairman Christopher Cox responsible for the crisis. Moreover, they proclaimed that the warnings about the growing market in credit derivatives were ignored for ideological reasons. To reinforce the idea that the free market is to blame for the crisis, interestingly enough, Alan Greenspan himself testified to Congress on October 23, 2008, that he had been "shocked" that self-interest (in the absence of paternalistic regulation) did not compel financial institutions to adopt adequate risk controls. Mr. Greenspan went so far as to say that he "found a flaw in the model that I perceived is the critical functioning structure that defines how the world works."[12]

Wherever the blame for the crisis might be, to restore the financial industry to a sound financial footing is vital, as the financial soundness of any economy depends on the strength of the whole banking system, which in turn depends on whether the failure of one financial institution can damage the entire industry. Thus, the government should limit the exposure of the whole banking industry to any single given financial institution. In this regard, in the past, the Japanese banking industry experience gave rise to the conventional wisdom that no bank would be able to compete with their international rivals unless they morphed into enormously big and powerful entities. It is evident that this strategy failed as bigger banks take too much risk. Also, US banks, like their Japanese counterparts, became *too big to fail*, which has now become synonymous for *too big to exist*. I don't vote for issuing a mandate to banks to break themselves up into smaller entities, but I think that creating the incentives that encourage them from becoming too big in the first place might be of consequence.

Overall, accounting rules are created to provide the interested parties with relevant and reliable to the decision-making information on the financial position of the entity. Accounting helps to identify the problematic business entities and helps users of the financial information recognize the areas of the most significant concern, assisting them in diagnosing the problem. Blaming accounting for economic failure is like blaming an X-ray for showing the tumor.

The Change in the IFRS After the Crisis

As a response to the widespread criticism of fair value accounting, in July 2009 the International Accounting Standards Board (IASB) proposed a new approach to the accounting for financial instruments by making changes to the financial instrument classification and their measurement. Since that point, IASB has been making amendments to the IAS 39 (Financial Instruments), and the change was finalized in the issuance of IFRS 9 that superseded all previous amendments to IAS 39. The IASB's main goal while working on IFRS 9 was to combine in one standard the classification, measurement, and impairment of the financial instruments, and hedge accounting to replace IAS 39.[13] Under the new approach, according to the IASB, the primary determinant of whether a financial instrument meets the test is the actual operation of a firm's business model, and not management's intention to trade or hold to maturity used in the past. In other words, the IASB's intent was to build IFRS 9 on one consistent classification and measurement methodology for financial assets that reflects the business model in which they are managed and their cash flow characteristics. IASB believes that this is a forward-looking expected credit loss model that applies to all financial instruments subject to impairment accounting and will result in the more timely recording of loan losses on the books. Also, IFRS 9 was designed to address the so-called own credit issue, which can be described as a chain of events triggered when financial institutions choose to measure their debt at fair value. In this case, when the value of their debt declines, they record their gains in the profit and loss account, impacting creditworthiness of financial institutions.

The IFRS 9 also includes an improved hedge accounting model to better link the economics of risk management with its accounting treatment. In particular, the initial measurement of the financial instruments under IFRS 9 is consistent with IAS 39. To simplify the subsequent accounting treatment for financial instruments, IASB eliminated available or held for sale securities (assets). This category of securities had a combined valuation approach, i.e., the change in the normal value of these securities was required to be recorded in either other comprehensive income or income statement, depending on whether the security itself was realized (sold) or not. Thus, with the elimination of the available or held for sale securities, all assets would be recorded at either fair (trading securities) value or historical cost (held-to-maturity securities). In other words, a financial instrument would be measured at its fair value unless it meets two criteria: (1) it has only "basic loan features" (contractual cash flows of principal and interest) and (2) it is "managed on a contractual yield basis" (an issuer's credit quality triggers a pre-specified loan rate reset).[14] Also, the IASB emphasized that "occasional sales of instruments with basic loan features would not trigger a wholesale switch to fair value accounting for all such instruments as long as these sales were consistent with a general 'originate and hold' business model."[15] This change triggered financial executives' concern that some assets will be reclassified under the new regulation and will be moved into the trading securities category, changing the fair market value of those assets, and hitting companies' income statements.

IFRS v. US GAAP: To Adopt or Not to Adopt? That Is the Question

Among professionals and academics alike the question about the future of accounting is worded straightforwardly: Should the US Stay US GAAP or Go IFRS or become financially bilingual? The July 2012 Final Staff Report, issued by the Office of the Chief Accountant at SEC, included an IFRS work plan. The staff provide no provision for adopting IFRS as an accounting regulation in the US. However, they did show a lot of optimism and opportunities for exploring other means of incorporating IFRS. They also demonstrate a substantial commitment to the "objective of a single set of high-quality, global accounting standards." Specifically, while communicating the opinion of the broad-spectrum investor constituency in the US on adopting of global standards, in the same Final Staff Report, the SEC identified that "investors do not believe that high-quality standards should be compromised for the sake of uniformity." In other words, SEC and FASB would grant their standard-setting authority to the IASB only when and if IFRS reach the high threshold established for them by the US. Moreover, the same Staff Report carries on to state that "further, investors noted that the FASB, in acting as an endorser, could serve an important role, ensuring that any standard incorporated into the US financial reporting system is of sufficient quality to maintain or improve on the financial reporting system."[16]

With no clear plan to adopt IFRS in the US, the discussion about the use of international accounting standards in the US continues. At the AICPA National Conference on Current SEC and PCAOB Developments in December 2016, the Chief Accountant of the SEC's Office of the Chief Accountant signified that while he does not anticipate the use of IFRS for domestic registrants in the near future, the FASB and IASB should carry on to collaborate to eliminate differences when in the best interest of the capital markets. In the same way, in a public statement issued in January 2017, the outgoing SEC Chair articulated support for the expansion of high-quality, globally accepted accounting standards, and recommended that the SEC support further efforts by the FASB and IASB to converge their accounting standards to enhance the quality and comparability of financial reporting.[17]

Among the main reasons for the lack of convergence, a political one can probably be listed at the top of the record. It seems that the US is disinclined to give up the GAAP standard-setting authority over domestic issuers to an international standard-setting body headquartered in London. Pronouncing (and lawfully so) that their primary goal is to protect US investors' welfare, the SEC notes that IFRS lacks reliable application, allows too much latitude with judgment, and is undersized in many specific areas. US GAAP, on the other hand, has detailed and accepted guidance and established practice regarding industry accounting and reporting, and many particular transactions, as can be seen in the August 2015 US GAAP "Guidance on the Presentation of Costs Related to Revolving Lines of Credit." The development of new guidance means that even in the relatively distant future when/if IFRS are finally adopted for the US issuers, international standards still will be reviewed and possibly customized to meet the specific needs of an American investor. It is not surprising that the Final Staff Report mentioned above did not provide any conclusions or recommendations to the SEC for the actions concerning IFRS in the US.

Most recently, the SEC's *Strategic Plan for Fiscal Years 2014–2018* stressed again that

- the SEC will continue to promote the establishment of high-quality accounting standards to meet the needs of investors. Due to the increasingly global nature of capital markets, the agency will work to promote higher quality financial reporting worldwide and will consider, among other things, whether a single set of high-quality global accounting standards is achievable.[18]

The New York State Society of Certified Public Accountants (NYSSCPA) became probably the first group of professional accountants to voice their concerns regarding IFRS adoption in their 2009 comments to the IASB Road Map. For instance, they specified:

- The SEC's plan for adoption lacked sufficient detail as to "the methodology and criteria expected to be applied to the milestones in assessing the adequacy of IFRS in meeting the needs of preparers, users, and auditors."
- The proposal did not recognize any tilting in the cost-benefit calculus that must surely have occurred as a result of the current economic environment:

> companies, investors and other participants in the U.S. capital markets have to face the continued dearth of capital at an economically feasible price. It would be reasonable to conclude that the monetary and human capital costs of the transition to IFRS could be burdensome to entities with limited resources and prohibitive for smaller entities, *even over a period of many years.*

- For a variety of technical, legal, and practical reasons, IFRS will not enhance comparability of financial statements across companies. As this is one of the purported benefits of IFRS adoption, if not the primary benefit being touted, a positive net benefit from adoption is somewhat illusory. Moreover, another benefit of IFRS adoption put forth in the proposing release is the added flexibility afforded to issuers to account for transactions and events by applying their judgment; the Society is concerned that opportunities for management judgment will result in *less* comparability.
- Recent events indicate that the IASB is inappropriately influenced by various national regulators and others "who promote the interests of their specific constituencies, as opposed to the needs of the worldwide community."[19]

In this context, the NYSSCPA cites as an example the modifications to IFRS (IAS 39 and IFRS 7) that have allowed companies to "'cherry pick' [financial] assets with significant losses and reverse those losses out of net income."

Fully acknowledging the extensive history of lobbying and political influence on US GAAP, it is still relevant to the IFRS adoption decision to recognize that by making that step the political pressure on accounting standard setting will intensify. Thus, the US capital market will be regulated by the standards that have been developed under the pressure, not just national but also international special interests. For example:

- *IFRIC 23*: the long-established and well-reasoned basis for "benchmark" alternative of expensing interest was abandoned. It is marked as merely the "allowed alternative" and capitalization of interests becomes a primary accounting treatment. The fact that no substantive basis was given for this change leaves little doubt that behind-the-scenes the IFRS issuers that are the most addicted to interest capitalization spearheaded the change.
- *IFRIC 15*: construction contract accounting treatment seems to be ingeniously crafted to provide the construction industry with the capability of managing its earnings. Looking back, the similar loopholes in US GAAP were closed decades ago. So, probably under the pressure of political interests, the IASB instead of converging to US GAAP decided to sustain theirs on regulation.
- *IAS 24 includes* a requirement on special disclosure of the information about related party transactions. The Chinese have never been big supporters of this requirement, and they continue to put pressure on the IASB to suppress it. It seems that they will be successful in changing it.

On a positive side, the IFRS 3R on business combinations is an example of the FASB's victory during the convergence project with IASB. IFRS 3R was not fully converged with SFAS 141R in the area of measuring the noncontrolling interests, so the final version of the international standard was ultimately changed to conform with the US standard fully. Overall, after more than 16 years of collaboration all the joint IASB/US FASB projects are complete or nearing their completion, but the convergence of IFRS and US GAAP has not been achieved, and the IFRS adoption in the US is not a part of a short-term plan.

It is both apparent and hopeless that politics has and will continue to play too significant a part in both US GAAP and IFRS standard-setting process. Aside from the academic inquiry as to who is guilty of yielding to politics more in the past, the pertinent issue when considering IFRS adoption is whether it will inflate or constraint the potential for politics to manipulate accounting standards used by American companies. With the expanded playing field and numerous added participants to the game of standard setting, the answer is a self-evident "yes."

Litigious Business Environment in the US

Among the general characteristics that make IFRS adoption even more problematic is the less prescriptive nature of IFRS. Under the assumption that *a matter of principle* maximizes the quality of financial reporting, it becomes complicated to assess the degree to which an accounting rule has been influenced inappropriately. Thus, it raises the concern about how the standard-setters intent to appease special interests can be recognized. To this end, a set of accounting standards lacking clarity in rules will not be operational in a highly litigious business environment like the US. In the American environment of "high professional liability," it is understandable and even justifiable that accountants and auditors demand a highly elaborate set of definite rules rather than "general principles" that "merely" declare neutrality and faithful representation, leaving the rest to preparer's decision. There is no reservation that professional opinion is essential and even critical for a high-quality reporting process. At the same time, it is difficult to disagree that in real life, along with judgment, come different and contradictory opinions, selections of estimations, and other "leeways" that may assist other interests.

That is why FASB carries on creating detailed reporting rules, which focus on particular accounting issues and business situations, thus generating widespread gaps with IFRS. Those detailed rules are instrumental in protecting accountants and auditors from being blamed and sued together with the company's preparers of financial reports for investor or creditor problems that are even tangentially related to reporting. So, it looks like the war between the "principles-based" IFRS and the "rules-based" US GAAP (as it is not very reasonably perceived by many) is far from over yet.

Notes

1. www.forbes.com/2009/02/23/mark-to-market-opinions-columnists_recovery_stimulus.html#3e5b481b738b
2. www.forbes.com/2010/02/13/wesbury-first-trust-intelligent-investing-economy.html#3b96bdfa512b
3. FASB 157 is a standard from the US Federal Accounting Standards Board, that went into effect in 2007, reintroducing mark-to-market accounting.
4. www.forbes.com/2009/02/23/mark-to-market-opinions columnists_recovery_stimulus.html#31ea8cf1738b
5. R. C. Posen, "Is It Fair to Blame Fair Value Accounting for the Financial Crisis?" *Harvard Business Review*, November 2009 issue (https://hbr.org/2009/11/is-it-fair-to-blame-fair-value-accounting-for-the-financial-crisis).
6. It must be noted here, that accounting rules for impairment that are paired up with the historical costs approach represent an attempt to report a permanent reduction in the fair value of an asset below its book value (carrying amount). Specifically, it compares an asset's book value with its fair market value by including in the test the total profit, cash flow, or other benefit that's expected to be generated by a specific asset.

7. www.fasb.org/jsp/FASB/Page/SectionPage&cid=1175801857762
8. https://fee.org/articles/did-deregulated-derivatives-cause-the-financial-crisis/
9. www.forbes.com/2010/02/13/wesbury-first-trust-intelligent-investing-economy.html#3b96bdfa512b
10. www.forbes.com/2010/02/13/wesbury-first-trust-intelligent-investing-economy.html#3b96bdfa512b
11. www.slate.com/articles/news_and_politics/the_big_idea/2008/10/the_end_of_libertarianism.html
12. www.gpo.gov/fdsys/pkg/CHRG-110hhrg55764/html/CHRG-110hhrg55764.htm
13. October 13, 2008 Amendment to IAS 39 for reclassifications of financial assets, effective date July 1, 2008.

    16 April 2009 IAS 39 amended for Annual Improvements to IFRS 2009, original effective date January 1, 2010.

    12 November 2009 IFRS 9 *Financial Instruments* issued, replacing the classification and measurement of financial assets provisions of IAS 39, original effective date January 1, 2013.

    28 October 2010 IFRS 9 *Financial Instruments* reissued, incorporating new requirements on accounting for financial liabilities and carrying over from IAS 39 the requirements for derecognition of financial assets and financial liabilities, original effective date January 1, 2013.

    24 July 2014 IFRS 9 *Financial Instruments* issued, replacing IAS 39 requirements for classification and measurement, impairment, hedge accounting and derecognition, effective for annual periods beginning on or after January 1, 2018 (www.iasplus.com/en/standards/ias/ias39).
14. Most financial derivatives would not meet the first test. Managing on a contractual yield basis usually means holding financial assets to their contractual maturity date.
15. 28 October 2010 IFRS 9 Financial Instruments reissued, incorporating new requirements on accounting for financial liabilities and carrying over from IAS 39 the requirements for de-recognition of financial assets and financial liabilities Original effective date 1 January 2013.

    24 July 2014 IFRS 9 Financial Instruments issued, replacing IAS 39 requirements for classification and measurement, impairment, hedge accounting and de-recognition Effective for annual periods beginning on or after 1 January 2018#(www.iasplus.com/en/standards/ias/ias39)
16. www.sec.gov/spotlight/globalaccountingstandards/ifrs-work-plan-final-report.pdf
17. www.sec.gov/about/secstratplan1418.htm
18. www.sec.gov/about/secstratplan1418.htm
19. ww2.cfo.com/gaap-ifrs/2011/08/ny-cpas-ifrs-still-not-ready-for-the-u-s/

2 Corporate Characteristics Motivating Convergence

International Sample

Victoria Krivogorsky

Introduction

Historically, financial accounting standardization follows market integration. This association is evidenced by the events in the US in the early twentieth century when the move to uniform accounting followed legislation to regulate the national capital markets. Similarly, the present impetus for a single uniform set of global accounting standards follows the accelerating integration of the world economy, accompanied by the struggle for economic growth and more efficient capital markets. The convergence process in accounting is part of a much larger global integration process. During the last few decades harmonization or convergence has been pursued in a variety of political and economic settings, including constituent territories of a political unit (United Kingdom), nations creating agreements for common welfare (NAFTA), and a single economic unit with institutional structures such as the European Union (EU). Within the boundaries of the theory of comparative advantage, scholarly literature embraces the idea of convergence as the mechanism which eliminates differences in institutional regimes and levels the playing field.[1] Thus, convergence can be viewed as removing an "artificial" source of a comparative advantage enjoyed by domestic companies. Convergence is not an end in and of itself. Rather, it is perceived as the means by which the end is achieved with greater efficiency. It should be noted here that convergence is a wide-ranging integration process and an example of accounting standardization by the EU as a part of it.

Both the value of convergence and the effectiveness of its implementation should be judged regarding an asserted objective. This objective determines the main benefits of convergence. It has already been reported in the literature that convergence reduces information processing costs (Chen et al., 2014), thus enhancing accounting conformity (Dong, 2014), the comparability and efficiency of financial statements, and promoting the integration of the global market. Also, Hail et al. (2010) demonstrated that the decision to adopt IFRS mainly involves a cost-benefit trade-off between (1) recurring comparability benefits for investors; (2) recurring future cost savings; and (3) one-time transition costs borne by all. Furthermore, Li (2010) finds that mandatory IFRS adoption in the European Union reduces the cost of equity, especially for countries with strong legal enforcement. Overall there is an extensive literature on IFRS adoption already in existence. However this research is the first I am aware of that uses the theory of network externalities in explaining a phenomenon of accounting standardization to be advantageous for a company. I conjecture that the companies with certain characteristics such as international exposure, for example, obtain additional value from employing the same financial reporting system as the rest of the network participants will continue to rise. To this end, these firms drive the standardization process by adopting the same set of standards rather early. To this purpose, instead of examining gains and losses associated with IFRS adoption, I identify firm-specific characteristics that associate with the likelihood of the adoption.

This study has relevance as standardization of International Auditing Standards took place not long ago. Also, in a period of globalization, it is important to understand better firm-specific characteristics associated with companies' decisions to standardize their business practices and financial reporting in particular. In this study a sample of companies have been grouped into three categories: (1) early adopters, (2) those that presumably lack the incentives to adopt early (2005-adopters);[2] and (3) those that did not perceive IFRS adoption advantages, and thus postponed the adoption (2007-adopters).[3]

The research on network externalities (David, 1985; Katz & Shapiro, 1985) and following the logic of the transaction cost/internalization theory, that there is no direct and general relationship between international diversification and performance (Hennart, 2007, 2011), provides us with useful insights into the prerequisites for a single set of standards to be advantageous for a company. In particular, the firm's positive externality from one set of standards increases, when no economically justified market demand for their variety and network effects stays unbounded (Arthur, 1989). Also, there should be no anti-competitive risk from using a common set of accounting standards. Therefore, members of smaller economic networks with no immediate intent to enter a worldwide integrated market have fewer incentives to adopt IFRS unless it is mandatory. Moreover, if the law offers an option to postpone the adoption of common standards, companies more bounded by national and sector-related limits will most likely use this opportunity to delay adoption. To this end, high business complexity raises the odds of the firm becoming an early IFRS adopter.

In addition to testing the impact of business complexity and firm-specific characteristics on the odds of earlier IFRS adoption, I also assess the extenuating effects of jurisdictions on the tested relationships. The importance of the institutions has been extensively addressed in the literature earlier (Ding et al., 2006; Krivogorsky & Grudnitski, 2010). Some studies, in particular (Ball et al., 2003; Hung, 2001), have identified a set of institutional characteristics important in explaining imperative determinants of the actual implementation of accounting standards. These characteristics include legal origin, which is measured by a dichotomous variable that indicates whether a country's laws originated from the common-law or code-law tradition. Consistent with the latest developments in the corporate governance literature, I use more precise identification than just common-law vs. code-law legal traditions by identifying German, French, and Scandinavian origins within code-law tradition (Botero et al., 2004; Djankov et al., 2002). I also test the national levels of bureaucratic formalities in business as a differentiating factor that reduces the likelihood of a company entering an integrated market. To my best knowledge, this variable has never been tested before in this type of analysis.[4]

The data has been collected from Thomson Financial-Worldscope and Thomson Bank One databases. The initial sample consisted of 3,196 firm-observations. After omitting companies with inconsistent or missing data, financial and utility companies, companies where the state is the dominant owner, and cross-shareholdings limited by shares, the final sample is comprised of 1,676 firm-observations for the period 2005–2007 from 14 EU countries, which makes us comfortable with the generalizability of the results.[5]

Overall, the results of the regression analysis support the initial conjecture that certain firms' characteristics are strongly associated with the likelihood of IFRS adoption and suggest strong extenuating effects of jurisdictions on the tested relationships. While the results for the overall sample of early (voluntary) adopters vs. non-adopters do not show the strong significant association for all tested regressands (only a number of foreign subsidiaries and a size have a significant impact on the odds of early adoption), after disaggregating the sample into four groups correlated with origins, the results become much stronger. In particular, the results show that for the British legal origin firms business complexity and Tobin's Q have a significant impact on the odds of early IFRS adoption, whereas the size is significant for the French and German legal origin firms, which is consistent with the market-oriented and government, tax, and law-based economies, respectively. Thus, consistent with the idea pinpointed by Harzing and Pudelko (2016), context country-specific characteristics, such as investment regulations, political risk, access to capital, etc. mostly exemplified by the national institutions such as jurisdictions and bureaucratic formalities have a significant impact on the managers' decisions, e.g., a likelihood of becoming an early adopter.[6] The additional test compares 2005-adopters vs. 2007-adopters after all voluntary adopters have been excluded; 2005-adopters have significantly higher company value, growth, and managerial efficiency in generating cash. The results of the logit regression for the sub-sample of 2005-adopters vs. 2007-adopters suggest that the percentage of foreign sales, Tobin's Q, and rate of growth have a significant impact on the likelihood of becoming a 2007-adopter.

Literature Review and Hypotheses

The scholarly literature identifies several main theoretical bases for common accounting standards to contribute to economic success. IFRS, as a set of common standards, helps to enable open markets and as a result increase competition (Reddy, 1987; Swann et al., 2000) by furnishing the user of financial information with an identical means of measurement, helping to identify the denotation of the information, improving the comparability of financial statements, and enhancing accounting quality (Barth et al., 2008; Dayanandan et al., 2016). The adoption of IFRS produced a vast debate on its economic consequences and the loss of "custom-made" national standards. Some argue that distinctive characteristics of national economies create diverse financial reporting needs, and therefore it will take a long time to erode the importance of national standards (Fearnley & Sunder, 2005). There are several arguments supporting diversity in accounting standards. First among them is that historically most Continental European economies have relied on means other than the US-UK arm's-length stock market as their main source of financing, instead of using such sources as bank debt. Second, financial standards suitable for developed economies may not be feasible in less-developed ones (Ball, 2006). On a related note, Daske et al. (2008), after examining the capital-market effects around IFRS adoption in 26 countries throughout the world, found that the capital-market benefit is more profound only in countries where firms have incentives to be transparent. Third, the poor quality of standard enforcement in some jurisdictions would make adoption and implementation of IFRS difficult (Ball, 2006; Daske et al., 2008). Fourth, there is an audit problem linked to the full implementation of IFRS that can be mitigated through market mechanisms by employing the services of Big Four auditors to verify the compliance with IFRS (just as private companies with local auditors sometimes turn to more prestigious auditors when going public).[7] And finally, there are the problems associated with transplanting accounting standards from common-law to code-law, especially about countries that have less respect for protecting shareholder value and minority rights (Ball, 2006; Reese & Weisbach, 2002).

On the other side of this debate, the main argument for common standards relates to the gains a company receives from integrating into a larger, more competitive market. Theoretically, the more closely the world's stock market approaches a single market, the lower the transaction costs for investors[8] and the cost of capital for firms in that market.[9] All things being equal, a larger, competitive market is more closely associated with (1) more competition between buyers and sellers, (2) more division of labor, and (3) more opportunities for risk sharing and risk matching (Maskus et al., 2005; Runyan & Smith, 2007). In particular, it is argued that companies switching to IFRS benefit from increased transparency (Ding et al., 2006), drop in earnings management (Cai et al., 2014), lower costs of financial statement reconciliation associated with multinational equity listings (Biddle & Saudagaran, 1989), enhanced comparability of financial reporting (Pownall & Schipper, 1999; Mohammadrezaei et al., 2015), and therefore lower informational asymmetry, and private benefits of managerial discretion in comparison to local GAAPs (Armstrong et al., 2010). However, there is mixed evidence for accounting quality improvements for firms that adopted IFRS as the result of a mandatory requirement (Christensen et al., 2007; Li, 2010). In related work, Ball et al. (2003) provide empirical evidence suggesting that accounting quality is being driven by incentives other than accounting standards, for example by the institutional setting. Furthermore, Ball and Shivakumar (2005) show that earnings quality is lower for private firms than for public firms, even though they are using common accounting standards. The benefits from having access to a larger pool of capital can be substantial for firms from underdeveloped economies, but the effect seems to diminish as national economic development increases (Hail & Leuz, 2006).[10] Therefore, gain from the decreased costs of capital might not be a plausible explanation as to why some EU companies early adopted IFRS. Crucial to these calculations is the estimated cost of penalties from operating in markets smaller than a single world market (unbounded network effect), or conversely, benefits arising from operating in a market that is not divided by different accounting standards, after all, costs of compliance have been covered. The importance of identifying these benefits is defined by the fact that they mostly outline the incentives (i.e., determinants) for convergence. Elusiveness of these unaccounted "benefits vs. costs" considerations contributes to the inconsistencies in measuring and identifying different explanatory variables when limited data is available, as well as an absence of consensus in the literature on the economic consequences of IFRS adoption.

While the results on economic benefits of IFRS adoption remain inconclusive, a different way to detect the determinants of IFRS adoption is to identify firm-specific characteristics that increase the likelihood that a firm earlier adopts IFRS. Company benefits received from integrating into a larger, more competitive market come from the economic theory, which provides some assurances that the additional value companies obtain from employing the same accounting system as the rest of the network participants will continue to rise as the network of users grows. In particular, for a company with fewer geographical and/or sector-related limits, this effect comes from two sources: (1) internal, as common standards help to reduce the intra-company costs associated with diversification (i.e., enhance the cross-border monitoring of management and contracting), there are no extra costs associated with entering the integrated market, and the only costs counter-weighting the benefits of adopting IFRS relate to the costs of compliance with new sets of rules;[11] and (2) external, as common standards furnish the users of financial information anywhere in the world, including potential investors, with the identical means of measurement, helping to identify the transparency of the information and improving comparability of financial statements, promoting trust. Following this line of reasoning, firms that benefit most from network effects probably operate in more complex business environments and employ distinct corporate governance practices to strengthen their competitive edge in the integrated market.[12]

In other words, following the logic of the theory on network externalities, I argue that a company with higher business complexity associated with fewer geographical or sector-related limits more likely falls into the category of firms benefiting the most from using a common set of standards, and therefore derives additional benefits from becoming a member of the international network of companies with a comparable, less impartial, and more open set of financial statements. This highly integrated company benefits from high synchronization value by doing business and raising capital far outside its national boundaries (Liebowitz & Margolis, 1994, 1996). Also, as already mentioned, a company with fewer geographical or sector-related limits to its interests usually operates in more competitive environments and presumably has enhanced corporate transparency and auditing.[13] Therefore, common accounting standards potentially assist those companies in sustaining *cross-border* portfolio and direct investments, and contracting and monitoring of management by shareholders. Otherwise the cost of all these activities may be needlessly inflated by complex translations. Furthermore, these firms represent potential advocates for convergence in all areas of business activities since they see no economically justified demand for the variety of standards, as they perpetually benefit from harmonization and experience no anti-competitive risk from using common standards. In addition, the use of standardized financial reporting can help to reduce transaction costs[14] (Hudson & Jones, 2003; Williamson, 1998), making it cost effective for companies to more extensively use the existing capital market, as well as extending the market geographically (Li, 2010; Maskus et al., 2005). Thus, a firm's complex business architecture and market value affect the likelihood of IFRS adoption. I state the hypotheses in alternative form:

> *H1: The likelihood of standardizing accounting rules earlier strongly associated with business complexity.*

H2: The likelihood of standardizing accounting rules earlier strongly associated with the equity value, measured as Tobin's Q.

Research Design

Data and Sample

To test the hypotheses, I collect data available on Thomson Financial-Worldscope and Thomson Bank One databases. Initially, I had more than 3,000 observations-publicly traded companies from 15 EU countries: Austria, Germany, UK, Greece, France, Ireland, Italy, The Netherlands, Luxembourg, Belgium, Denmark, Spain, Portugal, Sweden, and Finland. The decision to use only 15 developed countries in the test was instigated by the analysis originated in Ball, 2006, claiming that financial standards suitable for developed economies may not be feasible in less-developed ones (Ball, 2006). After omitting Luxembourg from the sample (only three companies were available for testing), as well as removing companies with incomplete data, financial and utility companies, companies with the state as dominant owner, and cross-listings,[15] the final sample included 1,884 firm-years observations of publicly traded companies from 14 countries during 2005–2007. However, the final sample comprised only 1,676 firms, because I eliminated 159 firms with fewer than three board members[16] and 49 other firms from regulated industries. The data selection procedure is described in Table 2.1, Panel A.

Panel B of Table 2.1 gives the country, the legal origin and the distribution of firms in the sample. While the whole sample is comprised of 14 EU countries, almost 75% of it came from five Western European economies: approximately 27% British firms, about 34% either German or French (distributed almost equally), almost 8% Italian, and about 6% Swedish.

Table 2.1 Data selection procedures and country distribution

Panel A: Data selection procedures

Initial sample	3,196
Minus financial and utility companies, companies with dominant state ownership, cross-shareholdings limited by share*	1,884
Remaining sample from 14 European countries	
Minus companies with board size less than three members	159
	1,725
Minus firms with missing financial data	
Final sample	49
	1,676

*All these companies are subjects for special regulatory environment

Table 2.1 (Continued)

Panel B: Country sample distribution

Country	*Number of Firms*	*Percentage*	*Legal Origin*
Austria (AT)	53	3.2%	German
Belgium (BE)	38	2.3%	French
Germany (DE)	285	17.0%	German
Denmark (DK)	50	3.0%	Scandinavian
Spain (ES)	37	2.2%	French
Finland (FI)	68	4.0%	Scandinavian
France (FR)	277	16.5%	French
United Kingdom (UK)	457	27.3%	British
Greece (GR)	81	4.8%	French
Ireland (IE)	16	1.0%	British
Italy (IT)	132	7.9%	French
Netherlands (NL)	79	4.7%	French
Portugal (PT)	9	0.5%	French
Sweden (SE)	94	5.6%	Scandinavian

Variables in the Model

To test the hypotheses, I draw on three sets of variables. The first set of variables represents the dependent variables defined as voluntary early adopters (firms that adopted IFRS before 2005), 2005-adopters (firms that adopted IFRS in 2005), and 2007-adopters (firms that adopted IFRS after 2005). The second set of independent variables comprises a variety of firm-specific characteristics, and the third is intended to control for national, institutional, industry, and corporate governance effects.

DEPENDENT VARIABLES

A voluntary early IFRS adopter (VOLUNTARY) is a company that filed its consolidated financial statement prepared according to IFRS before 2005 (i.e., in 2004).[17] All companies that filed their financial statements prepared according to IFRS for the first time in 2005 are defined as 2005-adopters (2005), the companies that decided to postpone IFRS adoption are defined as 2007-adopters (POSTPON). The logit model uses binary dependent variables, Y_i, defined so that, for example, if a firm was a voluntary IFRS adopter $Y_1 = 1$ and otherwise $Y_1 = 0$, if a firm was a 2005-adopter then $Y_2 = 1$ and otherwise $Y_2 = 0$.

INDEPENDENT VARIABLES

Business Complexity: Two variables have been used to measure the level of the geographic and sector-related limits to company interests: the number of foreign subsidiaries (SUBSIDIARY) and the percentage of foreign sales scaled by total sales (FRSALES).[18]

Tobin's Q and Firm Performance: Tobin's Q (TOBINQ) estimates company value (Yermack, 1996) by comparing a firm's market value to the cost of replacing the firm. In doing so, it reflects various company characteristics including (1) growth opportunities, (2) market sentiment (the market views regarding the company's prospects, or speculation such as bid rumors), and (3) the intellectual capital of the company. Daske et al. (2008) find that a company's Tobin's Q decreases in the year when IFRS reporting becomes mandatory, but it increases one year before the mandatory adoption date. Furthermore, they find that valuation effects for 2005-adopters are economically significant but generally smaller than the corresponding capital-market effects of early adoption. In this study, Tobin's Q is used to examine whether the firms with higher equity valuation (or growth opportunities) are more likely to become the earlier IFRS adopters.

Earnings under IFRS could be systematically smaller/larger than earnings under local standards, which lead to a higher/smaller Tobin's Q after the adoption of IFRS. Li (2010) compares earnings under IFRS vs. under local standards for mandatory adopters and finds that mean earnings are significantly smaller under IFRS but no difference in median earnings under two standards. Therefore, the percentage change of net income (CHGNI) is included as a control variable to examine whether the adoption of IFRS impacts a company's reported earnings during the first adopting year.

CONTROL VARIABLES

Various arguments related to the effectiveness of corporate governance mechanisms employed by a company have been addressed in prior research. In summation, there are two main lines of reasoning in analyzing the roles of external and internal corporate governance mechanisms. First, the external corporate governance mechanisms are believed to have a strong association with early IFRS adoption. For example, Ding et al. (2006) provide some evidence that countries with weaker investor protection are more likely to adopt IFRS. Ramanna and Sletten (2009), using 102 non-EU countries, find that countries with moderate governance standards have higher IFRS adoption rates than those with advanced governance standards. Second, internal corporate governance mechanisms are more likely to be associated with high-quality governance. According to Verriest and Gaerremynck (2008), better corporate governance is associated with early IFRS adoption and fewer earnings management. Therefore, I include corporate governance variables as control variables.

Board Size and Composition: The role and effectiveness of different internal corporate governance mechanisms remain inconclusive, in part because the debate on the effect of board size (BRDSZ) on governance effectiveness remains unresolved. First, some scholars (Lipton & Lorsch, 1992; Jensen, 1993) suggest that larger boards are less effective than smaller ones due to the difficulty of coordination and free-riding issues. Others (Yermack, 1996; Eisenberg et al., 1998) provide evidence that smaller boards are associated with higher firm's value, as measured by Tobin's Q. Conversely, Coles et al. (2008) indicate that, at the very least, larger boards and a higher fraction of insiders on the board do not necessarily reduce firm value, whereas others find that the previously documented negative effect of board size on Tobin's Q does not hold for diversified, large, and high-debt firms (Krivogorsky, 2006; Krivogorsky & Burton, 2012). Overall, as Bhagat and Black (2002) suggest, inside and independent directors play valuable roles that may be lost in a single-minded drive for greater board independence.

Second, there is no consensus on the role outside (independent) and inside directors play on firm value. There is a whole spectrum of findings, from strongly positive, suggesting that outside (independent) directors represent a positive force in a company (Yermack, 1996; Eisenberg et al., 1998; Black & Kim, 2012), to weak, suggesting that there is no evidence on the relationship between the percentage of outside (independent) directors and Tobin's Q (Hermalin & Weisbach, 1991; Bhagat & Black, 2002). To control for the impact of independent directors on the company's decisions, I use IND_DIR% variable, measured as the proportion of independent directors on board.

The role of inside directors is also not completely clear. Although common wisdom suggests that a large number of inside directors deepens the agency problem, results of some studies suggest that in cases where firm-specific knowledge of insiders is relatively important, the addition of an insider on the board increases stock price, or the fraction of insiders on investment and finance committees is associated with an increase in various measures of firm performance (Rosenstein & Wyatt, 1997; Klein, 1998; Coles et al., 2008). To control for the impact of the executive directors on the company's decisions, I use EXE_DIR% variable, measured as the proportion of executive directors on board.

To control for other distinctive characteristics in corporate governance, several variables have been employed: (1) the number of inside (executive) directors (EXDIR) with properly disclosed identity; (2) the number of independent directors (INDIR) with adequately disclosed identity; and (3) the number (GRDIR) and the proportion (GREY_DIR) of directors whose identity was not properly disclosed, and therefore remains questionable, referred to here as "grey" directors. This last variable is used as a proxy for the level of corporate governance disclosure, following previous findings that disclosure may reduce information asymmetry and therefore have a positive effect on firm value (Lang & Lundholm, 2000).

Ownership Concentration: Concentration of ownership is an essential element of corporate governance. Concentrated shareholdings and predominance of controllership seem to be the norm in EU countries (Krivogorsky & Burton, 2012). Following the argument that large owners may or may not be good company stewards, I include the immediate largest owners (OWNERSHIP) to examine their association with a firm's decision to adopt IFRS earlier.

Firm Size and Growth: Fama and French (1995) document that on average small firms have lower earnings (scaled by book value of equity) than do large firms. To control for the size effect, this study uses the natural logarithm of total assets (SIZE).

Previous studies indicate that fast-growing firms are more often subject to underinvestment (Myers, 1977) and asset substitution, as they have more flexibility in their choice of investment (Titman & Wessels, 1988). In this study, I use the logarithm of the difference between year t and t-1 (i.e., two subsequent years') sales to control for the short-term growth opportunities (GROWTH).[19]

Auditor: To validate the financial information augment the trust of the users, and amplify market reaction, I control for the fact that these companies employ a Big Four auditor to authenticate their financial statements. Teoh and Wong (1993) provide evidence that investors perceived (then) Big Eight auditing firms as those that provided better audit quality, and thereby ensured greater credibility (trust) in accounting information, and Chang and Sun (2009, 2010) support those findings. Eshleman and Peng (2014) suggest that Big Four auditors do perform higher quality audits. Thus, following this logic, it is assumed that Big Four services are instrumental in raising trust, i.e., lowering the cost of capital in different security markets. So, a BIG4 variable is used to capture the choice of employing a Big Four auditor. BIG4 is a binary variable that has a value of one if a company uses one of the Big Four firms and is zero otherwise.

Leverage and Cash Turnover: Two variables, leverage and cash-flow turnover, are used to address the facts that in Europe, (1) reserves represent a considerable part of total shareholders' funds (total equity), and are an important source of investments (with various degrees of importance for different European countries), (2) bank debt remains a significant source of capital, and (3) liabilities include accounts payable and provisions arising from national labor-market contracts or specific regulations with no importance for financing decisions. To control for the level of bank debt, I define LEVERAGE as the ratio of total long-term bank debt scaled by net assets.

The significance of tax effects on all European companies' decisions stems from the fact that all financial statements filed for accounting purposes are simultaneously used by tax authorities to verify companies' tax liabilities. Previous studies (e.g., MacKie-Mason, 1990) find that the adverse tax effect holds only for firms with low cash flow, which are more likely to be close to tax exhaustion. Tax effects and sales have been found to be negatively correlated with leverage (Kim & Sorensen, 1986; Lang et al., 1996). Following the previous arguments, cash flow turnover (CFTURN) is used as an indicator of managerial operating efficiency to generate cash flows and the capability to pay off debt and taxes. It is defined as the ratio of annual end of cash balances to yearly turnover (net sale).

Industry: The decision to control for the industry is based on two reasons. First, firm value, growth, risk, and cash flow may be more or less severe in specific industries due to differences in competitive intensity and industry maturity (Demsetz & Lehn, 1985; Fama & French, 1997). Second, Lang and Stulz (1994) showed that the Tobin's Q of diversified firms tends to be lower, and that industry effects account for a significant fraction of the diversification discount; i.e., after correcting for industry effects, the diversification discount was positive and significant every year in their sample. To control for possible differential industry effects, I use a variable (INDUSTRY) that follows Fama and French's (1997) industrial classifications.[20]

Classification of Countries: To validate the results of the tests performed for the whole sample, I also test for the impact of the existing contextual diversities in the various nations within which firms operate (Harzing et al., 2016). Jurisdiction and level of bureaucratic (administrative) formalities are two ways to classify similar countries.[21] The first classifying measure is based on the hypothetical classification of financial-reporting measurement practices, which supposedly constitute the long-run fundamental differences between a country's business environment and the importance of the influence of law and economics. Following the logic of this classification, the decision-making in the countries from British origin is mostly

> determined by the impact of those decisions on company market value. The decision-making in the countries from government tax or law-based groups are significantly associated with the quality of information provided to the government and governmental agencies. According to this classification, the sample consists of four distinct groups associated with the following origins: (1) British (pragmatic, business practice); (2) French (government, tax-based); (3) German (government, law-based); and (4) Scandinavian (governmental economics).

The second classifying measure to test the extenuating effect of institutions is a level of bureaucratic formalities, which is also associated with the level of political risk in a country. The relationship between the managers' choices and a level of political risk in a country has been established in the literature (Datta et al., 2015). Thus, the theory/logic behind using a level of bureaucratic formalities is very similar to any other argument regarding the palliative effects of institutions. The government, as opposed to the market, is associated with higher bureaucracy and therefore makes market-related measurements of less significance. The national levels of bureaucratic (administrative) formalities were identified and measured as a part of the research project conducted by the French Research Centre in International Economics in 2006. The indexes are available at the Database of the Institutional Characteristics of 85 Developing and Developed Countries/2006.[22] It is expected that the higher the level of bureaucratic formalities in a country, the more the increase in the procedural complexity becomes an impediment to effective convergence. Indeed, within the European Union, the economic and financial policy remains first and foremost a competency belonging to each of the member states; there is no centralized EU economic policy institution, or a common EU accounting or financial services regulator. Although some economic coordination takes place at the EU level, notably under the framework of the Stability and Growth Pact, the unity of action is still dependent on agreement by the representatives of the member states who sit on the Economic and Financial Affairs Council.

Following the previous investigation of bureaucratic formalities, three levels of administrative formalities have been identified. The bureaucratic (administrative) formalities level was assigned to each country based on the overall score, which in turn was measured as the aggregated score using sub-scores such as (1) level of government involvement in businesses, (2) the allocation of financial funds available for companies, and (3) the existence and observance of business legislation and measures. Countries included in Level 1 belong to the most rigid administrative environment with strong governmental involvement in business and capital allocation and strongly enforced national business legislatures. Level 3 countries represent a very relaxed business environment, mostly dependent on the market for capital redistribution. The countries included in Level 2 were in the middle third of the score.

Results

Descriptive Statistics

The differences in the key variables have been examined in two steps. First, I detected the voluntarily adopters in the overall sample (630 firms, almost 38% of the sample) in 2004 and ran the Wilcoxon non-parametric median test to identify the significance of differences in firms' characteristics between the voluntarily adopters and non-adopters, i.e. the rest of the sample (Panel A of Table 2.2).[23] The general descriptive statistics presented in Panel A show that the early adopters, similarly to non-adopters, are highly leveraged firms with high ownership concentration, one-third of the boards comprising executive directors, and a low level of corporate disclosure (on average about two-thirds of directors' identities have not been disclosed). Consistent with the hypotheses, the results of the Wilcoxon test for the overall sample show a significantly higher (1) number of foreign subsidiaries (SUBSIDIARY), (2) percentage of foreign sales (FRSALES), and (3) Tobin's Q during the year t-1 (TOBINQ). As expected, I also report a significant difference in total assets (TA$), the rate of growth of sales, cash flow turnover (CFTURN), and Big Four auditor (AUDITOR) for voluntary adopters. No differences in board size were detected. The same test showed a significantly lower number of inside (executive) directors (EXEDIR/EXE_DIR), marginally significant difference for independent directors (INDDIR/IND_DIR), and level of ownership concentration (OWNERSHIP) for voluntary adopters. These results can be attributed to two possibilities. First, there can be an unaccounted number of independent directors with undisclosed identity, which I identified as grey directors. Second, the board independency institution and defused ownership are less pronounced in the code-law countries.

The same test performed for different legal origins (Panel B of Table 2.2) shows that British-origin firms (BO) on average have the lowest ownership concentration, smallest board size, the highest proportion of independent directors and level of corporate disclosure. The results from the British sub-sample consistently support the hypotheses, as voluntary adopters there have a significantly higher percentage of foreign sales, a Big Four auditor, smaller board size, fewer executives on board, a higher percentage of independent directors on board, size, and rate of growth. Similarly, voluntary adopters of German origin (GO) also tend to have a higher number of foreign subsidiaries, size, and rate of growth, but unlike voluntary adopters of British origin, those of German origin have lower levels of foreign sales. The latter can be attributed to the

Table 2.2 Descriptive statistics

Panel A: Voluntarily adopters vs. non-adopters, 2004 n = 1,676

Variable	*Early (Voluntary) Adopters n = 634*			*Non-adopters n = 1,042*			*Wilcoxon Test Pr.*
	Mean	*Median*	*Std Dev*	*Mean*	*Median*	*Std. Dev*	
Independent Variables							
SUBSIDIARY	145	45	372	82	29	295	0.01***
FRSALE (%)	33.78	26.52	32.99	30.12	19.49	33.2	0.02**
TOBINQ	1.36	0.57	2.56	0.79	0.43	1.65	0.01***
BIG4	83.12	100	37.48	70.83	100	45.48	0.01***
Control Variables							
BRDSZ (#)	9.07	8	4.29	9.38	8	5.04	0.65
INDDIR (#)	0.55	0	1.5	0.57	0	1.43	0.07*(–)
IND_DIR (%)	6.36	0	15.9	6.93	0	15.58	0.07*(–)
EXEDIR (#)	3.12	3	2.26	3.3	3	2.42	0.07*(–)
EXE_DIR (%)	36.02	33.33	18.54	36.67	33.33	18.54	0.12
GRDIR (#)	5.4	5	3.61	5.51	4	4.16	0.19
GREY_DIR (%)	57.62	60	24.43	56.4	60	22.62	0.15
OWNERSHIP (%)	12.36	0	23.37	14.94	0	25.88	0.12
CHGNI (%)	–20.10	9.14	570.9	93.29	6.53	1170.2	0.42
SIZE ($ mil)	12,446	645	52,156	4,475	265	29,716	0.01***
SALE ($mil)	3,529	532	11,101	2,406	273	9,868	0.01***
LEVERAGE (%)	14.78	9.32	23.62	13.93	8.49	23.13	0.23
CFTURN	6.71	5.5	8.9	5.54	4.27	9.73	0.01***

(*Continued*)

Table 2.2 (Continued)

Panel B: Voluntarily vs. non-adopters by legal origin, 2004 n = 1,676

Variable	*GO*			*FO*			*BO*			*SO*		
	Voluntary Adopters n = 38	*Non-adopters n = 300*	*Wicoxon Test Pr.*	*Voluntary Adopters n = 296*	*Non-adopters n = 357*	*Wicoxon Test Pr.*	*Voluntary Adopters n = 153*	*Non-adopters n = 320*	*Wicoxon Test Pr.*	*Voluntary Adopters n = 147*	*Non-adopters n = 65*	*Wicoxon Test Pr.*
	Mean	*Mean*		*Mean*	*Mean*		*Mean*	*Mean*		*Mean*	*Mean*	
Independent Variables												
SUBSIDIARY	52	22	0.01***	34	29	0.2	78	39	0.01***	39	26	0.01***
FRSALE (%)	1.04	34.43	0.01***(–)	18.08	17.13	0.97	37.41	4.73	0.01***	48.33	30.24	0.18
TOBINQ	0	0.42	0.01 ***	0.49	0.46	0.73	0.56	0.38	0.04**	2.28	1.7	0.66
BIG4	100	100	0.04**	100	100	0.01***	100	100	0.01***	100	100	0.33
Control Variables												
BRDSZ (#)	8	9	0.39	9	9	0.38	7	7	0.04**	8	8	0.58
IND_DIR (%)	0	0	0.03**	0	0	0.02**(–)	12.5	12.5	0.91	0	0	0.67
EXE_DIR (%)	28.57	30.38	0.73	33.33	37.5	0.22	28.57	34.85	0.01***(–)	37.5	37.5	0.49
EXEDIR (#)	3	3	0.63	3	3	0.05**(–)	2	2	0.17	3	3	0.28
INDDIR(#)	0	0	0.03**	0	0	0.02**(–)	1	1	0.6	0	0	0.67
GRDIR (#)	5.5	6	0.8	5	5	0.99	3	3	0.11	5	5	0.82
GREY_DIR (%)	667.71	68.59	0.99	64.29	61.11	0.24	50	50	0.12	62.5	60	0.32
OWNERSHIP (%)	0	0	0.29	0	0	0.02**(–)	0	0	0.09* (–)	0	0	0.13
CHGNI (%)	6.01	5.78	0.99	12.35	5.55	0.04**	2.75	10.32	0.10*	14.15	9.07	0.88
SIZE ($ mil)	9,941	268	0.01***	704	347	0.01***	831	199	0.01***	413	230	0.01***
SALE ($mil)	1,626	289	0.01***	502	296	0.01***	662	231	0.01***	401	213	0.3
LEVERAGE (%)	0	9.02	0.01***(–)	10.37	9.11	0.51	9.1	6.21	0.09*	11.94	8.6	0.3
CFTURN	0	4.88	0.01***	5.28	3.27	0.02***	6.93	4.27	0.01***	5.96	5.47	0.3

Panel C: 2005-adopters vs. postponers, 2005 n = 1,163

Variable	*2005-adopters n = 657*			*2007-adopters n = 506*			*Wilcoxon Median Pr.*
	Mean	*Median*	*Std Dev*	*Mean*	*Median*	*Std. Dev*	
Independent Variables							
SUBSIDIARY	79	33	144	85	25	393	0.01***
FRSALE (%)	36.79	34.37	32.3	25.58	2.53	33.38	0.01***
TOBINQ	1.2	0.62	2.2	0.63	0.44	0.89	0.01***
BIG4	71.53	100	45.16	73.91	100	43.95	0.37
Control Variables							
BRDSZ (#)	10.08	8	5.55	8.04	7	3.51	0.01***
IND_DIR (%)	5.29	0	13.81	9.03	0	17.6	0.01***(–)
EXE_DIR (%)	36.81	33.33	18.69	36.55	33.33	19.23	0.63
EXEDIR (#)	3.54	3	2.63	2.8	2	1.81	0.01***
INDDIR(#)	0.46	0	1.37	0.71	0	1.46	0.01***(–)
GRDIR (#)	6.08	5	4.49	4.53	4	3.22	0.01***
GREY_DIR (%)	57.9	60	22.15	54.42	57.14	23.38	0.02***
OWNERSHIP (%)	16.88	0	27.06	11.33	0	22.96	0.01***
CHGNI (%)	52.02	11.11	1200.86	107.51	0.69	1871.4	0.01***(–)
SIZE ($mil)	4,790	379	19,587	4,735	280	39,334	0.02**
SALE ($mil)	3,110	385	11,769	1,836	273	8,100	0.01***
LEVERAGE (%)	17.07	11.66	27.14	14.99	8.16	31.3	0.01***
CFTURN	7.62	6.06	9.1	6.19	3.94	10.35	0.01***

(Continued)

Table 2.2 (Continued)

Panel D: 2005-adopters vs. 2007-adopters by legal origin, 2005 n = 1,163

Variable	*GO*			*FO*			*BO*			*SO*		
	Adopters n = 226	*Non-adopters n = 74*	*Wicoxon Test Pr.*	*Adopters n = 253*	*Non-adopters n = 189*	*Wicoxon Test Pr.*	*Adopters n = 130*	*Non-adopters n = 225*	*Wicoxon Test Pr.*	*Adopters n = 48*	*Non-adopters n = 18*	*Wicoxon Test Pr.*
	Median	*Median*		*Median*	*Median*		*Median*	*Median*		*Median*	*Median*	
Independent Variables												
SUBSIDIARY	24	13	0.02**	41	18	0.01***	45	37	0.63	27	20	0.58
FRSALE (%)	39.16	13.42	0.02**	31.72	0	0.01***	20.6	6.5	0.07*	49.44	0	0.01***
TOBINQ	0.53	0.47	0.28	0.64	0.43	0.01***	0.58	0.48	0.07*	3.93	0	0.01***
BIG4	100	100	0.55	100	100	0.78	100	100	0.34	100	100	0.42
Control Variables												
BRDSZ (#)	9	9	0.44	10	7	0.01***	7	7	0.96	9	8	0.36
IND_DIR (%)	0	0	0.62	0	0	0.44	14.28	10	0.05**	0	0	0.99
EXE_DIR (%)	33.33	26.14	0.11	36.36	38.46	0.42	33.33	33.33	0.57	37.98	37.5	0.74
EXEDIR (#)	3	2	0.01***	3	3	0.01***	2	2	0.81	3	3	0.89
INDDIR (#)	0	0	0.62	0	0	0.44	1	1	0.05**	0	0	0.92
GRDIR (#)	6	6	0.78	6	4	0.01***	3	3	0.79	5	5	0.85
GREY_DIR (%)	66.67	72.07	0.11	61.54	60	0.39	50	50	0.6	60	59.03	0.83
OWNERSHIP (%)	0	0	0.2	0	0	0.42	0	0	0.3	0	0	0.92
CHGNI (%)	12.17	0	0.01***	10.11	0.81	0.04**	12.93	4.23	0.11	4.98	7.18	0.28

SIZE ($ mil)	357	148	0.11	482	316	0.01***	275	275	0.97	260	165	0.58
SALE ($mil)	379	150	0.02**	492	290	0.01***	361	296	0.48	264	97	0.27
LEVERAGE (%)	11.97	4.08	0.11	13.11	9.33	0.07*	8.23	8.62	0.86	10.45	0	0.03**
CFTURN	6.04	5.4	0.59	5.08	3.74	0.15	7.64	4.47	0.01***	7.99	0	0.01***

*, **, and *** represent the traditional significance level of 10%, 5%, 1%, respectively.

Note that the voluntary adopters are excluded from Panel C and Panel D subsamples.
Early (voluntary) adopters are defined as the firms that have already adopted IFRS in 2004 before the mandatory date. 2005-adopters are defined as the firms that have adopted IFRS under mandatory requirement 1606/2002 in 2005. Non-adopters are those companies, which were not using IFRS in 2004. 2007-adopters are those companies, which postponed the date of adoption. TOBINQ is a firm's [(long-term debt + market value of equity – book value of common equity)/ total assets] in t-1. LEVERAGE is a firm's long-term debt scaled by total assets in t-1. SALE is the firm's sale in the year t-1, and TA is total assets in the year t-1. CFTURN is the cash flow turnover rate that is year-end cash balance scaled by net sales in the year t-1. CHGNI is the percentage change of net income before taxes (IBT) of in the year of adopting IFRS minus the net income before taxes of last year of adopting local GAAP (i.e., (NIIFRSt—NIoldGAAPt-1) / NIoldGAAPt-1). SUBSIDIARY is a number of operating foreign subsidiaries of a firm. BRDSZ is the board size of the firm. EXEDIR is the number of executive directors—insiders. GREYDIR is the number of directors who are not identified as an insider or an independent director in the ORBIS database. INDDIR is the number of independent outsiders. EXE_DIR is the percentage of EXEDIR scaled by BRDSZ. GREY_DIR is the percentage of GREYDIR scaled by BRDSZ. IND_DIR is the percentage of INDDIR scaled by BRDSZ. OWNERSHIP is a percentage of a firm's shares owned by the immediate owners. BIG4 is a dummy equal to 1 if a firm's auditor is Big Four accounting firm during the year prior to the adoption.

strong position of unions and employees within German companies' corporate governance who tend to vote against outsourcing. There are no significant differences in the characteristics of voluntary adopters vs. non-adopters between the companies of Scandinavian origin (SO), except one: voluntary adopters of SO have a significantly larger number of foreign subsidiaries. Thus, in accord with others, SO firms are more likely to adopt IFRS when they have fewer geographical limits. The voluntary adopters of French origin (FO) are significantly larger measured as both sales and total assets. Second (Panel C of Table 2.2), I tested differences between the 2005-adopters (657 firms) vs. 2007-adopters (506 firms) in 2005.[24] The Wilcoxon test showed that the 2005-adopters have a significantly higher (1) percentage of foreign sales (FRSALES), (2) number of foreign subsidiaries (SUBSIDIARY), (3) Tobin's Q (TOBINQ), (4) total assets (SIZE), and (5) cash flow turnovers (CFTURN) than postponers. 2005-adopters also have larger boards (BRDSZ), a higher number of inside directors (EXEDIR), a lower level of corporate disclosure (higher number and percentage of "grey" directors), and a higher level of ownership concentration (OWNERSHIP). There is no significant difference in BIG4 between 2005-adopters and postponers.

The descriptive statistics presented in Panel D of Table 2.2 suggest that, whereas 2005-adopters from all legal origins consistently show higher percentages of foreign sales, the results for Tobin's Q are ambiguous, ranging from insignificant for the 2005-adopters of German origin to marginally significant for the 2005-adopters of British origin, and strongly significant for 2005-adopters of French (FO) and Scandinavian (SO) legal origins.

Pearson Correlation

The results of Pearson correlations among the variables used in the tests are reported in Table 2.3. Results presented in Panel A of Table 2.3 show that voluntary adopters have a significantly positive correlation with a higher number of foreign subsidiaries, percentage of foreign sales, Tobin's Q, employment of a Big four auditing firm, size, rate of growth, and cash flow turnover, while significantly negatively correlating with ownership concentration. There is no significant correlation with board composition or level of corporate disclosure (inside, independent, and grey directors). Interestingly, highly diversified firms employ Big Four auditors more often, have larger boards, fewer executives, more independent directors on board, and lower ownership concentration, but they have lower Tobin's Q, which is consistent with the Lang and Stulz (1994) findings.

Panel B of Table 2.3 presents Pearson correlation results for 2005- vs. 2007-adopters. It shows that 2005-adopters are associated with higher percentage of foreign sales, Tobin's Q, ownership concentration, rate of

Table 2.3 Pearson correlation

Panel A: Voluntarily adopters vs. non-adopters, 2004 n = 1,676

	TOBIN	*LEVERAGE*	*GROWTH*	*FRSALE*	*CFTURN*	*CHGNI*	*SIZE*	*SUBSIDIARY*	*BRDSZ*	*EXE_ DIR*	*GREY_ DIR*	*IND_ DIR*	*OWNERSHIP*	*AUDITOR*
Mandatory	0.158***	0.035	0.061**	0.167***	0.073***	−0.017	0.001	−0.012	0.207***	0.007	0.076***	−0.119†	0.108***	−0.026
TOBINQ		0.212***	−0.029	0.122***	0.201***	−0.019	−0.041	−0.010	0.040	−0.035	0.026	0.004	0.005	0.040
LEVERAGE			0.015	0.008	0.088***	0.213***	−0.015	0.028	0.092***	−0.077***	0.045	0.028	−0.002	0.025
GROWTH				0.152***	0.049*	−0.010	0.391***	0.28***	0.321***	−0.086***	0.064**	0.011	−0.012	0.098***
FRSALE					0.094***	−0.036	0.036	0.064**	0.116***	−0.095***	0.047	0.047	−0.041	0.132***
CFTURN						0.001	0.034	0.016	0.076***	−0.093***	0.014	0.091***	−0.034	0.115***
CHGNI							−0.007	−0.007	0.017	−0.050*	0.056*	−0.021	0.048*	−0.039
SIZE								0.803†	0.234***	−0.071	0.070*	−0.014	−0.021	0.077***
SUBSIDIARY									0.246***	−0.115***	0.071**	0.036	−0.076***	0.089***
BRDSZ										−0.164***	0.200***	−0.093***	0.050*	0.072***
EXE_DIR											−0.731***	−0.145***	0.081***	−0.159***
GREY_DIR												−0.568***	0.040	0.051*
IND_DIR													−0.157***	0.118***
OWNERSHIP														−0.187***

(*Continued*)

Table 2.3 (Continued)

Panel B: 2005-adopters vs. postponers, 2005 n = 1,163

	TOBIN	*LEVERAGE*	*GROWTH*	*FRSALE*	*CFTURN*	*CHGNI*	*SIZE*	*SUBSIDIARY*	*BRDSZ*	*EXE_DIR*	*GREY_DIR*	*IND_DIR*	*OWNERSHIP*	*AUDITOR*
Mandatory	0.158***	0.035	0.061**	0.167***	0.073***	−0.017	0.001	−0.012	0.207***	0.007	0.076***	−0.119†	0.108***	−0.026
TOBINQ		0.212***	−0.029	0.122***	0.201***	−0.019	−0.041	−0.010	0.040	−0.035	0.026	0.004	0.005	0.040
LEVERAGE			0.015	0.008	0.088***	0.213***	−0.015	0.028	0.092***	−0.077***	0.045	0.028	−0.002	0.025
GROWTH				0.152***	0.049*	−0.010	0.391***	0.28***	0.321***	−0.086***	0.064**	0.011	−0.012	0.098***
FRSALE					0.094***	−0.036	0.036	0.064**	0.116***	−0.095***	0.047	0.047	−0.041	0.132***
CFTURN						0.001	0.034	0.016	0.076***	−0.093***	0.014	0.091***	−0.034	0.115***
CHGNI							−0.007	−0.007	0.017	−0.050*	0.056*	−0.021	0.048*	−0.039
SIZE								0.803†	0.234***	−0.071	0.070*	−0.014	−0.021	0.077***
SUBSIDIARY									0.246***	−0.115***	0.071**	0.036	−0.076***	0.089***
BRDSZ										−0.164***	0.200***	−0.093***	0.050*	0.072***
EXE_DIR											−0.731***	−0.145***	0.081***	−0.159***
GREY_DIR												−0.568***	0.040	0.051*
IND_DIR													−0.157***	0.118***
OWNERSHIP														−0.187***

*, **, and *** represent the traditional significance level of 10%, 5%, and 1%, respectively.

GROWTH is the log of the difference between net sales for two subsequent years (t-1 and t), SIZE03 and SIZE04 take natural log of the book value of total assets for 2003 and 2004, respectively. Other variables are defined as in Table 2.2.

growth, and cash flow turnover, but there were no significant associations with a number of foreign subsidiaries or size. As far as corporate governance characteristics, 2005-adopters are significantly associated with larger boards (BRDSZ), lower level of corporate disclosure (higher proportion of grey directors on board (GREY_DIR), and a lower proportion of independent directors on their board (IND_DIR)).

Logit Test Results

To test the hypotheses, I employ the logistic regression model, and the results of the tests are presented in the panels of Table 2.4.[25] In particular, the results of the logistic regression in Panel A of Table 2.4, consistent with the Wilcoxon test, show that number of foreign subsidiaries, the choice of auditor, and size have a significant effect on the odds of becoming a voluntary adopter, but significantly smaller reported earnings and no significant results for the value and the percentage of foreign sales were found after controlling for industry and country fixed effects.[26] The results for corporate governance characteristics are not significant, except early adopters have smaller boards.

To check the results from Table 2.4, Panel A for the extenuating effects of national institutional environments on firm's characteristics, the sample has been partitioned into subsamples and then the differences in all tested firms' characteristics for different jurisdictions have been examined. When it comes to early adopters, the consistent significant support for the hypotheses can only be detected for British firms (Panel B of Table 2.4). The outcomes of the tests for voluntary adopters from other legal origins are conflicting. For example, for companies of Scandinavian origin, only number of foreign subsidiaries raises the odds of voluntary adoption, whereas for companies of French and German origins, the choice of auditor and size significantly affect the odds of voluntary adoption. French-origin early adopters also have smaller board size. Contrary to the results for companies of British origin, the Tobin's Q measured a year prior to the adoption remains insignificant for all companies of Continental European legal origins. These disparities are partly due to at least two factors. First, previously documented differences in how effectively national stock markets incorporate accounting information. Indeed, the findings reported by Morck et al. (2000) and Jin and Myers (2006) illustrate that stock markets around the world are not equally effective in incorporating firm-specific information. Second, as agency literature suggests (Himmelberg et al., 2004), in a case of highly concentrated inside ownership and imperfect investor protection, managers have strong ex-ante incentives for self-dealing (assets stripping) and assign a lower value to stochastic profits because they discount for idiosyncratic risk.

The analyses of the incremental effects of company characteristics of early IFRS adopters from both Panel A and Panel B of Table 2.4 provide

Table 2.4 Logistic regression results

Panel A: Voluntary adopters vs. non-adopters, 2004

Dependent Variable: Voluntary Adopters: 634 and Non-adopters: 1,042 n = 1,676

Variable	*Model 1*	*Model 2*	*Model 3*	*% Change in the Odds*
1	*2*	*3*	*4*	*5*
INTERCEPT	0.061	0.163	0.133	
	–0.01	–0.06	–0.04	
SUBSIDIARY	0.188	0.187	0.187	12.9
	(9.49**)	(9.42**)	(9.43**)	
FRSALES	0.185	0.18	0.185	0.7
	–0.62	–0.63	–0.65	
TOBINQ	0.028	0.028	0.023	
	–0.54	–0.53	–0.56	17.2
BIG4	0.3	0.295	0.296	61.3
	(3.06**)	(2.98*)	(3.00*)	
BRDSZ	–0.627	–0.631	–0.632	–21.8
	(12.22***)	(12.40***)	(12.48***)	
EXE_DIR	0.135			47.7
	–0.16			
IND_DIR			–0.097	
			–0.05	

GREY_DIR		−0.050		7.1
		−0.03		
OWNERSHIP	−0.001	−0.001	−0.001	
	−0.01	−0.01	−0.01	
CHGNI	−0.027	−0.027	−0.027	
	(7.26**)	(7.22**)	(7.19**)	
SIZE	0.187	0.187	0.187	
	(10.26***)	(10.19***)	(10.20***)	27.1
GROWTH	−0.018	−0.019	−0.019	-9.3
	−0.17	−0.1	−0.1	
LEVERAGE	0.194	0.194	0.194	
	−0.6	−0.6	−0.6	
CFTURN	0.006	0.006	0.006	0.7
	−0.76	−0.75	−0.76	
INDUSTRY	Y	Y	Y	
COUNTRY	Y	Y	Y	
Wald Chi-Square	356.62***	356.73***	356.75***	

(Continued)

Table 2.4 (Continued)

Panel B: Voluntary adopters vs. non-adopters by legal origin, 2004

Dependent Variable: Voluntary Adopters: 634 and Non-adopters: 1,042 n = 1,676

	German Origin	*% Change in the Odds*	*French Origin*	*% Change in the Odds*	*British Origin*	*% Change in the Odds*	*Scandinavian Origin*	*% Change in the Odds*
1	*2*	*3*	*4*	*5*	*6*	*7*	*8*	*9*
Voluntary Adopters (n)	38		296		153		147	
Non-adopters (n)	300		357		320		65	
INTERCEPT	–3.659		–0.070		–3.729		3.065	
	(7.59***)		–0.01		(11.86***)		–2.37	
SUBSIDIARY	0.375	35.1	0.051	4.8	0.241	24	0.394	46.8
	(2.92*)		–0.36		(4.97**)		(3.49*)	
FRSALE	–2.281	–66.2	–0.534	–42.3	0.852	145.2	1.016	66.2
	(5.56**)		–2.53		(4.20**)		–2.16	
TOBINQ	–1.233	–55.5	–0.134	–12.6	0.477	54.7	0.012	16.1
	(2.96*)		–1.69		(6.45***)		–0.06	
BIG4	0.936	115.11	0.477	62.9	0.376	48.6	0.46	47
	(2.64*)		(5.80**)		–0.74		–0.44	
BRDSZ	–0.294	–22.7	–1.003	–63.3	–0.529	–36.8	–1.943	–82.0
	–0.4		(21.56***)		–1.62		(4.77**)	
IND_DIR	–4.464×	2358	–1.080	–64.6	–0.016	–5.4	–2.076	–86.5
	–0.22		–1.37		–0.01		–1.67	
OWNERSHIP	0.011	0.7	–0.005	0.6	–0.014	–1.5	0.021	0.2
	–2.46		–2.51		–1.67		(3.82**)	

CHGNI	−0.019		−0.016		−0.059		−0.092	
	−0.66		−1.2		(3.39*)		−1.2	
SIZE	0.232		0.262		0.165		0.295	
	(2.96*)		(8.44***)		−1.91		−2.12	
GROWTH	0.062		−0.069		−0.042		−0.220	
	−0.17		−0.58		−0.13		−1.52	
LEVERAGE	−8.459		0.783		0.063		1.039	
	(6.31**)		(3.63*)		−0.01		−0.42	
CFTURN	−0.026	1.4	0.016	1.6	0.006	0.1	0.004	0.6
	−0.68		−2.24		−0.24		−0.02	
INDUSTRY	Y		Y		Y		Y	
Wald Chi-Square	49.36***		89.95***		76.54***		32.05	

(*Continued*)

Table 2.4 (Continued)

Panel C: 2005-adopters vs. postponers, 2005

Dependent Variable: 2005-adopters: 657 Postponers: 506 n = 1,163

Variable	*Model 1*	*Model 2*	*Model 3*	*% Change in the Odds*
1	*2*	*3*	*4*	*5*
INTERCEPT	–1.273	–1.094	–1.244	
	(3.95**)	–1.74	–2.3	
SUBSIDIARY	0.082	0.078	0.072	8.2
	–1.21	–1.09	–0.95	
FRSALE	0.521	0.48	0.502	148.4
	(3.23*)	(2.77*)	(3.00*)	
TOBINQ	0.297	0.293	0.293	26.6
	(14.03***)	(13.83***)	(13.79***)	
BIG4	0.117	0.096	0.09	–25.6
	–0.34	–0.23	–0.2	
BRDSZ	0.177	0.18	–0.196	142.8
	–0.63	–0.66	–0.78	
EXE_DIR	0.751			64.5
	(2.79*)			

IND_DIR			–0.270	–80.5
			–0.26	
GREY_DIR		–0.387		53
		–1.07		
OWNERSHIP	0.004	0.004	0.004	
	–1.11	–1.27	–1.28	
CHGNI	–0.005	–0.005	–0.006	
	–0.92	–0.99	–1.1	
SIZE	–0.114	–0.115	–0.112	
	–2.36	–2.41	–2.28	
GROWTH	0.22	0.215	0.214	
	(8.58***)	(8.32***)	(8.26***)	
LEVERAGE	–0.081	–0.087	–0.086	
	–0.07	–0.08	–0.08	
CFTURN	0.023	0.023	0.023	9.4
	(6.70***)	(6.56***)	(6.61***)	
INDUSTRY	Y	Y	Y	
COUNTRY	Y	Y	Y	
Wald Chi-Square	280.28***	280.60***	280.57***	

(Continued)

Table 2.4 (Continued)

Panel D: 2005-adopters vs. 2007-adopters by legal origin, 2005 n = 1,163

Dependent Variable: 2005-adopters: 657 Postponers: 506 n = 1,163

	German Origin	*% Change in the Odds*	*French Origin*	*% Change in the Odds*	*British Origin*	*% Change in the Odds*	*Scandinavian Origin*	*% Change in the Odds*
1	*2*	*3*	*4*	*5*	*6*	*7*	*8*	*9*
Mandatory Adopters (N)	226		253		130		48	
2007-adopters (N)	74		189		225		18	
Intercept	0.093		−2.241		−2.342		3.375	
	−0.01		(3.12*)		(5.17**)		−0.25	
SUBSIDIARY	0.131	15.3	0.493	61.1	0.082	5.2	−0.275	−1.7
	−0.64		(16.95***)		−0.57		−0.15	
FRSALES	0.749	84.2	0.883	41.3	0.141	42.5	−1.262	−6.3
	−1.59		(4.07**)		−0.08		−0.42	
TOBINQ	−0.032	−139.0	0.247	28.4	0.001	89.6	0.745	95
	−0.03		(3.31*)		−0.01		(3.57*)	
BIG4	−0.172	168.8	−0.496	−38.9	0.121	16.8	−1.067	−80.0
	−0.24		(3.51*)		−0.1		−0.27	
BRDSZ	−0.343	−30.9	1.33		−0.155	−25.69	−2.744	−8.92
	−0.84		(20.95***)		−0.13		−0.54	
IND_DIR	−3.388	−9.7	−1.912	−85.1	0.067	−6.6	−3.078×	−96.1
	−2.25		−2.34		−0.01		−0.98	
OWNERSHIP	0.005	4.1	0.008	0.8	0.005	6.18	−0.013	−5.8
	−0.81		(3.62*)		−0.21		−0.16	
CHGNI	−0.009		0.01		−0.014		0.068	
	−0.95		−0.1		−0.58		−0.26	
SIZE	−0.117		−0.286		−0.093		0.84	
	−0.67		(4.86**)		−0.4		−2.08	

GROWTH	0.35		0.254		0.116		−0.168	
	(6.11***)		(4.00**)		−0.67		−0.08	
LEVERAGE	1.101		−0.434		−0.467		5.711	
	−0.2		−1.11		−0.34		−1.83	
CFTURN	0.044	4.7	0.001	0.1	0.026	2.6	0.351	42.3
	(4.45**)		−0.01		(3.39*)		(4.86**)	
INDUSTRY	Y		Y		Y		Y	
Wald Chi-Square	40.10*		81.35***		34.39		10.37	

Upper number in each panel represents the coefficient estimate while the parenthetic number represents the statistic significance of the chi-squared test. *, **, *** represent traditionally statistic significance levels of 10%, 5%, 1%, respectively.

Dependent variable is a dummy variable as value one if a firm was an early or 2005-adopter and zero otherwise.

Voluntary adopters are defined as the firms that had already adopted IFRS in 2004 before the mandatory date.

Non-adopters are those companies that were not using IFRS in 2004.

2005-adopters are defined as the firms that adopted IFRS under mandatory requirement 1606/2002 in 2005. 2007-adopters are those companies that postponed the date of adoption until 2007 (Article 9, regulation (EC) 1606/2002).

Note that voluntary and 2005-adopters can be considered early in comparison with non-adopters and 2007-adopters, respectively.

TOBINQ is a firm's [(long-term debt + market value of equity – book value of common equity)/total assets] in t-1. LEVERAGE is a firm's long-term debt scaled by total assets in t-1. GROWTH is the log of the difference between net sales for two subsequent years (t-1 and t). SIZE03 and SIZE04 take natural log of the book value of total assets for 2003 and 2004, respectively. CFTURN is the cash flow turnover rate that is year-end cash balance scaled by net sales in the year t-1. SUBSIDIARY is a number of operating foreign subsidiaries of a firm. BRDSZ is the board size of the firm. EXEDIR is the number of directors—insiders. GREYDIR is the number of directors who are not identified as an insider or an independent director in the ORBIS database. INDDIR is the number of independent outsiders. EXE_DIR is the percentage of EXEDIR scaled by BRDSZ. GREY_DIR is the percentage of GREYDIR scaled by BRDSZ. IND_DIR is the percentage of INDDIR scaled by BRDSZ. OWNERSHIP is a percentage of a firm's shares owned by the immediate owners. BIG4 is a dummy equal to 1 if a firm's auditor is a Big Four accounting firm during a year prior to the adoption.

× We replace IND_DIR with GREY_DIR because annual reports of "postponers" identify no independent directors for the binary logistic model.

† To identify the incremental quantitative effects of the one unit increase in independent variables on the odds of becoming an early/2005-adopter, we used the following algorithm:

The odds of early adoption (EA) = probability of EA / 1 – probability of EA
The odds ratio = e^{coeff}
The percentage of increase in the odds of EA = (odds ratio – 1) × 100

For example, adding one foreign subsidiary will increase the logit of EA by .159 (Panel A), therefore
Odds ratio = e^{159} = 1.172, thus the percent of increase in the odds of early adoption by adding one foreign subsidiary is
= (1.172 – 1) × 100 = 17.2%. The results of this exercise are summarized in the columns of Table 2.4 identified as "% increase in odds."

evidence that (1) adding one foreign subsidiary is positively associated with becoming an early IFRS adopter by 12.9% for the overall sample, from the highest percentage for the firms of Scandinavians origin (46.21) to the lowest percentage for the firms of French origin (4.81); (2) a one unit increase in the Tobin's Q ratio increases the likelihood of early IFRS adoption by 17.2% for the overall sample, from the highest percent for the firms of British origin (about 55) to the lowest percent for the German-origin firms; and (3) using a Big Four auditor increases the likelihood of early IFRS adoption by 61.3% for the overall sample, with the highest percent for firms of German origin (115.11), and the lowest percent for firms of Scandinavian origin (46.96).

The results of the logit regression for the 2005- vs. 2007-adopters provided in Panel C of Table 2.4 report that the coefficients of FRSALE, TOBINQ, and GROWTH are statistically significant, but I did not detect any significant effect of the number of foreign subsidiaries and firm size on the odds of becoming a 2005-adopter.

The results of the tests on the extenuating effects of jurisdictions, provided in Panel D, show that for companies of French origin, higher business complexity, Tobin's Q, board size, and growth increase the likelihood of becoming a 2005-adopter, in contrast to firms of German origin. Higher managerial operating efficiency in generating cash flow raises the odds of becoming a 2005-adopter in all legal origins except French.

The analyses of the incremental effects of company characteristics on the likelihood of being a 2005- vs. a 2007-adopter show that adding one foreign subsidiary raises the odds of becoming 2005-adopter by 8.2% for the overall sample, from the highest percent for the firms of French origin (61.1) to the lowest percent for the firms of Scandinavian origin (–1.65); one unit increase in the Tobin's Q ratio raises the odds of 2005 adoption by 26.6% for the overall sample, from the highest percentage for the Scandinavian-origin firms (about 95) to the lowest percentage for the German-origin firms; using a Big Four auditor increases the likelihood of early IFRS adoption, from the highest percent for the firms of German origin (168.8), and the lowest percent for firms of Scandinavian origin (about 80).

Additional Tests

In the set of additional tests, I examine the effects of the levels of bureaucratic formalities in a country on previously received results (Table 2.5, Panels A and B). For the test, the overall sample has been divided using the levels of bureaucratic (administrative) formalities in business, measured on a scale from 1 to 3, as assigned by the Database of the Institutional Characteristics of 85 Developing and Developed Countries/2006. Following the grouping from this database, I assembled

Table 2.5 Level of bureaucratic formality

Panel A: Voluntary adopters vs. non-adopters by 2004 n = 1,676

	LEVEL 1	*% Change in the Odds*	*LEVEL 2*	*% Change in the Odds*	*LEVEL 3*	*% Change in the Odds*
1	*2*	*3*	*4*	*5*	*6*	*7*
Voluntary Adopters (n)	140		231		263	
Non-adopters (n)	29		580		433	
INTERCEPT	−1.916		−0.714		−3.414	
	−1.33		−1.42		(16.99***)	
SUBSIDIARY	0.87	138.7	0.129	13.7	0.214	22
	(7.40***)		−2.37		(6.22***)	
FRSALE	−1.895	−84.5	0.094	–	0.342	33.8
	−1.99		−0.09		−1.16	
TOBINQ	1.928	586.2	−0.061	−5.9	0.229	25.9
	(3.61*)		−0.43		(29.65***)	
BIG4	−0.605	−45.8	0.312	36.2	0.847	136.6
	−0.64		(2.78*)		(5.37**)	
BRDSZ	1.256	251.1	−0.836	−56.7	−0.425	−35.1
	−2.21		(16.59***)		−1.8	
IND_DIR	−2.617×	−92.6	0.192	21.3	−0.036	−7.9
	(2.96*)		−0.05		−0.01	
OWNERSHIP	−0.002	−2.0	−0.003	−3.0	0.001	−1.0
	−0.02		−0.69		−0.02	

(*Continued*)

Table 2.5 (Continued)

	LEVEL 1	*% Change in the Odds*	*LEVEL 2*	*% Change in the Odds*	*LEVEL 3*	*% Change in the Odds*
1	*2*	*3*	*4*	*5*	*6*	*7*
CHGNI	0.007		–0.003		–0.055	
	–0.01		–0.05		(4.41**)	
SIZE	–0.060	–43.4	0.119	12.7	0.214	23.9
	–0.11		–2.1		(6.69***)	
GROWTH	0.322		–0.017		–0.089	
	(3.08*)		–0.04		–1.28	
LEVERAGE	8.596		0.313		0.164	
	(3.63*)		–0.83		–0.08	
CFTURN	–0.011	–1.1	0.009	9.4	0.002	1
	–0.06		–0.69		–0.04	
INDUSTRY	Y		Y		Y	
Wald Chi-Square	24.38		81.54***		111.07***	

Panel B: 2005-adopters vs. postponers, 2005 n = 1,163

	LEVEL 1	*LEVEL 2*	*% Change in the Odds*	*LEVEL 3*	*% Change in the Odds*
1	*2*	*4*	*5*	*6*	*7*
2005-adopters (N)	8×	436		213	
2007-adopters (N)	97	154		255	
Intercept		−0.461		−1.206	
		−0.39		−1.73	
SUBSIDIARY		0.361	42.3	0.097	9.6
		(10.94***)		-0.97	
FRSALES		1.439	357.2	0.299	36.2
		(9.91***)		-0.61	
TOBINQ		0.35	46.5	0.451	57.5
		(4.68**)		(14.69***)	
BIG4		0.125	15.6	0.084	9.5
		-0.3		-0.06	
BRDSZ		0.166	16.4	-0.358	−135.5
		-0.4		-0.94	
IND_DIR		-4.288	-97.9	-1.009	-62.7
		(13.59***)		(3.26*)	
OWNERSHIP		0.004	4.1	0.009	0.9
		-1.1		-1.54	
CHGNI		-0.001		-0.010	
		-0.03		-0.45	
SIZE		-0.168		-0.007	
		(2.63*)		-0.01	
GROWTH		0.28		0.084	
		(6.68***)		-0.53	

(Continued)

Table 2.5 (Continued)

1	*LEVEL 1* 2	*LEVEL 2* 4	*% Change in the Odds* 5	*LEVEL 3* 6	*% Change in the Odds* 7
LEVERAGE		−0.410		−0.536	
		−1.18		−0.6	
CFTURN		0.014		0.011	
		−1.1		−0.93	
INDUSTRY		Y		Y	
Wald Chi-Square		94.00***		54.26*	

Upper number in each panel represents the coefficient estimate while the parenthetic number represents the statistic significance of the chi-squared test. *, **, and *** represent statistic significance levels of 10%, 5%, and1%, respectively.

The classification is based on the level of bureaucratic (administrative) formalities and by the number of entry barriers and labor-market regulations that affect a company's decisions to enter into an integrated market. Level of bureaucratic formalities is measured on a scale from 1 to 4. We used these scores in grouping countries by the level of administrative formality, Level 4 being countries with minimum or no formalities at all. Initially all scores are assigned by the Database of the Institutional Characteristics of 85 Developing and Developed Countries/2006. Institutional Profiles Database (www.cepii.fr/institutions/EN/ipd.asp). In our tests Level 1 consists of Spain and Italy, Level 2 includes Austria, Belgium, Finland, France, Germany, Greece, and Portugal, and Level 3 is comprised of Demark, Ireland, UK, Netherlands, and Sweden.

Dependent variable is a dichotomous variable with value one if a firm was an early or 2005-adopter or zero otherwise. Independent variables are previously defined in Table 2.4.

x Level 1 has only eight 2005-adopters vs. 97 postponers; it caused a quasi-completion in logistic regression, when many variables have no matched pair.

† To identify the incremental quantitative effects of the one unit increase in independent variables on the odds of becoming an early adopter, we used the following algorithm:

The odds of early adoption (EA) = probability of EA / 1 − probability of EA
The odds ratio = e^{coeff}
The percentage of increase in the odds of EA = (odds ratio − 1) x 100

For example, adding one foreign subsidiary will increase the logit of EA by .159 (Panel A), therefore
Odds ratio = $e^{.159}$ = 1.172, thus the percent of increase in the odds of early adoption by adding one foreign subsidiary is
= (1.172 − 1) x 100 = 17.2%. The results of this exercise are summarized in the columns of Table 2.4 identified as "% change in the odds."

countries in the subsamples by the levels of administrative formalities in business, where Level 3 includes countries with minimal or no formalities at all and minimum governmental involvement in business and capital allocation, and Level 1 includes countries on the other end of the continuum, with Level 2 in the middle. The results of the tests performed after disaggregating the sample by the levels of bureaucratic formalities in a country[27] suggest that in the countries with the least-rigid administrative environment (Level 3), a company with higher business complexity, Tobin's Q, choice of auditor, and size is more likely to become a voluntary IFRS adopter (Table 2.5, Panel A). Adding one foreign subsidiary increases the odds of early IFRS adoption for the Level 1 and Level 3 firms by 138.7% and 22.0%, respectively; a one unit increase in the Tobin's Q ratio increases the odds of early IFRS adoption by 586.2% for the Level 1 (highest level of bureaucratic formalities) firms and only by 25.86% for the Level 3 firms.

The results for the 2005-adopters vs. 2007-adopters (Table 2.5, Panel B) suggest that the majority of firms operating in the most rigid administrative environment (Level 1) postponed IFRS adoption until 2007 (97 firms out of 105). It caused a quasi-completion of the logistic regression, and thus the logit tests were performed only for Level 2 and Level 3 firms. A higher number of foreign subsidiaries, level of foreign sales, Tobin's Q, smaller size, and lower level of corporate disclosure significantly increased the probability of becoming a 2005-adopter for Level 2 firms. Only higher Tobin's Q was significant for 2005 adoption for Level 3 firms.

Other robustness tests not tabulated here include (1) the test without the UK and (2) the test without UK, Germany, and France, as they represent the three largest subsamples in the test. The results of all additional tests are consistent with those in Table 2.4.

Conclusions

This study examines the effects of corporate characteristics of firms in 14 EU countries on the timing of IFRS adoption. By the economic theory, I recognized three main purposes of accounting convergence: compatibility, interoperability, and promotion of economies of scale by efficient variety reduction. Thus, I identified the main characteristics of firms which would benefit from accounting standardization, that is, adopting a single set of accounting standards, such as IFRS, as (1) firms with fewer geographic or sector-related limits; (2) firms that do business everywhere in the world, raise capital from multiple stock exchanges, and have higher Tobin's Q; and (3) have better corporate governance practices. I hypothesize that the environment the firms operate in has an impact on the firm's decision to adopt IFRS vs. deferring the adoption. The results of this investigation support the initial conjecture. The number of foreign subsidiaries and Tobin's Q increase the likelihood of early IFRS adoption. In addition to the main findings, several additional findings related to the extenuating effects of jurisdictions and the levels of administrative formalities hold special importance. First, the results of the tests for the firms of British origin consistently support the hypotheses, which are mostly derived from theories emphasizing the decision-making needs of capital-market shareholders. British-origin early adopters have more foreign subsidiaries, a larger proportion of foreign sales, and larger Tobin's Q. Also, the level of corporate disclosure is the highest for firms of British origin (the proportion of grey directors is the lowest).

Results for Continental European firm origins are diverse. Among all variables tested, the following three appear to have a consistently positive effect on the chance of IFRS adoption in the manner and degree outlined: (1) adding a foreign subsidiary increases the likelihood of early IFRS adoption by 35, 4.8, and 46.8% for German-, French-, and Scandinavian-origin firms, respectively; (2) a Big Four auditor increases the likelihood of early IFRS adoption by 115, 62.9, and 47% for German-, French-, and Scandinavian-origin firms, respectively; and (3) increase in ownership concentration raises the likelihood of early adoption for the firms of a shared origin. There are mixed results for firm value as measured by Tobin's Q: higher Tobin's Q decreases the likelihood of early IFRS adoption for firms of German origin. Contrastingly, higher Tobin's Q has no impact on the likelihood of early IFRS adoption by firms of Scandinavian or French legal origin.

The analysis of the effects of bureaucratic formality levels on companies' choices regarding early IFRS adoption indicates that in countries with the strongest bureaucratic rules (Level 1), no explanatory variables have a positive effect on the odds of early adoption, except for the number of foreign subsidiaries and the Tobin's Q. It is consistent with previous findings suggesting that heavier regulatory environments are negatively correlated with firms' business decisions to enter the global market (Desai et al., 2003). The strong effect of Tobin's Q ratio on the odds of early IFRS adoption is consistent with the notion that Level 1 countries predominantly represent regulated markets with less competition, a division of labor, and opportunities for risk sharing and risk matching, and therefore higher costs of financial statement reconciliation associated with multinational equity listings. As a result, potential benefits from enhanced comparability of financial statements, and therefore incentives for convergence, are stronger.

In addition to the findings for early adopters, there is also evidence that firm characteristics also play a role in determining whether firms adopt IFRS in 2005 or delay the adoption. The results suggest that 2005-adopters have a higher percentage of foreign sales, Tobin's Q, and have a larger amount of total assets (Wilcoxon Median Pr. are significant on 0.01, 0.01, and 0.02 risk levels, respectively). For 2005- vs. 2007-adopters, a higher percentage of foreign sales, Tobin's Q, and rate of growth have statistically significant effects on the likelihood of adopting IFRS on time. Furthermore, higher managerial efficiency to generate cash increases the likelihood of 2005-IFRS adoption vs. postponing it. It is consistent with the initial prediction that a firm's business complexity and higher value positively impact the likelihood of IFRS adoption.

In conclusion, this study provides evidence that increases the understanding of a wide range of firm and environmental characteristics affecting accounting standardization. With these results in mind, policymakers can now better understand what companies benefit most from a positive network effect. And, thus, these findings should be helpful for regulators, exchanges, and jurisdictions to prepare for the increasing global convergence.

Notes

1. The theory of comparative advantage is generally attributed to David Ricardo's work *On the Principles of Political Economy and Taxation*. This theory received a great deal of attention during last several decades due to economic globalization (Carlton & Klamer, 1983; Fox, 1991; Bebchuk, 1992; etc.).
2. According to Accounting Regulation 1606/2002 EU companies were given an *option* to postpone IFRS adoption in two cases: (1) those that are listed on EU and non-EU stock exchanges and used US GAAP as a primary accounting standard, and (2) companies that trade only debt securities. The sample analysis shows that numerous firms that meet criterion 2 of Article 9 decided against the possibility of postponing IFRS adoption. Alternatively, the result obtained here suggests that a group of companies that had to adopt the IFRS in 2005 decided to postpone the adoption until later.
3. There are companies in the EU (some legal business forms or companies trading on the alternative market) that are not subject to the Accounting Regulation 1606/2002. Each member state could also extend the application of the IFRS Regulation through national law to permit or require the use of IFRS by the legal entity.
4. National levels of bureaucratic formalities are measured on a scale from 1 to 3. It assists in grouping countries by the level of administrative formalities (Level 3: countries with minimum or no formalities at all). The scores are assigned by the Database of the Institutional Characteristics of 85 Developing and Developed Countries/2006. Institutional Profiles Database (www.cepii.fr/institutions/EN/ipd.asp).
5. Countries included in the sample belong to the EU 15: Austria, Germany, UK, Greece, France, Ireland, Italy, Sweden, The Netherlands, Luxembourg, Belgium, Denmark, Spain, Portugal, and Finland. I omitted Luxembourg from the sample due to insufficient number of observations—only three public companies were available.
6. Level 1 (high level of bureaucratic formalities) includes Spain and Italy. Level 2 (average level of bureaucratic formalities) includes Austria, Belgium, Finland, France, Germany, Greece, and Portugal. Level 3 (low level of bureaucratic formalities) includes Denmark, Ireland, UK, The Netherlands, and Sweden.
7. Regulation (EC) 1606/2002 was effective on July 19, 2002 for the application of international accounting standards (IFRS).
8. Leuz and Verrecchia (2000) demonstrate that German firms that switch to either IAS or US GAAP exhibit lower percentage bid-ask spreads and higher

share turnover than firms using German GAAP. Daske (2006), however, following Leuz and Verrecchia (2000), fails to document lower expected cost of equity capital for German firms using IAS/IFRS or US GAAP in the period 1993–2002.

9. Previous studies (Leuz & Verrecchia, 2000; Daske, 2006; Daske et al., 2008) report mixed results related to the lower cost of capital and higher equity value for the firms that adopted IAS/IFRS or US GAAP.
10. Hail and Leuz (2006) calculated the implied cost of equity capital for different national markets. Raw data show very insignificant differences across the developed economies—the estimates for the US, UK, and German markets were 10.2%, 10.6%, and 10.1%, respectively. However, much more substantial differences emerge for smaller, less-developed economies such as Sri Lanka and Egypt, with figures of 17.0% and 25.3%, respectively.
11. Much of the early impetus for global accounting standards came from multinational companies whose subsidiaries had to report for some purposes (tax, local borrowing, local benchmarking) using local accounting regulations, but then convert and consolidate their statements into a different framework for reports on global operations in the market(s) where they were listed. I know no estimates of the costs of translation in such circumstances, but for companies such as ExxonMobil or HSBC, which operate in 40 and 79 countries, respectively, they must have been considerable when many of these countries operated idiosyncratic standards.
12. There is no consensus, however, on the effect of corporate governance practices on firms' values. Some studies (e.g., Comper et al., 2003; Cremers & Nair, 2005; Brown & Caylor, 2006) find positive association between corporate governance and firm equity valuation. Others, however (e.g., Paananen & Parmar, 2008), find that investors rely more on the book value of shareholders' equity and find no change in the overall increase accounting information's ability to predict future equity values after IFRS adoption by UK firms.
13. Following previous findings (Ding et al., 2006), I control for various firm-level internal corporate governance (CG) mechanisms for each group of adopters, presuming that CG mechanisms, which perceived to be instrumental in affecting companies' values (board composition: number and percentage of inside and independent directors; level of corporate disclosure: number and percentage of directors with undisclosed identity (grey directors); and the perceived quality of audit: employing a Big Four auditing firm as a company auditor) will probably show a significant association with early IFRS adopters. Such an inquiry can yield the important insights into the interpretation of the economic consequences of IFRS adoption studies.
14. Transaction costs describe the costs that two parties incur in doing business with each other. Transaction costs can take several forms, including the costs of ensuring that a particular supplier produces exactly what the customer wants.
15. This study tests the decision to adopt a new set of standards. Companies subject to the special regulatory environment should be omitted, as their decision making may be affected by certain rules and regulations.
16. Companies with fewer than three board members have no executive power.
17. I am aware of and accounted for the fact that 2005-adopters were required to restate their 2004 financial statements according to IFRS, when they filed their 2005 reports.
18. Initially, I also tested percentage of foreign assets as an identifier of geographical diversity and received significant results in all models. The results, not tabulated here, were consistent with those received for the percentage of foreign sales.

Because in the final run I use total assets as a measurement of a firm size, I had to exclude percentage of foreign assets variable from the final testing.

19. Initially, I also controlled for one-year market-to-book (MTB) ratio, five-year average MTB ratio, and ROA, net income before taxes (IBT), shares turnover, and market volatility in the logistic models, and I found no significant likelihood that any of these variables significantly associated with the company's decision to adopt IFRS early.
20. I also used country and individual countries' GDP growth to test fixed effect. The logistic results are qualitatively similar to the tabulated results.
21. These two factors are designed to operate for developed EU countries that share certain economic features. Including Eastern European EU countries requires the inclusion of other discriminating factors, such as degree of economic development, inflation, etc.
22. Institutional Profiles Database (www.cepii.fr/institutions/EN/ipd.asp). The database was built by researchers based at the French Ministry for the Economy, Industry and Employment (MINEIE) and the French Development Agency (AFD) based on a survey conducted by MINEIE and AFD agencies in the countries covered. It was then calibrated with the leading existing indicators (Transparency International corruption indicator, Reporters Without Borders indicators, Freedom House indicators, etc.) as regards common subject coverage. It was also compared with the views of experts who know the countries concerned. It was then amended accordingly.
23. For the descriptive statistics, I use two measures of a firm's size: sale (SALE) in million dollars, and total assets (TA) in million dollars.
24. The number of non-adopters in Panel A of Table 2.2 is different from the total number of the firms tested in Panel C of Table 2.2. The difference of 121 companies is due to the fact that those companies switched back to using their national GAAPs and postponed IFRS adoption until 2007.
25. These exploratory data analyses included tests for multicollinearity and normality. The results show no significant multicollinearity existing for the set of independent variables. The sample was also checked for normality using the Shapiro-Wilk W-test. It did not identify the presence of a "fat tailed" error distribution.
26. I also tested country and GDP/capita fixed effects. The results are qualitatively similar.
27. Level 1 (high level of bureaucratic formalities) includes Spain and Italy. Level 2 (average level of bureaucratic formalities) includes Austria, Belgium, Finland, France, Germany, Greece, and Portugal. Level 3 (low level of bureaucratic formalities) includes Denmark, Ireland, UK, The Netherlands, and Sweden.

References

Armstrong, C. S., M. E. Barth, A. D. Jagolinzer, and E. J. Riedl (2010), "Market Reaction to the Adoption of IFRS in Europe", *The Accounting Review*, Vol. 85, No. 1, 31–61.

Arthur, W. B. (1989), "Competing Technologies, Increasing Returns, and Lock-in By Historical Events", *Economic Journal*, Vol. 99, 116–131.

Ball, R. (2006), "International Financial Reporting Standards (IFRS): Pros and Cons For Investors", *Accounting and Business Research International Accounting Policy Forum*, 5–27.

Ball, R., and R. Kothari (2000), "The Effect of International Institutional Factors on Properties of Accounting Earnings", *Journal of Accounting and Economics*, Vol. 29, 1–51.

Ball, R., A. Robin, and J. Wu (2003), "Incentives versus Standards: Properties of Accounting Income in Four Asian Countries", *Journal of Accounting and Economics*, Vol. 36, 235–270.

Ball, R., and L. Shivakumar (2005), "Earnings Quality in U.K. Private Firms", *Journal of Accounting and Economics*, Vol. 39, 83–128.

Barth, M. E., W. R. Landsman, and M. H. Lang (2008), "International Accounting Standards and Accounting Quality", *Journal of Accounting Research*, Vol. 46, No. 3, 467–498.

Bebchuk, L. (1992), "Federalism and the Corporation: The Desirable Limits on State Competition in Corporate Law", *Harvard Law Review*, Vol. 105, 1435–1510.

Bhagat, S., and B. Black (2002), "The Non-Correlation Between Board Independence and Long-Term Firm Performance", *Journal of Corporation Law*, Vol. 27, No. 2, 231–273.

Biddle, G. C., and S. M. Saudagaran (1989), "The Effects of Financial Disclosure Levels on Firms' Choices among Alternative Foreign Stock Exchange Listings", *Journal of International Financial Management and Accounting*, Vol. 1, 55–87.

Black, B., and Kim, W. (2012), "The Effect of Board Structure on Firm Value: A Multiple Identification Strategies Approach Using Korean Data", *Journal of Financial Economics*, Vol. 104, No. 1, 203–226. DOI: 10.1016/j.jfineco.2011.08.001

Botero, J. C., S. Djankov, R. La Porta, F. Lopez-De-Silanes, and A. Shleifer (2004), "The Regulation of Labor", *Quarterly Journal of Economics*, Vol. 119, No. 4, 1339–1382.

Brown, L. D., and M. L. Caylor (2006), "Corporate Governance and Firm Valuation", *Journal of Accounting and Public Policy*, Vol. 25, 409–434.

Burgstahler, D., L. Hail, and C. Leuz (2006), "The Importance of Reporting Incentives: Earnings Management in European Private and Public Firms", *The Accounting Review*, Vol. 81, No. 50, 983–1016.

Cai, L., A. Rahman, and S. Courtenay (2014), "The Effects of IFRS Adoption Conditional Upon the Level of Pre-Adoption Divergence", *The International Journal of Accounting*, Vol. 49, 147–178.

Carlton, D., and J. Klamer (1983), "The Need For Coordination Among Firms With Special Reference to Network Industries", *University of Chicago Law Review*, Vol. 50, 446–465.

Chang, J., and H. Sun (2009), "Cross-Listed Foreign Firm's Earning Informativeness, Earnings Management and Corporate Governance Under SOX", *The International Journal of Accounting*, Vol. 44, No. 1, 1–32.

Chang, J., and H. Sun (2010), "Does the Disclosure of Corporate Governance Structures Affect Firms' Earnings Quality", *Review of Accounting and Finance*, Vol. 9, No. 3, 212–231.

Chen, C. J. P., Y. Ding, and B. Xu (2014), "Convergence of Accounting Standards and Foreign Direct Investment", *The International Journal of Accounting*, Vol. 49, 53–86.

Christensen, H. B., E. Lee, and M. Walker (2007), "Cross-Sectional Variation in the Economic Consequences of International Accounting Harmonization: The Case of Mandatory IFRS Adoption in the UK", *The International Journal of Accounting*, Vol. 42, No. 4, 341–379.

Coles, J. L., N. D. Daniel, and L. Naveen (2008), "Boards: Does One Size Fit All?", *Journal of Financial Economics*, Vol. 87, 329–356.

Comper, P., J. Ishii, and A. Metrick (2003), "Corporate Governance and Equity Price", *Quarterly Journal of Economics*, Vol. 118, No. 1, 107–155.

Cremers, K. J. M., and V. B. Nair (2005), "Governance Mechanisms and Equity Prices", *Journal of Finance*, Vol. 60, 2859–2894.

Daske, H. (2006), "Economic Benefits of Adopting IFRS or US-GAAP-Have the Expected Costs of Equity Capital Really Decreased?", *Journal of Business Finance & Accounting*, Vol. 33, Nos. 3–4, 329–373.

Daske, H., L. Hail, C. Leuz, and R. Verdi (2008), "Mandatory IFRS Reporting around the World: Early Evidence on the Economic Consequences", *Journal of Accounting Research*, Vol. 46, No. 5, 1085–1142.

Datta, D. K., M. Musteen, and D. A. Basuil (2015), "Influence of Managerial Ownership and Compensation Structure on Establishment Mode Choice: The Moderating Role of Host Country Political Risk", *Management International Review*, Vol. 55, No. 5, 593–613.

David, P. A. (1985), "Clio and the Economics of QWERTY", *American Economic Review*, Vol. 75, 332–337.

Dayanandan, A., H. Donker, M. Ivanof, and G. Karahan (2016), "IFRS and Accounting Quality: Legal Origin, Regional, and Disclosure Impacts", *International Journal of Accounting & Information Management*, Vol. 24, No. 3, 296–316, available at: https://doi.org/10.1108/IJAIM-11-2015-0075

Demsetz, H., and K. Lehn (1985), "The Structure of Corporate Ownership: Causes and Consequences", *Journal of Political Economy*, Vol. 93, No. 6, 1155–1177.

Desai, M., P. Gompers, and J. Lerner (2003), "Institutions, Capital Constraints and Entrepreneurial Firm Dynamics: Evidence from Europe", NBER Working Paper No. w10165.

Ding, Y., O. K. Hope, T. Jeanjean, and H. Stolowy (2006), "Differences between Domestic Accounting Standards and IAS: Measurement, Determinants, and Implications", *Journal of Accounting and Public Policy*, Vol. 26, 1–38.

Djankov, S., R. La Porta, F. Lopez-De-Silanes, and A. Shleifer (2002), "The Regulation of Entry", *The Quarterly Journal of Economics*, Vol. 117, No. 1, 1–37.

Dong, M. (2014), "Discussion of 'Convergence of Accounting Standards and Foreign Direct Investment'", *The International Journal of Accounting*, Vol. 49, 87–96.

Eisenberg, T, S. Sundgren, and M. Wells (1998), "Large Board Size and Decreasing Firm Value in Small Firms", *Journal of Financial Economics*, Vol. 48, 35–54.

Eshleman, J. D., and G. Peng (2014), "Do Big 4 Auditors Provide Higher Audit Quality after Controlling for the Endogenous Choice of Auditor?", *Auditing: A Journal of Practice & Theory*, Vol. 33, No. 4, 197–219.

Fama, E. F., and K. R. French (1995), "Size and Book-to-Market Factors in Earnings and Returns", *Journal of Finance*, Vol. 50, 131–155.

Fama, E. F., and K. R. French (1997), "Industry Costs of Equity", *Journal of Financial Economics*, Vol. 43, 153–193.

Fearnley, S., and S. Sunder (2005), "The Headlong Rush to Global Standards Stella Fearnley and Shyam Sunder Suggest a Monopoly Process May Not Be Most Efficient", *Financial Times* (October 27), 14.

Fox, E. M. (1991), "Harmonization of Law and Procedures in Globalized World: Why, What and How?", *The Antitrust Law Journal*, Vol. 60, 593–599.

Hail, L., and C. Leuz (2006), "International Differences in the Cost of Equity Capital: Do Legal Institutions and Securities Regulation Matter?", *Journal of Accounting Research*, Vol. 44, No. 3, 485–531.

Hail, L., C. Leuz, and P. Wysocki (2010), "Global Accounting Convergence and the Potential Adoption of IFRS by the U.S. (Part 1): Conceptual Underpinnings and Economic Analysis", *Accounting Horizons*, Vol. 24, No. 3, 355–394.

Harzing, A. W., and M. Pudelko (2016), "Do We Need to Distance Ourselves from the Distance Concept? Why Home and Host Country Context Might Matter More Than (Cultural) Distance", *Management International Review*, Vol. 56, No. 1, 1–34.

Hennart, J.-F. (2007), "The Theoretical Rationale for a Multinationality-Performance Relationship", *Management International Review*, Vol. 47, No. 3, 423–452.

Hennart, J.-F. (2011), "A Theoretical Assessment of the Empirical Literature on the Impact of Multinationality on Performance", *Global Strategy Journal*, Vol. 1, 135–151. DOI: 10.1002/gsj.8

Hermalin, B. E., and M. S. Weisbach (1991), "The Effects of Board Composition and Direct Incentives on Firm Performance", *Financial Management*, Vol. 20, No. 4, 101–112.

Himmelberg, C. P., R. G. Hubbard, and I. Love (2004), "Investor Protection, Ownership, and the Cost of Capital", World Bank Policy Research Working Paper No. 2834.

Hudson, J., and P. Jones (2003), "International Trade in 'Quality Goods': Signaling Problems for Developing Countries", *Journal of International Development*, Vol. 15, No. 8, 999–1013.

Hung, M. Y. (2001), "Information and Trading Risks in Global Investing: An Empirical Analysis of Research Location and Pacific Mutual Fund Performance", *Journal of International Financial Management and Accounting*, Vol. 12, 1–23.

Jensen, M. (1993), "The Modern Industrial Revolution, Exit, and the Failure of Internal Control Systems", *The Journal of Finance*, Vol. 48, 831–880.

Jin, L., and S. C. Myers (2006), "Around the World: New Theory and New Tests", *Journal of Financial Economics*, Vol. 79, 257–292.

Katz, M., and C. Shapiro (1985), "Network Externalities, Competition, and Compatibility", *American Economic Review*, Vol. 75, 424–440.

Kim, W. S., and E. H. Sorensen (1986), "Evidence on the Impact of Agency Costs of Debt in Corporate Debt Policy", *Journal of Financial and Quantitative Analysis*, Vol. 21, 131–144.

Klein, A. (1998), "Firm Performance and Board Committee Structure", *The Journal of Law and Economics*, Vol. 41, No. 1, 275–303.

Krivogorsky, V. (2006), "Ownership, Board Structure and Performance in Continental Europe", *The International Journal of Accounting*, Vol. 41, No. 2, 176–197.

Krivogorsky, V., and F. G. Burton. (2012), "Dominant Owners and Financial Performance of Continental European Firms", *Journal of International Accounting Research*, Vol. 2, No. 1, 191–221.

Krivogorsky, V., and G. Grudnitski (2010), "The Influence of Continental European, Country-Specific Institutional Effects on the Relationship Between Ownership Concentration and Company Performance", *Journal of Management and Governance*, Vol. 14, No. 1, 163–193.

Lang, L. H., and R. M. Stulz (1994), "Tobin's Q, Corporate Diversification, and Firm Performance," *Journal of Political Economy*, Vol. 102, No. 6, 1248–1280.

Lang, L. H. P., E. Ofek, and R. M. Stulz (1996), "Leverage, Investment, and Firm Growth", *Journal of Financial Economics*, Vol. 40, 329–356.

Lang, M. H., and R. J. Lundholm (2000), "Voluntary Disclosure and Equity Offerings: Reducing Information Asymmetry or Hyping the Stock?", *Contemporary Accounting Research*, Vol. 17, No. 4, 623–663.

Leuz, K., D. Nanda, and P. Wysocki (2003), "Earnings Management and Investor Protection: An International Comparison", *Journal of Financial Economics*, Vol. 69, 505–527.

Leuz, K., and R. Verrecchia (2000), "The Economic Consequences of Increased Disclosure", *Journal of Accounting Research*, Vol. 38 (supplement), 91–124.

Li, S. (2010), "Does Mandatory Adoption of International Financial Reporting Standards in the European Union Reduce the Cost of Equity Capital?", *The Accounting Review*, Vol. 85, No. 2, 607–636.

Liebowitz, S. J., and S. E. Margolis (1994), "Network Externality: An Uncommon Tragedy", *Journal of Economic Perspectives*, Vol. 8, No. 2, 133–150.

Liebowitz, S. J., and S. E. Margolis (1996), "Market Processes and the Selection of Standards", *Harvard Journal of Law and Technology*, Vol. 9, 283–318.

Lipton, M., and J. W. Lorsch (1992), "A Modest Proposal for Improved Corporate Governance", *Business Lawyer*, Vol. 48, 59–77.

MacKie-Mason, J. K. (1990), "Do Taxes Affect Corporate Financing Decisions?", *Journal of Finance*, Vol. 45, No. 5, 1471–1493.

Maskus, K. E., T. Otsuki, and J. S. Wilson (2005), "The Cost of Compliance with Product Standards for Firms in Developing Countries: An Econometric Study", Policy Research Working Paper Series 3590. The World Bank.

Mohammadrezaei, F., N. Mohd-Saleh, and B. Banimahd (2015), "The Effects of Mandatory IFRS Adoption: A Review of Evidence Based on Accounting Standard Setting Criteria", *International Journal of Disclosure and Governance*, Vol. 12, No. 1, 29–77.

Morck, R., B. Yeung, and W. Yu (2000), "The Information Content of Stock Markets: Why Do Emerging Markets Have Synchronous Stock Price Movements?", *Journal of Financial Economics*, Vol. 58, 215–238.

Myers, S. C. (1977), "Determinants of Corporate Borrowing", *Journal of Financial Economics*, Vol. 5, 147–175.

Paananen, M., and N. Parmar (2008), "The Adoption of IFRS in the UK", Working Paper, Available at SSRN: http://ssrn.com/abstract=1275805.

Pownall, G., and K. Schipper (1999), "Implications of Accounting Research for the SEC's Consideration of International Accounting Standards for U.S. Securities Offerings", *Accounting Horizons*, Vol. 13, (September), 259–280.

Ramanna, K., and E. Sletten (2009), "Why Do Countries Adopt International Financial Reporting Standards?", Working Paper. Harvard Business School Accounting & Management, Unit No. 09–102. Available at SSRN: http://ssrn.com/abstract=1357674.

Reddy, M. N. (1987), "Technology Standards and Markets: A Market Institutionalization Perspective", edited by H. L. Gabel, *Product Standardization and Competitive Strategy*, North-Holland, Amsterdam, 47–66.

Reese Jr., W. A., and M. S. Weisbach (2002), "Protection of Minority Shareholder Interests, Cross-Listings in the United States, and Subsequent Equity Offerings", *Journal of Financial Economics*, Vol. 66, No. 1, 65–104.

Rosenstein, S., and J. Wyatt (1997), "Inside Directors, Board Effectiveness, and Shareholder Wealth", *Journal of Financial Economics*, Vol. 44, No. 2, 229–250.

Runyan, B., and L. M. Smith (2007), "The Effect of Multinationality on the Precision of Management Earnings Forecasts", *International Journal of Accounting, Auditing & Performance Evaluation*, Vol. 4, No. 6, 572–588.

Swann, G. M. P., P. Temple, and M. Shurmer (2000), "The Economics of Standardization. Report for Department of Trade and Industry", Report available at: www.berr.gov.uk/files/file11312.pdf and References at: www.berr.gov.uk/files/file11316.pdf.

Teoh, S. H., and T. J. Wong (1993), "Perceived Auditor Quality and the Earnings Response Coefficient", *The Accounting Review*, Vol. 68, No. 2, 346–366.

Titman, S., and R. Wessels (1988), "The Determinants of Capital Structure", *Journal of Finance*, Vol. 43, No. 1, 1–19.

Verriest, A., and A. Gaerremynck (2008), "The Impact of Governance on IFRS Restatement Quality", Working Paper.

Williamson, O. E. (1998), "Transaction Cost Economics: How It Works; Where It Is Headed", *De Economist*, Vol. 146, 23–58.

Yermack, D. (1996), "Higher Market Valuation of Companies with a Smaller Board of Directors", *Journal of Financial Economics*, Vol. 40, 185–211.

Table 2.6 Description of variables

Variable	*Description*	*Comments*
Dependent Variables		
VOLUNTARY	Firm used IFRS before 2005	
2005	Firm adopted IFRS in 2005	
POSTPON	Firm postponed IFRS adoption after 2005 (2007-adopters)	
Independent Variables		
Business Complexity Proxies:		
SUBSIDIARY	Number of foreign subsidiaries	
FRSALE (%)	% of foreign sale scaled by total assets	
Firm Value:		
TOBINQ	Firms market value to the book value	Firm's [(long-term debt + market value of equity – book value of common equity)/total assets] in t-1.

Variable	*Description*	*Comments*
Control Variables		
Auditor:		
BIG4	Big Four auditor	Binary variable measured a year prior to the adoption = 1 if a firm uses Big Four auditor and = 0 otherwise
Board Size and Composition:		
BRDSZ (#)	Total number of directors	
INDDIR(#)	Number of independent directors	
IND_DIR (%)	% of independent directors	Number of independent directors to the total number of directors
EXEDIR (#)	Number of executive directors	
EXE_DIR (%)	% of executive directors	Number of executive directors to the total number of directors
GRDIR (#)	Number of directors with undisclosed identity	Used as a proxy for the level of CG disclosure
GREY_DIR (%)	% of unidentified directors	Number of unidentified directors to the total number of directors
OWNERSHIP (%)	Ownership concentration	
Other Variables		
CHGNI (%)	Measure of the impact of IFRS adoption on reported earnings	% change in NI during first year after IFRS adoption
SIZE	To measure the size of a company	As the descriptive statistics size is measured in $mln, for the regressions it is measured as Ln of Total Assets
SALE	To measure the size of a company	As the descriptive statistics size is measured in $mln, for the regressions it is measured as Ln of Sale
GROWTH	Growth	Ln {Sale in year t- (t-1)}
LEVERAGE (%)	Long-term bank debt scaled by net assets	Proxy to measure bank power
CFTURN	Cash flow turnover	Annual end of cash balances to annual net sale
INDUSTRY	Control for industry	

3 Change in Business Objective

Shareholder Value vs. Stakeholder Value Primacy Concepts

Victoria Krivogorsky

Introduction

The financial crisis of 2008 reinvigorated the discussion on business objective, and as a result, "enlightened shareholder value" (ESV) has been introduced as an alternative vision of the corporate purpose. Under ESV the attention to corporate stakeholders, including employees, creditors, customers, and local communities, is seen as critical to generating long-term shareholder wealth as a direct emphasis on serving shareholders' interests. Thus, this study re-examines a vision of the business objective and directors' duties that define the division between the shareholder-stakeholder models that have traditionally existed in the literature. With the initiation of the ESV approach, which has been statutorily introduced in the UK, the previously well-defined partition between two traditional models becomes blurry. Until not long ago, both the UK and the US were recognized as the countries where maximization of shareholder value (SV) has continuously been the traditional business objective for years. In this respect, the current departure from the shareholder model observed in the UK presents a unique opportunity to analyze changes in the corporate purpose.

This situation is especially exceptional for several reasons. First, the transformation of the shareholder welfare supremacy presumption became worthy of note when the notion of "customer-driven capitalism" was named in the business literature as a competitive model 40 years ago or so. Advocates of the customer-driven capitalism model have argued that SV maximization should give way to customer-driven capitalism, in which firms "should instead aim to maximize customer satisfaction" (Martin, 2010).[1] In this regard, Paul Polman, the CEO of Unilever, a consumer-goods giant, said to the *Financial Times* in March 2010, "I do not work for the shareholder, to be honest; I work for the consumer, the customer . . . I'm not driven, and I don't drive this business model by driving shareholder value." Second, because the new ESV model (adopted into UK law in the Companies Act 2006) does not represent a full departure from previously utilized SV model, nor does it exemplify an arrival to the stakeholder value (STV hereafter) model. Rather it remains in the middle position, bringing together goals and responsibilities of both models. In particular, it states that "corporations should pursue shareholder wealth with a long-run orientation that seeks sustainable growth and profits based on responsible attention to the full range of relevant stakeholder interests."[2] At the same time, it keeps shareholders' interests at the forefront of business objectives.

It seems that the ESV model was designed with the intention to be instrumental in overcoming managers' myopia in decision-making consistent with the SV model. Essentially, it focuses on generating SV, while having regard to the long-term external impacts of wealth generation (Keay, 2013). Third, this particular shift in UK corporate governance is exceptional because the law now impacts the organization of the corporate decision-making process in a way that it has not been seen before. The overriding goal of the law is to ensure that, when making decisions, directors are heedful of all matters which could feasibly have a bearing on the going concern of their company. To this end, the importance of the analysis presented here is much broader than just to record and acknowledge the institutional changes in the UK. This analysis is closely linked to the change in the business objective, and thus, directors' obligations associated with the introduction of ESV embedded in the law with far-reaching policy implications. For the most part, in this paper discussions on the pros and cons of SV vs. STV models in different institutional environments, and whether the SV model really failed, have been left aside.

In the world of normative theories of corporate social responsibility that define the role of a corporation, the question "Should companies seek shareholder value maximization or strive to serve the often-conflicting interests of all stakeholders?" has been debated for quite a while now. By extension, this question can also be seen as one that belongs to a normative theory of business ethics, since under the assertion of the stakeholder model dominant in Continental European relational markets, managers and directors are agents of *all* stakeholders and hence have a responsibility to ensure that the rights of no stakeholder are violated.[3] In other words, they have to offset the legitimate interests of all stakeholders when making decisions. The business objective, in this case, is not just profit maximization, but to balance profit maximization with the corporation's *long-term* capacity to remain in business, i.e., the going concern. In accord with this line of thought, Continental European countries show a long history of emphasis on the stewardship function of managers and directors and extend the decision-making power to the employees, called co-determination.

Contrary to this approach, under the premise of the shareholder theory, executives and managers of a corporation should make decisions rooted in the presumption of shareholder welfare supremacy that is not necessarily aligned with the other stakeholder's interests. The shareholder model dominated the Anglo-American (market-centered) type of market economies until recently. For the first time, along with SV maximization, the importance of stakeholder value was acknowledged and classified in *The UK's Company Law Review* (CLR) in 2001. The importance of this concept was reiterated when it was adopted into law in the Companies Act 2006 (CA2006),[4] and directors and managers were identified as company stewards. This change represents an important development in UK corporate governance (CG) and a clear move away from the shareholder model. All modifications in the concept of CG that came after enacting CA2006 have been consistent with the change in the perception of directors and managers role, and therefore their duties in a company.

The relevance of UK regulatory innovations analysis to American scholars and policymakers was established a long time ago. Indeed, the US and the UK share a common legal heritage, and their markets share important similarities historically characterized by dispersed ownership. Also, like in the US, the CG in the UK has traditionally been grounded in shareholder primacy. So, it was logical to see that the UK experience has served as a source for some recommendations published in the US in favor of increased shareholder voice (Bebchuk, 2005) with subsequent incorporation into the *NYSE: Corporate Governance Guide* in 2014.[5]

The Development of the ESV Concept: Timetable

Company Law Review Steering Group (CLRSG), established in 1998 by the UK Secretary of State for Trade and Industry, conceived the ESV concept while reviewing UK company law. CLRSG was in charge of developing the CLR project that consisted of four stages. In 1998 CLRSG published the scope of the CLR project with the first noticeable move toward the ESV model in it. In their pronouncements (1999, 2000a, and 2000b), CLRSG has offered several drafts of the CLR project for public discussions and published a final CLR Report in 2001. Before incorporating the ESV model into law, CLRSG summarized the proposed changes and later condensed them all in the CA2006, section 172.[6] Notwithstanding the ESV model's prompt development, the ESV approach did not see the legislative light of the day until late 2007. At that time, CA2006 was brought into force in stages, with the final provision commenced in October 2009. Financial crisis slowed down the work on regulatory changes related to the new approach. In November of 2016, the UK Department for Business, Energy, and Industrial Strategy (DBEIS) published the green paper *Corporate Governance Reform* (CGR) and once again endorsed the ESV model stipulations.[7] The green paper further discusses a "new approach to strengthen big business through better CG" and points out the inconsistencies in the existing conceptual framework (Department for Business, Energy & Industrial Strategy, 2016; CGR, 2016, p. 2).

The UK Financial Reporting Council (FRC)[8] in its response to the green paper, published in February 2017, proclaims its full support for the new developments in the area of "the interests of major stakeholders."[9] Also, in January 2017, FRC published *Developments in Corporate Governance and Stewardship, 2016* addressing the implementation of the ESV approach into CG. In particular, in this document, "FRC presents its assessment of the UK Stewardship Code and Engagement and spells out its future actions to foster the ESV model enactment."[10]

Corporate Objectives and Directors' Duties Under the SV and STV Models

The shareholder primacy and stakeholder models are two theories of corporate objectives, which have a far-reaching impact on CG and management responsibilities. These two theories are the normative doctrines of corporate social responsibility because they dictate a company's role in the economy. Also, they are also called the normative theories of business ethics, as the directors should make decisions which are consistent with the right judgment. Each method is designed to be applied in a distinctive economic setting of a "stock market" vs. a "social market" form of capitalism. In this regard, the literature has always explicitly recognized the existence of different "varieties of capitalism," with a particularly significant dichotomy between the Anglo-American (or "Anglo-Saxon," "stock market," or "shareholder") model and the "social market" (or "welfare," "relational," "stakeholder," or "Rhine") model (Albert, 1993; Hutton, 1995; Dore, Lazonick and O'Sullivan, 1999; Dore, 2000; Hutton, 2003). The two models have also been referred to as "liberal market economies" (associated with SV model) and "coordinated market economies" (associated with STV model), respectively (Hall and Soskice, 2001, p. 8). According to Hall and Gingerich (2009, p. 452) these terms describe a spectrum "where relations between firms and other actors are coordinated primarily by competitive markets" at one end, and "where firms typically engage in more strategic interaction with trade unions, suppliers of finance and other actors" at the other end. The notion of shareholder superiority, therefore, is that companies are private property, so directors should run a business to increase shareholders' wealth (sole objective) (Berle and Means, 1923, 1930). Contrariwise, the stakeholder theory assumes that companies are social institutions. Thus, directors should consider all stakeholders' interests by balancing conflicting interests between stakeholders and augmenting their benefits in their entirety (multiple objectives). There is no consensus in the literature so far on the advantages and disadvantages of sole vs. multiple objective approaches, and a subject of the directors' opportunism associated with either of them is still being debated. Advocates of the STV model argue that companies' activities have a strong impact on all elements of the society, and therefore it is not sufficient for companies to operate single-mindedly in the economic interests of only one interest group—shareholders—and to be accountable to them exclusively. In other words, companies as social institutions should have responsibilities not just to their shareholders but also to their employees, customers, and the general public. This philosophy came to be associated with the "social model" regimes of Continental Europe, with their insistence on incorporating the concerns of non-shareholder interest groups into the corporate decision-making process.

Traditionally, the literature equated liberal market economies with the Anglo-American model of capitalism, affirming that the US and the UK present "relatively 'pure' cases" of liberal market economies with clear defined solo company objective (Hall and Gingerich, 2009, p. 459). The disparity in goals between the SV and STV models decides the differences in CG, such as directors' duties. The financial crisis of 2008 reinvigorated the discussion on companies' and directors' responsibilities, causing certain reservations in the literature regarding the relative *laissez-faire* approach that existed before. The example of the UK that partially departed from the SV maximization model draws significant interest. The initial optimistic view of the robustness of the Anglo-American model evident in the business periodical publications right after the crisis was slowly changing to a discussion on potential changes in that model of CG consistent with the STV model. It seems that over a short period the discussion in the Anglo-American business literature became more receptive to the idea that the stakeholders' interests are also very important.

The Development of ESV Model

This evolution of the law on a company's objectives and directors' duties has happened because a conscious attempt was made, via the CLR process, to re-think the legal position of a company within the wider business and social environment. Traditionally in the UK SV maximization has been a primary objective with other objectives being ancillary to this core purpose. As a departure from this point of view, it was acknowledged that a company has an expansive impact on other elements in society, and thus, it is impossible to continue operating single-mindedly in the economic interests of their shareholders only and to be accountable only to them. In seeking a suitable model for the future, initially, two options had been considered: an ESV approach and a "pluralist" approach.

The pluralist approach covers much bigger ground when it comes to the companies' and directors' responsibilities in relation to external matters. This concept implies that companies and their directors should be kept accountable not only to their shareholders but to other, external stakeholders' interests, which might include environmental pressure groups and trade unions. Thus, under this approach, directors would be required to act in the interests of and be liable to a whole variety of interest groups that possibly could be given a priority over the interests of the company's shareholders. This approach, if it had been adopted, would have considerably modified the character of the companies as it would have compelled them to play an active role in the pursuit of broader social policy goals, by forgoing their own business objectives. In the end, the pluralist approach was deemed to be unreasonable because it subjected the interests of shareholders (owners) to external groups (non-owners) and impractical because it would expose the directors to the decision on how to balance often competing and conflicting interests.

The concept of ESV acknowledges that maximizing shareholder value was and should be the ultimate aim of a company. Nonetheless, corporate social responsibility and the role of company directors with regard to it should be adjusted within that concept. The ESV concept implies that shareholders should be entitled to expect that their interests are protected, and that companies, acting through their directors, should pay close attention to and address all issues that are likely to associate with good management. The concept concedes that a limited approach to the pursuit of SV, by means of immediate profit (manager myopia), was sought after at the expense of long-standing value and it was not conducive to "sustainable" wealth creation (Adams, 2017). The ESV concept is viewed as an attempt to reconcile shareholder and stakeholder interests while arguing that a wealth creation goal will be better served if companies are responsive to a wider group of dynamics than the single-minded pursuit of profit (Beattie and Smith, 2013). Accordingly, the legitimate SV maximization objective should be tempered by a direct recognition that any company's likelihood of success is dependent on its effective managing of the various risks that confront it.

The CLR Steering Group ultimately has developed its proposal for the reform based on the ESV concept that was subsequently endorsed by the British government (CLRSG, 2000a, 2000b, 2001). The new statutory provisions regarding the duty of directors to act in the best interests of their company are fully rooted in the ESV concept. Following the main premises of the ESV model, directors are expected to manage their companies' affairs in the interests of the shareholders and other related parties (stakeholders), not consider external parties (interest groups). With that being said, to satisfy the ESV "enlightened" component, the new law stipulates that directors' perception about "the best interest of their company" construct is anticipated to be affected by the consideration of a variety of "environmental" factors (Christopher, 2010; Barth, Cahan, Chen and Venter, 2017). In other words, the strategic framework laid down in CLR does not reject the shareholder value model, but concurrently defines a much broader, all-inclusive long-term view on managers' and directors' duties. In particular, it says

> It is in our view clear, as a matter of policy, that in many circumstances directors should adopt the broader and longer-term ("inclusive")

> view of their role. . . . But we do not accept that there is anything in the present law of directors' duties which require them to take an unduly narrow or short-term view of their functions. Indeed, they are obliged honestly to take account of all the considerations which contribute to the success of the enterprise. There is nevertheless considerable evidence that the effect of the law is not well recognized and understood.
>
> (The Strategic Framework, CLRSG, 1999, p. 40)

The Strategic Framework also outlines some of the options and the potential challenges waiting on the way to new directors' duties. It articulates the pros and cons of a new concept of directors' responsibilities in the context of British business culture, as well as the nature and extent of any changes required for implementation of the proposed modifications.

Reform of the Directors' Duties

According to CA2006, the primary way in which companies account for the conduct of their affairs to their shareholders and to broader society is via the legal requirements to prepare and publish annual accounts and reports. A company's directors are responsible for ensuring that it complies with its responsibilities in this regard. The CA2006 requires all private and public companies to prepare annual accounts (which should comprise a profit and loss account and balance sheet, with notes on those statements) together with a directors' report. Public companies that have a full listing in the UK or elsewhere in the EAA must, additionally, prepare a remuneration (compensation) report containing specified information on the company's policies and practices on the remuneration of their directors and senior staff. Companies are also allowed to prepare a summary financial statement based on the main accounts as an additional voluntary disclosure.[11]

During the discussion of the new duties in Parliament, numerous opponents of the new law argued that when directors comply with their long-standing legal obligation to act in the best interests of their companies, they always have sought to pay attention to all matters which could affect their company's long-term health. The ESV approach was already, therefore, *de facto* effectively practiced by responsible companies and there was no need to spell out specific responsibilities in this area in the law. They also argued that imposing strict rules on the decision-making process would introduce undesirable bureaucracy and increase the risk that directors might be sued for non-compliance with procedural obligations. A discrete view that acknowledges a change in society's expectations of responsible corporate behavior prevailed after all. In particular, it recognizes that no project to modernize a company law would be complete if it did not provide for some accommodation of the principles of corporate social responsibility.

CA2006 replaces and codifies certain existing common-law principles, such as those relating to directors' duties, and implements the EU's Takeover and Transparency Obligations Directives. The codified principles clarify company law in the interests of the great majority of directors as well as reflecting society's changing ideas of responsible corporate behavior. In particular, in all cases, directors should be aware that their decisions as to what course of action is in the best interests of their company are now to be made in the light of a standard set of "environmental" factors (Al-Tuwaijri, Christensen and Hughes II, 2004) This approach has been embraced in the statement of general duties. For those companies that already implemented this "inclusive" decision-making approach, the reform may mean little more than a need to ensure the proper documentation of the fact that the board has paid due regard to the matters in question.

The traditional notion of corporate benefit has been replaced with corporate social responsibility, one of the most controversial aspects of the new legislation. Under the old law, the duties imposed on company directors fell under three principal headings: the fiduciary duty, the duty of skill and care, and the statutory duty. The new provisions that codify the long-standing common-law duties of company directors are presented in sections 170–177 of CA2006. In these eight sections (which are referred to collectively as the statement of general responsibilities, here) common-law rules and principles are established and condensed into a series of concise statements. Most of them appear familiar, but there are some important innovations. Among them, S172 requires directors to promote the success of the company in a way that benefits shareholders, but there is now an additional list of non-exhaustive factors, such as the long-term consequences of their decisions on the interests of others (Section 172, CA2006).[12]

The provisions on directors' general duties do not, however, limit themselves to a simple re-statement of existing common-law principles. It would be fair to say, therefore, that the provisions of the Act in this area not only codify the more fundamental aspects of the established law on directors' duties but develop them further.

General Statement (Section 170, CA2006)

Section 170 defines that the various duties set out in the statement are owed by directors to their company. Each aspect of the report, therefore, needs to be viewed as signifying the directors' duty to their company as a collective body: no duty is owed under the statement to individual shareholders or to persons outside the company. This point is of particular consequence for the duty to promote the success of the company under section 172. Section 170(3) and (4) explain how the new statutory statement of duties is intended to relate to the established legal framework.

Sub-section (3) says that the new statement has effect in place of "certain" common-law rules and impartial principles as they apply to directors. By virtue of this, rules and principles, which for many years have defined directors' duties, are superseded by the corresponding provisions of the new statutory statement. This notwithstanding, sub-section (4) says that the duties which are set out in the statement are to be "interpreted and applied in the same way as common-law rules or equitable principles and regard shall be had to the corresponding common law principles and equitable principles in interpreting and applying the general duties."

Accordingly, while the conventional rules and principles that are superseded by the statement of general duties no longer have a direct impact, the accrued knowledge of the courts in defining directors' responsibilities over many years is likely to remain dominant for the way that the courts choose to interpret the new statutory provisions. The statement also makes clear that, while in general a person who ceases to be a director no longer has obligations under it, this will not be the case in two circumstances (section 170(2)). The first of these relates to section 175 (duty to avoid conflicts of interest) and the second to section 176 (obligation not to accept benefits from third parties). Both those exceptions are discussed in the following section.

Duty to Act Within Their Powers (Section 171 CA2006)

Section 171 says that a director must (a) act by the company's charter and (b) only exercise powers for the purposes for which they are conferred. The definition of the company's charter in section 17 of the CA2006 includes not only the company's articles of association but the resolutions and agreements specified in section 29. These include special resolutions passed by the company and any recommendations or contracts that have been agreed to or which otherwise bind classes of shareholders.

Section 171(a) requires a company's directors to (1) follow all the directions as to how the company's affairs should be organized and administered that are set down in the company's constitution (charter), and (2) to comply with any limitations laid down in the Constitution on what activities a company may validly engage in. The passage implies that it is essential that all directors familiarize themselves with the detailed contents of their own company's constitution.

Section 171(b) sets out the long-standing common-law rule (known as the "proper purposes doctrine") that directors' powers should be used only for the purposes for which they were bestowed. This doctrine was developed to ensure that directors, as agents of their companies with extensive powers to manage their affairs, apply their powers only to the great benefit of a company's principal, and for no other, improper purposes which are inconsistent with the interests of the company.

Duty to Promote the Success of the Company (Section 172 CA2006)

This is the single most fundamental requirement of the statement of general duties and is crucial to the performance of directors' responsibilities under the new legislation. The precise wording of section 172 caused more discussion than virtually any other clause in the bill during its passage through Parliament and its full effect will, inevitably, only become known after it has been tested in the courts. The following paragraphs review its essential content. Although section 172 is presented in the legislation as a single, integrated measure, there are effectively two, but interlinking, parts to it. These two parts are discussed separately next.

Part 1, statement of objective 6.31, states that a director must act in the way that he or she considers, in good faith, would be most likely to promote the success of the company for the benefit of its members as a whole. This passage codifies, but with some potentially significant changes to terminology, the long-standing common-law position that directors must act in a way that they themselves, acting in good faith, consider to be conducive to the interests of their company. Authentic ("in good faith") business oversights or failures will not give grounds for claims of negligence against them. The intention of the government in formulating the new statutory statement was to reiterate this basic position.

There are three critical elements in Part 1 of the statement. The first is the phrase "considers, in good faith." The latter suggests that, as long as they act honestly and in a way which is mindful of their responsibilities, directors have the right to use discretion and judgment in the exercise of their decision-making powers. The second key element is the reference to directors' obligation to make decisions that are most likely to promote the "success" of their company. This term, which is not defined in the Act, was chosen to appear in the statement rather than the long-standing common-law concept of acting in the company's "interests." Some have voiced doubts as to whether the two concepts are the same, and whether the new term will be interpreted as such by the courts in due course. But "success" would appear to imply, at least, the achievement of whatever objectives the company concerned has set for itself, whether they be financial, strategic, or otherwise. Explanatory notes prepared by the Department of Trade and Industry (DTI) and published along with the Act convey the government's intention that "the decision as to what will promote the success of the company, and what constitutes such success, is one for the director's good faith judgment." The third key element of Part 1 of the statement is that directors must seek the success of their company "for the benefit of its members as a whole." This suggests that the aim should be to achieve "success" for the company—however this is determined—which can be viewed as such and shared in by the generality of the company's membership, and not just by some of them.

Part 2 of section 172 incorporates the gist of the ESV concept (the ESV provisions), recommended by the CLR and already discussed. As already stated, the first and second parts of section 172 need to be looked at as an integrated whole. This part of the statement gives rise to two practical questions. First, what does "have regard" to the various factors mean? And second, how are directors supposed to resolve any conflict which might arise from the specified factors?

The term "have regard" is, again, not defined in the Act and no indication is provided as to what weight should be given to individual factors. The explanatory notes only make the point that "it will not be sufficient to pay lip service" to the specified factors. They add, however, that in "having regard to" the specified factors their conduct must meet the test of reasonable care, skill, and diligence which is set out in section 174. There is, therefore, no instruction as to exactly what treatment is expected to be given to these factors in the decision-making process. What seems clear, however, is that directors cannot be expected to make decisions that favor all of the specified interests at all times, because in some cases interests may conflict with each other. For example, a decision to size down an inefficient company in an area of high unemployment might have an adverse impact on the local community where the factory was situated; it could damage the economic interests of suppliers, and it would certainly be against the interests of the company's employees. The directors' decision to cut the company's losses, however, might be in the long-term economic interests of the company and safeguard the position of the remainder of the company's workforce.

Second, companies which are involved in ethically controversial lines of business should "have regard" to maintaining high standards of business conduct. As those companies also have shareholders, employees, and suppliers, their interests must be taken into account too. So, it seems that the term "have regard" in this context is meant to require directors to be systematically aware of and take into account all factors that may affect the company's interests in respect of a particular matter, and in the decision-making process. But this should not be done in isolation and should always be done in the broader context of deciding whether a particular course of action would be likely to promote the success of the company.

Directors might become at most risk of violating their duty under section 172 if, as a result of failing to pay adequate attention to any of the factors addressed in Part 2, they make decisions that prove evidently unsuccessful in business terms. For example, a company may fail to put in place adequate environmental protection controls, which results in pollution, death, or injury to employees or third parties and, consequently, loss of revenue and consumer confidence in the company. Directors might also be at risk of breaching their responsibilities if they allow their company to engage in illicit business practices that lead to bad publicity for the company, regulatory or criminal action against it and, thus, adverse consequences for the company's business interests.

Complying with the new decision-making procedure is a very important aspect of section 172 as far as individual directors are concerned. The Act, though, is not explicit about how directors should record the fact of their compliance for future reference and how boards of directors should reflect their agreement (or otherwise) in board minutes. There are two distinct opinions on these issues. One suggests that since minutes of board meetings will usually only record decisions, and seldom record every single factor that was considered in the course of arriving at those decisions, section 172 will have no effect on the amount of detail recorded in minutes. The second opinion argues that as the purpose of the Act is to introduce a more significant measure of structure and formality into the decision-making process: the directors should defend their actions by producing evidence that they were striving to comply with the statutory procedure. Thus, companies may find it safer to include at least a standard reference to the fact that they have followed the decision-making provisions in section 172 in respect of their deliberations in their minutes. As a number of factors discussed in section 172 are competing and mutually exclusive, the minutes become a source document for directors' defense of their actions. For example, consider the interests of the company's employees against the impact of the company's operations on the environment. Directors may feel it useful to record the reasons why that particular option was considered to be more likely to promote the success of the company.

Duty to Exercise Independent Judgment (Section 173 CA2006)

This section says that a director must use independent discretion. There are two caveats to this basic position. First, the duty to exercise independent judgment is not infringed if the director acts by an agreement duly entered into by the company which restricts the future exercise of discretion by the directors. And second, the duty is not infringed if the directors act in a way that is authorized by the company's constitution. These two caveats enable a company's shareholders, if they see fit, to exert some measure of control over the directors' powers of discretion.

Duty to Exercise Reasonable Care, Skill, and Diligence (Section 174 CA2006)

This is the section of the obligations that identifies the standard of competence, which directors are expected to meet in the course of carrying out their functions. While, as with other areas of the statement of general duties, the Act codifies existing principles of the common law, this section is noteworthy because in addition to diligence it incorporates into the Act a higher standard of skill and care, as a developing theme of the common-law in recent years.

The duty to exercise diligence (a term which equates to conscientiousness and attentiveness) was a part of directors' duties for a long time. It is used in this context to refer to the responsibility of directors to take an active interest in ensuring that the affairs of their company are properly looked after. The wrongful trading provisions have had obvious ramifications for the standard of diligence. Those provisions reflect the rule that directors owe a personal responsibility to their company's creditors where they allow their company to continue trading beyond the point where they know that their company will not be able to avoid insolvent liquidation. Directors who take such little interest in the ongoing financial state of their company are considered incapable of making informed decisions about its affairs and will accordingly put themselves at risk of assuming personal liability.

Very relevant to the issue of diligence over the years has been the extent to which the law expects directors to attend to matters themselves, as opposed to delegating responsibilities to others. This is clearly a crucial matter for all directors, whatever the size of their company. In large, multinational companies, the scale and complexity of the business, the need for quick decision-making, and the high level of regulatory supervision make it impractical for directors to function effectively without there being a substantial delegation of authority downwards from the board. The directors of small companies will invariably know a great deal about their particular line of business but may not know much about other areas of business management. So, they will be dependent on the services of others. Accordingly, the law has long accepted that it is permissible for directors to delegate at least some responsibilities to others. In any situation whereby directors place reliance on the input of others, the provision requires them to take adequate steps to ensure the competence and trustworthiness of a person(s) they delegated to their functions.

In addition to diligence, section 174(1) now states that a director must exercise reasonable care and skill. It also adds that the requirement means that care, skill, and diligence should be exercised by a reasonably diligent person. Accordingly, there is a basic obligation under the Act for directors to carry out their duties consistent with the broadly framed benchmark set out in section 174(1) named a "reasonable" level of care, skill, and diligence. The use of the term "reasonable" ensures that the benchmark of conduct is not set unrealistically high and does not discourage people from forming companies and becoming directors. Thus, a director will be expected to act according to the knowledge, skills, and experience that he or she actually has. It allows the same basic test to be applied to all individual directors, who probably come from many different backgrounds, and judge them by the reference to his or her background, qualifications, and experience. Under this test, where a director has particular professional or business skills, for example as a qualified accountant, that will have a bearing on whether the standard of skill and diligence he or she displays in practice, both generally and in respect of specific matters, is "reasonable" and thereby meets the statutory test. According to section 174(2)(a), a director will be expected to act in a way which is appropriate for the position he or she occupies. The standards expected of a director under both the objective and subjective criteria will be subject to the "reasonably diligent person" test. Directors who have no specialist knowledge, skills, or experience will not be entitled to use that fact as a justification for not showing a measure of diligence in the way that they approach the conduct of their functions.

In summary, the duty in section 174 is sufficiently flexible for a modest test of skill and care to be applied to all directors, albeit one which incorporates at the same time scope for individual directors to be judged by reference to their backgrounds, circumstances, and specific functions.

It should be noted that, while much of CA2006 is concerned with creating differential rules as between public companies and private companies, section 174—as with the other elements of the statement of general duties—applies equally to directors of all companies, regardless of the size or type of their company or the nature of the business that a company carries on. The terms of the section are designed to be sufficiently broad and capable of application to directors of vastly different backgrounds and functions and to the full range of limited companies. As already stated, there is no basis by which persons are tested on their knowledge or competence before they are allowed to be appointed as directors; subject to the restrictions on eligibility, any person may be a director of a company.[13] Once a person becomes a director, however, the law will expect him or her to act by the legal standard. Thus, all prospective directors should ensure that they are aware of what the law requires them to do and the rule of conduct which is expected of them.

Duty to Avoid Conflicts of Interest (Section 175 CA2006)

Under this section, a director must avoid a direct or indirect conflict of interest with the company. This provision faithfully incorporates the long-standing common-law rule that directors, as persons with fiduciary responsibilities, must respect and never abuse the trust and confidence a company places in them. In other words, directors should strive to ensure that the collision of interests never transpires, but in case it does, the interests of the company must be placed first. Section 175 requires a director to avoid not only adverse situations but also a condition that "possibly may conflict" with the director's duty to the company. Thus, the director is obliged to consider whether his outside interests are likely to give others the impression that there may be a conflict. The common-law rule on avoiding conflict of interest has been applied many times over the years in cases involving directors that profit from business opportunities undermining their company's success.

A director may not resolve a conflict of interest by merely resigning—this principle is now expressly incorporated into the statement of general duties. Under section 170(2)(a), the duty to avoid conflicts continues to apply to a director after retirement from office "as regards the exploitation of any property, information or opportunity of which he became aware at a time when he was a director." Accordingly, after leaving a company, directors still owe that company a duty not to profit from property, information, or opportunity that came their way during their time in office, and the company may again take legal action against any director it believes to be in breach.

There are two exceptions to the primary duty in section 175(1) to avoid conflicts. First, it does not apply to conflicts of interest arising about a director's transactions or arrangements with his or her own company; these specific situations are addressed separately in sections 177 and 182 CA2006. Second, the duty will not be breached by the director if the case "can't reasonably be regarded as being likely to give rise to a conflict of interest" or if the matter has been authorized by the directors by the provisions of section 175(5).[14]

The procedure for authorization of potential breaches of section 175 is different for private and public companies. In the case of a private company, the directors may authorize their involvement in a situation that risks breaching section 175 as long as there is nothing in the company's constitution that invalidates their giving such authorization. In a public company, the directors may give approval only if the company's law expressly gives power to them to do so. So, in the case of a private company, if the articles are silent on this matter, the directors may grant authorization, while in a public company silence means that they may not. In both cases, a director who is the subject of a proposed authorization resolution must not be taken into account for quorum purposes, and neither may his or her vote be taken into account.

Duty Not to Accept Benefits From Third Parties (Section 176 CA2006)

Under section 176, a director must not receive a benefit from a third party which is conferred because of (a) his or her being a director or (b) his or her doing (or not doing) anything as a director. This rule is intended to ensure that a director is not distracted from performing his or her duty to the company by rewards offered for doing general things. By virtue of section 176(4), however, there will be no breach of duty if the acceptance of the benefit by the director cannot reasonably be regarded as likely to give rise to a conflict of interest, so immaterial benefits and those which are entirely unrelated to the affairs of the company may be accepted. For section 176 CA2006, a third party is any person other than the company, an associated company, or a person acting on behalf of the company or the associated company.

Duty to Declare an Interest in Proposed Transactions or Arrangements (Section 177 CA2006)

A director must announce to the other directors any situation in which he or she is in any way, directly or indirectly, interested in a proposed transaction or arrangement with the company. This rule is intended to reinforce the rule against conflicts of interest by ensuring that directors are transparent about personal interests which might affect their judgment or which might be seen to modify it. Any declaration required under section 177 must be made in advance of the company entering into the transaction or arrangement. The director may make it at a formal meeting of the directors or by written notice of an interest in a transaction or arrangement given to fellow directors. A director is not required to declare a benefit under section 177 of the other directors are aware of it (or ought reasonably to be aware of it) and if the interest concerns the terms of his or her service contract which have been or are to be considered by the directors or a committee of the board set up for the purpose (such as a Remuneration Committee). Disclosure, where required, must be made to all the other directors.

Conclusions on the Statement of General Duties

The introduction of the statement of general duties, as discussed in this chapter, is highly significant for the way that directors are expected to act and for how they account for their actions to their company. This is for two reasons. First, the Act introduces new rights for shareholders to take legal action against the directors of their company for alleged breach of their duties to the company. The courts will approach any such actions, in part, by weighing up whether the directors concerned have lived up to their duty to promote the success of their company under section 172. Second, companies (other than small companies) are required under the Act to prepare and publish a "business review" as part of their annual accounts and report. The overriding purpose of this review is to help the company's members to assess how the directors have performed their duty under section 172. Accordingly, the combination of section 172 and the duty to report via the business review becomes the essential yardstick of corporate accountability. The exercise of codifying the common-law duties may or may not make it easier for companies and their directors to operate as the law expects them to.

On the one hand, the general rules on directors' duties have been set out succinctly and in one place. This is consistent with the Law Commissions' original aim for the codification process to serve an educational purpose. On the other hand, the way that the government has gone about the process of codification has led to the adoption, in some cases, of different terminology to that used in the established common-law rules, and there is also some unhelpfully loose wording—for example, in section 172 directors are legally obliged to have regard to "other matters." In due course, it can only be for the courts to determine the real extent to which the new provisions have resulted in substantial changes to what the law requires from directors.

Notes

1. Martin, R. 2010. *Harvard Business Review*. January-February 2010 issue. https://hbr.org/2010/01/the-age-of-customer-capitalism
2. Paul Polman, Financial Times in March 2010, www.ft.com/content/2209d63a-d6ae-11e7-8c9a-d9c0a5c8d5c9
3. The two alternatives are defined as "enlightened shareholder value" and "pluralism."
4. The Company Law Review (CLR) began in March 1998. The Final Report was issued in June 2001 but continued through various parliamentary stages before the new act became law in November 2006. Provisions relating to directors' duties, which are a main area of interest of this study, came into force on October 1, 2007.
5. See www.nyse.com/publicdocs/nyse/listing/NYSE_Corporate_Governance_Guide.pdf
6. The Company Law Review (CLR) began in March 1998. The Final Report was issued in June 2001 but continued through various parliamentary stages before the new act became law in November 2006. Provisions relating to directors' duties came into force on October 1, 2007.
7. A green paper is a consultation paper designed to initiate feedback on broad policy proposals. The green paper *Corporate Governance Reform* is the latest government effort to use corporate governance reform as a vehicle to bolster trust and accountability between businesses, shareholders, and stakeholders. Specifically, the DBEIS position focuses on strengthening three aspects of corporate governance: transparency and accountability surrounding executive pay; business engagement with a wider group of stakeholders; and corporate governance in large privately held businesses. The deadline for public responses to the *Corporate Governance Reform* green paper was set for February 17, 2017.
8. FRC is the UK's independent regulator responsible for promoting high-quality corporate governance and reporting to foster investment. The FRC sets the UK Corporate Governance and Stewardship Codes and UK standards for accounting and actuarial work; monitors and takes action to promote the quality of corporate reporting; and operates independent enforcement arrangements for accountants and actuaries. As the Competent Authority for audit in the UK, the FRC sets auditing and ethical standards and monitors and enforces audit quality.
9. See www.frc.org.uk/news/february-2017/frc-responds-to-green-paper-on-corporate-governance.
10. "The FRC is prepared to assist the government by considering ways in which it can support legislative changes the government makes on these topics. We

also plan to consult on revisions to the UK Corporate Governance Code, the Guidance on Board Effectiveness and the Guidance on the Strategic Report. The consultations will take into account our work on culture and succession planning, the EU Non-Financial Reporting Directive and wider corporate governance changes in light of feedback to the government's Green Paper, 2016." See www.frc.org.uk/directors/corporate-governance-and-stewardship/uk-corporate-governance-code; www.frc.org.uk/getattachment/ca1d9909-7e32-4894-b2a7-b971b4406130/Developments-in-Corporate-Governance-and-Stewardship-2016.pdf#page=10&zoom=auto,-158,842.

11. In keeping with the aim behind the company law reform process of achieving a clearer distinction between the law as it applies to small private companies and the law that applies to other companies, the Act creates a separate reporting regime for "small companies," as well as reserving the most extensive reporting and disclosure requirements for "quoted companies."
12. See www.legislation.gov.uk/ukpga/2006/46/pdfs/ukpga_20060046_en.pdf.
13. Note that listed companies are required by the Listing Rules of the London Stock Exchange to ensure that the directors collectively have appropriate expertise and experience for the management of the business.
14. Either of these avenues might be used to validate a director's dealings post-retirement so as to enable him or her to avoid infringing the basic duty.

References

Adams, C. A. (2017). Conceptualising the Contemporary Corporate Value Creation Process. *Accounting, Auditing & Accountability Journal*, *30*(4), 906.

Albert, M. (1993). *Capitalism against Capitalism*. Retrieved from https://books.google.com/books?id=dBDsAAAAMAAJ

Al-Tuwaijri, S. A., Christensen, T. E., & Hughes II, K. E. (2004). The Relations among Environmental Disclosure, Environmental Performance, and Economic Performance: Simultaneous Equations Approach. *Accounting, Organizations, and Society*,*29*(5-6), 447–471.

Barth, M. E., Cahan, S. F., Chen, L., & Venter, E. R. (2017). The Economic Consequences Associated with Integrated Report Quality: Capital Market and Real Effects. *Accounting, Organizations and Society*, *62*, 43–64.

Beattie, V., & Smith, S. J. (2013). Value Creation and Business Models: Refocusing the Intellectual Capital Debate. *British Accounting Review*, *45*(4), 243–254.

Bebchuk, L. A. (2005). The Case for Increasing Shareholder Power. *Harvard Law Review*, *118*(3), 836–884.

Berle, A. A., & Means, G. C. (1923). *The Modern Corporation and Private Property*. (2nd ed.). New York: Harcourt, Brace, and World, 1967.

Berle, A. A., & Means, G. C. (1930). Corporation and Public Investor. *The American Economic Review*.

Christopher, J. (2010). Corporate Governance: A Multi-Theoretical Approach to Recognizing the Wider Influencing Forces Impacting on Organizations. *Critical Perspectives on Accounting*, *21*(8), 683–695.

CLRSG (Company Law Review Steering Group). (1999). *Modern Company Law for a Competitive Economy: The Strategic Framework*. London: Department of Trade and Industry.

CLRSG. (2000a). *Modern Company Law for a Competitive Economy (5): Developing the Framework*. London: Department of Trade and Industry.

CLRSG. (2000b). *Modern Company Law for a Competitive Economy (8): Completing the Structure*. London: Department of Trade and Industry.

CLRSG. (2001). *Modern Company Law for a Competitive Economy: Final Report*. Volumes 1 & 2. London: Department of Trade and Industry.

Department for Business, Energy & Industrial Strategy. (2016). *Corporate Governance Reform*. Retrieved from: https://assets.publishing.service.gov.uk/government/uploads/system/uploads/attachment_data/file/584013/corporate-governance-reform-green-paper.pdf

Dore, R. (2000). *Stock Market Capitalism and Welfare Capitalism: Japan and Germany versus the Anglo-Saxons*. Oxford: Oxford University Press. 280 pages.

Dore, R., Lazonick, W., & O'Sullivan, M. (1999). Varieties of Capitalism in the Twentieth Century. *Oxford Review of Economic Policy*, *15*(4), 102–120.

Hall, P. A., & Gingerich, D. W. (2009). Varieties of Capitalism and Institutional Complementarities in the Political Economy: An Empirical Analysis. *British Journal of Political Science*, *39*, 449–482.

Hall, P. A., & Soskice, D. W. (2001). *Varieties of Capitalism: The Institutional Foundations of Comparative Advantage*. Oxford, England; New York: Oxford University Press.

Hutton, W. (1995). *The State We're in*. London: Jonathan Cape.

Hutton, W. (2003). *The World We're in*. London: Abacus.

Keay, A. (2013). *The Enlightened Shareholder Value Principle and Corporate Governance*. New York: Routledge.

4 The Impact of Crisis on the Determinants of Leverage

European Evidence

Victoria Krivogorsky

Introduction

The contribution to the literature is an empirical analysis of the change in the role of institutions and macroeconomic indicators in determining firms' leverage before and after the financial shocks in Europe in 2008.[1] I believe that the heterogeneity of economic environments among European countries magnified by the crisis presents an acute test for corporate financing decisions, even though macroeconomic variables supposedly play little role in most capital structure models otherwise. The importance of this investigation stems from the current state of the global economy, where market confidence has been severely impacted in virtually every area. The scarcity of capital and increased risk aversion drive investors and lenders to focus on the relevance and reliability of the information utilized to make lending decisions. Thus, the estimation of the risk associated with a firm is more challenging now than at any time in recent history, and the prolonged elevated level of uncertainty over the last years will only continue to add complexity to valuation conjectures. Therefore, apart from the theoretical point of view, the findings have practical implications for predicting European firms' leverage, pertinent to the focus of financial statement analysis on a company's risk. The meaning of such analysis for investors around the world stems from the ongoing global integration of financial markets, a phenomenon that empirically manifests in the organization of exchange groups such as NYSE-Euronext exchange. As a result of this integration, European markets increase in their impact on their peers globally.

For this study, the period under investigation is bifurcated into two sub-periods, classifying 2005–2007 as pre-crisis and 2008–2011 as the crisis period. The decision to choose 2008 as the beginning of the crisis period is based on the facts that the banking crisis and bailout, as well as the most substantial decrease in Eurozone economic sentiment,[2] were reported in 2008 (down to 62 from 100 in 2007). All hypotheses are tested for pre- and post-2008 periods separately, measuring the difference in their significance between those two periods.

Most previous studies focus on the importance of a firm's characteristics while examining financing choices within individual countries during economically stable periods. The empirical evidence on the use of debt after 2008 is very fragmented and inconsistent so far, so the inquiry was extended to test the conjecture that the financial crisis impacts the bearing of institutional factors and macroeconomic indicators on the utilization of debt. This study builds on the already published literature in two ways. First, whether the changes in institutional factors result in different financing patterns due to the crisis is analyzed. In particular, the variation in debt utilization between pre- and post-2008 periods due to the preferences of capital suppliers (foreign investors), state of the credit environment and banking industry across European countries, as well as primary indicators used to gauge the economic health of national economies are identified. Second, these issues are considered within a panel that includes both firm- and time-specific fixed effects together as there are two sources of dependence in the data (Thompson, 2011). This approach allows capturing the correlation in the capital structure of the same firm across years and the correlation between observations on different firms in the same year. The decision to utilize clustering was instigated by the criticism originated in Petersen (2008), claiming that archival research based on linear statistical models does not produce correct results.

Several recent developments in the European economy have aided in shaping this study. First is the crisis that challenged the viability of the European (and global) economy by spreading into several economic areas (Shambaugh, 2012). It started as a banking crisis, followed by the sovereign debt crisis, where most European countries faced rising bond yield accompanied by the challenge of self-funding. Later it penetrated the real economy, impacting corporate bonds and manifesting itself among others as slow GDP growth and a decrease in corporate sales. Second, the adoption of IFRS by all EU members in 2005 and the recent alleged changes in the traditional bank-company relationship all around Europe have supposedly promoted more homogeneity between Continental Europe and the UK, all as the European market allegedly switches to the arm's-length system.

Three leverage ratios are used as dependent variables in this study. The choice of the leverage measures has been determined by their association with the areas heavily impacted by the crisis: banking industry and bond market. To capture the impact of the crisis on (1) the utilization of bank loans, bank loans ratio is used; (2) the use of bonds in the capital structure, the bond debt ratio is employed; and (3) the total debt ratio, as the total debt ratio is traditionally used in this type of research. To check for robustness of the findings, regressions with and without a UK sub-sample were run. The final sample includes financial data of the listed companies from 29 European countries collected from Worldscope and consists of 21,703 firm-year observations.

The primary findings of this paper are as follows: first, all three leverage ratios significantly decreased from pre- to post-2008 periods in almost equal proportions (Table 4.2, Panel A). Consistent with procyclical tendencies in the time of crisis, companies display an acute change in risk-taking behavior by cutting down on fixed obligations, which has significant implication for liquidity and risk. Second, contrary to the results previously reported in the US literature, this study finds no foreign investors' extreme risk aversion before 2008 apparently manifesting itself as a negative association between the level of debt utilization and aggregated level of foreign investment (Dahlquist and Robertson, 2001). However, it finds strong foreign investors' preference against using bank loans after 2008. Yet bond utilization after 2008 remains unaffected by the level of aggregated foreign investment. Third, after 2008 the impact of the size of the high-tech sector on all three leverage ratios significantly increased, and in the economies with larger high-tech sectors (measured as a proportion of high-tech sector net assets in the total net assets of all firms in the same country), companies have lower total liabilities and bank loan ratios. Also, the stringency of collateral and bankruptcy laws has a strong inverse association with both bank loan and bond ratios, especially after 2008, suggesting that in times of economic distress, the design of collateral and bankruptcy laws has a limiting effect on financing decisions associated with the proliferation of risk. Among other prominent outcomes are the findings that the level of bank funds available to the firms influences the overall use of debt, and when/if bank loans becomes less attractive, investors allocate their attention to the long-term bonds. Overall, the use of bank loans is more sensitive to the crisis compared to bonds, probably at least partially because the crisis started as a downturn in the banking industry, creating panic among the customers followed by the loss of confidence.

The control variables run in the test include the level of inflation, budget deficit, level of market capitalization, and tax system across countries and country risk. The results suggest that these variables jointly explain a significant portion of differences in financing decisions. Moreover, the country-specific risk (defined as the countries' variability in return on assets) is negatively correlated with a firm's use of bank loans, which is consistent with the logic that the variability of the firms' profitability is an essential factor in *ex-ante* estimates of their ability to meet fixed obligations. Furthermore, variability in return on assets estimates the probability of financial distress, and, thus, increase in ROA variability implies an increase in operational component of business risk that makes banks loans more costly. Besides, country risk has a strong positive correlation with the bond ratio, possibly because higher variability in profitability is connected to higher earnings volatility, amplifying the decline on the equity market, accompanied by substantial reductions in the market value of equities. So, having only a limited number of sources of capital, when equity market declines and banks experience a significant loss of consumer confidence accompanied by the high cost of bank loans, firms turn to the bond market for capital.

There is also evidence concerning the importance of firm-specific variables such as return on assets, market-to-book value, and asset tangibility in debt utilization before and after 2008. However, there is no significant impact of financing deficit on leverage during pre- or post-2008 periods. In addition, the results document a significant decrease in profitability and growth and increase in interest coverage ratio (risk), financing deficit ratio, and level of long-term tangible assets after 2008. As companies experience larger operating risk, they strive for a higher level of tangible assets, which are easier to collateralize. They also suffer a smaller loss of value in times of distress, so they are associated with lower agency costs of debt.

Literature and Hypotheses

Extensive use of debt as the primary source of capital in Europe is attributed to the importance of banks in European economic systems (IMF, Global Financial Stability Report, October 2012). These issues were addressed in Rajan and Zingales (2003), who stressed the differences between the two financial systems as the institution-heavy, relationship-based system, more prevalent in Europe, and the market-intensive, arm's-length system, more prevalent in the US. Distinct from those used in the US, legal capital rules are designed to reflect the unique position of creditors in Europe, especially in the Continental European countries.[3] To mimic what is achieved in the US through contractual bargaining and the use of bond covenants (Day et al., 2004), firms in Continental Europe are subject to less flexible legal capital rules intended to provide a ready-made, off-the-shelf solution to reduce transaction costs (Kubler, 2004). In fact, some advocates of the legal model in Continental Europe view legal capital rules as means of addressing the collective interests of creditors, mitigating agency problems, and shielding them from opportunistic behavior that cannot be easily replicated contractually (Armthe, 2000; Schoen, 2004). With the development of the equity market in Europe during the last decade, legal capital rules are allegedly losing their ground to arm's-length relationships.[4]

Most previous research on capital structure has focused on American publicly traded firms, as US capital markets and institutions provide an excellent field for it. Thus far, the very limited cross-country studies on capital structure conducted in Europe have mostly been surveys (Brounen et al., 2005, Bancel and Mittoo, 2004; Gaud et al., 2007; Frydenberg, 2011). Among country-specific studies, no consensus has been reached on the determinants of leverage. For instance, Bevan and Danbolt (2001), after analyzing the capital structure of UK public companies, report that firms' indebtedness is explained by firm-specific characteristics: growth estimate, size, performance, and tangibility of assets; whereas Miguel and Pindado (2001), using a sample of 133 Spanish companies, show that current debt level is only dependent on the previous debt level.

In the American literature, the question on the determinants of leverage was identified as essential for investment and financing decisions, as leverage has a profound impact on the risk associated with a firm, and thus on firm's value. Numerous studies have addressed the bearing of firm characteristics on the utilization of debt, reporting that they partially explain the variation in firm leverage (Titman and Wessels, 1988; Rajan and Zingales, 1995; Frank and Goyal, 2009, just to name a few). Recent international studies on the determinants of firms' leverage conducted in the US corroborate previous findings for the most part, supplementing them with reports on the importance of country-specific institutional environments and the structure of corporate ownership (Fan et al., 2012; Booth et al., 2001; Faccio et al., 2010). They do not examine, however, the role of the crisis in explaining the variation in firms leverage.

Crisis Impact on Leverage

Among financial crisis origins discussed in the literature, several stand out as related to the topic of this study. The combination of off-balance sheet investment vehicles, derivatives, and repurchase agreements initially originated in the US house market, and created what has been termed the "shadow banking system" (Gorton, 2010; Gorton and Metric, 2010). Once problems began to accumulate in the US house market, it became impossible for outside investors to penetrate this shadow banking system and to determine where the actual risks were located. Thus, the financial crisis introduced (among other problems) acute agency conflict into the European system, conflict mitigated before by prudent regulations (legal capital laws), concentrated ownership, and distinct relationship between firms and banks.[5] With all these features losing their ground to the market intensive, arm's-length relationships more susceptible to the agency problem, the impact on investors' confidence was severe (Tweedie, 2008).

Faced with this classic example of information asymmetry and moral hazard problem, customers overreacted by refusing to deal with banks, and banks refused to deal with each other. So, the crisis proliferated rapidly, causing a global economic shock, and the failure of a number of European banks followed. Global (and European) stock markets declined, accompanied by large reductions in the market values of equities and commodities. Financial institutions de-levered to pay back obligations, credit spreads widened, and a global liquidity crisis began as banks refused to lend to one another and to customers. Almost immediately a global financial shock was transmitted to the real economy. In other words, the downward slide in the business sector followed sliding in the financial sector, showing the synchronization in both cycles (procyclicality). Economic and financing decisions underlying the two cycles are not independent. They are inherently linked by the risk-taking behavior of economic agents, behavior which is prone to change in response to incentives, regulations, new information, and perceptions of risk. The change in risk-taking behavior explains large swings in investor sentiment, from a period of economic stability when risk is almost disregarded to a crisis period defined by extreme risk aversion. It also underscores the abrupt change in financing behavior and in the direction and momentum of economic activities. Thus, in addition to numerous economic problems, the crisis caused an increase in volatility, uncertainty, and heterogeneity in investors' beliefs and elevated risk aversion.

As mentioned, the crisis started as a classic example of information asymmetry and moral hazard in the banking industry and rapidly impacted other areas of the real economy. The idea of procyclicality is instrumental in understanding the relationship between the crisis and debt utilization, and implies that three reinforcing cycles (financial, business, and the cycle associated with the swing in risk-taking behavior), moving in tandem, define the amplitude and the momentum of the cyclical fluctuations, as well as the risk (or the perception of thereof) associated with crisis. So, a period of low macroeconomic volatility usually brings about an expansionary phase of the business cycle, resulting in escalated demand for credit and a rise in asset prices, which is followed by economic downturn accompanied by a decrease in demand for credit. It is believed that institutions can somewhat reduce the procyclicality effect by lessening the economic agents' overreaction to the cycles (Barth et al., 2012). For instance, creditors' protection laws (if complemented by strong enforcement) promote greater awareness of risk and improve risk assessment, so the extreme shifts in sentiment and confidence related to a crisis can be at least in part avoided. Also, a strong (more liquid) and well-developed banking sector can give economic agents some level of confidence in the sustainability of an economy. Also, in the time of crisis foreign investors will probably be more risk sensitive, as it has also been long documented that in general investors tend to be more risk-averse when investing internationally compared to their domestic investments. It manifests itself as foreign investors' preference to invest in large, more liquid, and less levered companies (Dahlquist and Robertson, 2001).

Another dimension of this issue—the relationship between financing structure and uncertainty—was explored by Knight (1921), who pointed out the impact of institutional maturity on the level of "indeterminate uncertainty" (or "immeasurable risk") making the connection between the latter and the cost of capital. Following this logic, an immeasurable risk, whether associated with the state of national institutions or the economic stability of the business environment, should have an impact on debt utilization. In compliance with this statement, Beck et al. (2008) report that firms in countries with better-developed banking systems are less likely to use equity finance and thereby increase the proportion of bank credit, simultaneously decreasing the proportion of residual financing from other sources in the financing mix of firms.

Assuming for a moment that European companies are more inclined to use debt during relatively stable economic periods, the final decision on the source of debt capital would be, at least in part, determined by the laws and regulations and presumption of risk associated with each given a choice. By taking a loan, a company enters a rigid contract, where the interest rate, the principal, and the likelihood of a bank's demand to increase security will depend on whether a firm meets the lending terms, including a requirement of security. The latter is measured by the firm's financial position and a history of its relationship with the bank. The cost of bond issuance also depends on the firm's financial position, as potential investors will be looking among other things at the level of default risk and marketability risk (ease in subsequent disposal of the bond), while deciding on the initial investment. Each leverage choice, therefore, is supplemented by risk situated on both debtor and creditor sides of the transaction, which in time of economic calamity comes with an additional immeasurable risk emanating from an extra uncertainty related to the crisis. Thus, I make a conjecture that in times of economic distress firms should reduce their overall dependence on debt, as debt is the source of additional risk for issuers and investors; and among the alternatives, the source of debt is associated with higher costs, i.e., the risk is less desirable.

As Miller (1977) shows, the debt ratio in the economy is at least in part determined by aggregate investor preferences for holding various debt vs. equity. The effect of investors' preferences on the capital structure was further discussed by Titman (2002). Follow this logic, I incorporate foreign direct investment ratio in the test as a proxy for foreign investors' penetration (i.e., the size of investment by foreign investors) to examine the aggregated foreign investors' inclination to use leverage. I expect that after 2008 foreign investors will display higher sensitivity to the risk associated with their investment, and thus, I will observe both an increased impact of foreign direct investment ratio on use of debt and a negative association between the size of foreign investment into corporations and the use of debt.

H1. The size of foreign investment has a strong inverse association with leverage during the post-2008 period.

To proxy for the national variations in the use of debt in capital structure I use the size of high-tech industries in a country. Demirgüç-Kunt and Huizinga (1999) and Fan et al. (2012) report that countries with larger high-tech sectors require a considerable amount of external capital, making equity financing of a more significant consequence. Toward that point, I expect that after 2008 the impact of high-tech sector size on debt utilization will amplify, as the additional risk associated with the crisis should be factored in. Thus, as the debt itself is connected with the risk, I make a conjecture that:

> *H2. The size of the high-tech sector has a strong inverse association with leverage during the post-2008 period.*

As the recent crisis has mainly been a crisis of confidence, the design of collateral and bankruptcy law is essential in reestablishing this confidence. To estimate the role of the credit environment in debt utilization, I use the index, which measures the strictness of collateral and bankruptcy laws developed by the World Bank. I conjecture that strict credit laws will have a limiting effect on the use of debt. Also, procyclicality may affect the association between the credit environment and leverage, causing collateral and bankruptcy laws to become a predicament in lending by imposing an additional stratum of regulations on the firms.

> *H3. The strength of creditors' rights protection laws has a strong negative association with leverage during the post-2008 period.*

To address a concern presented in De Jong et al. (2008) and Fan et al. (2012) regarding the role of solvency of the national banking systems in defining firms' leverage I use the bank's net assets ratio. As an impact of crisis varied by country, I think that it had a diverse effect on banks' solvency across European countries, contributing to the diversity in banking industry financial conditions. For instance, in some countries, private debt arising from a property bubble was transferred to sovereign debt, and because European banks own a significant amount of sovereign debt, the banks' ability to loan was severely impacted. In other countries, like Spain, some unsustainable public sector wages and pension commitments drove the debt increase partially absorbed by banks. Also, the extents of banking system bailouts were different across countries. Potentially there are unobserved factors, which affect both the inclination on the part of investors to deposit funds with banks and the bank's disposition to provide long-term funding to firms, creating possible spurious correlations between available funds and capital structure. Also, one might argue that the financing needs of the firms affect the funds available to other investor sectors. Also, if for any reason bank loans become less attractive relative to long-term bonds, investors will allocate their money to long-term bonds. While this creates a potential endogeneity problem, in the test, it is mitigated by the presence of other institutional variables and probably has a minor influence on the estimates. Thus, a reasonable conjecture is that firms use more debt in the countries where banks have more available funds.

H4. The banks' net assets ratio has a strong positive association with leverage.

To estimate the bearing of macroeconomic indicators of economic health in explaining variations in leverage ratios I use the national level of public debt and GDP growth. In a time of economic stability, none of these variables display too much variation across years. As a result of the crisis and due to the array of responses to it across countries the variations in these macroeconomic indicators over time and among countries have increased. In some cases, public debt is absorbed by the banks, and slow GDP growth is associated with an elevated level of uncertainty. So, I conjecture that the level of public debt scaled by GDP and the level of GDP growth in the time of crisis will have an inverse association with leverage.

H5. The levels of public debt and GDP growth have a strong inverse association with leverage.

Research Design

Data and Sample

The sample comes from Worldscope and Worlds Bank's Doing Business Survey databases. Initially, I collected almost 28,000 observations of publicly traded companies from 29 European countries (Table 4.1, Panel A). The sample period starts in 2005, after IFRS adoption, through 2011. It covers two sub-periods: before and after 2008, the year when the financial crisis started. After removing (1) companies which are not consistently public during the investigated period; (2) firms with incomplete data; (3) companies that report unreliable data (i.e., negative debt or negative sales); (4) utility companies (code 8200–8280), financial companies (code 60–69), and aerospace (military) firms (code 1310–1350), as they operate in a different regulatory environments; and (5) firms with non-positive market-to-book value ratio, I ended up with a sample of 21,722 firm-year observations tested in the analysis. Almost 70% of the sample comes from six European countries: approximately 20% are British firms, about 13% are German, 15% are French, nearly 10% are Swiss, almost 5% are Italian, and about 6% are Swedish. I excluded Estonia, Greece, Malta, Slovakia, and Slovenia from the test because after the financial crisis most public companies in those countries were delisted and/or reported unreliable financial data (negative sale, equity, or nonfinancial liabilities). The difference between pre- and post-2008 periods in the number of the firm-year observations is due to (1) more extended period covered after 2008, and (2) the larger number of financial reports with reliable financial data from Poland, Portugal, Sweden, Lithuania, Latvia, Austria, and Denmark available for us. The composition of the final sample by country is detailed in Table 4.1.

Table 4.1 Distribution of the sample by country

Country	*Pre-2008 (2005–2007)*	*Post-2008 (2009–2011)*	*Total Sample*
Austria	147	258	405
Belgium	170	277	447
Bulgaria	89	403	492
Cyprus	4	125	129
Czech Republic	21	19	40
Denmark	474	771	1245
Finland	266	401	667
France	1,150	1,803	2953
Germany	1,048	1,835	2883
Hungary	43	52	95
Ireland	65	101	166
Italy	449	744	1193
Latvia	17	76	93
Lithuania	23	92	115
Luxembourg	47	72	119
Netherlands	230	337	567
Norway	175	298	473
Poland	407	1,102	1509
Portugal	168	492	660
Romania	8	21	29
Spain	16	40	56
Sweden	378	808	1186
Switzerland	673	1,174	1847
United Kingdom	1,567	2,735	4302
Total	7,635	14,036	21,671

*Initial sample also included Malta, Estonia, Slovakia, Greece, and Slovenia. After 2008, I was unable to identify publicly traded companies with reliable data domiciled in any of these countries, so I omitted them from the sample.

Definition of Leverage

The book measure of leverage has traditionally been preferred in European research due to (1) the belief that investors rely more on the book value measurements (Paananen and Parmar, 2008); and (2) the fact that neither debt nor equity markets were historically well developed (Rajan and Zingales, 2003). Thus, I operationalize the first leverage measure to indicate the efficiency of capital employed as bank debt to total assets (BLTA) (Rajan and Zingales, 1995; Fan et al., 2012): BLTA = Bank Loan / Total Assets. I use book values in the ratio because the optimal allocation of bank credit in Europe is mostly based on the formal screening process using *pro forma* balance sheet values as assets and liabilities to define final loan terms. To speak to the importance of the bond market in Europe I use leverage determined as an amount of bonds liabilities scaled by total assets[6] (FLTA): FLTA = Bonds Liabilities / Total Assets.[7] I also use total debt ratio measured as a total debt scaled by total debt plus book value of equity—TLTA (Rajan and Zingales, 1995; Fan et al., 2012): TLTA = Total Debt / Total Assets. The denominator in all three ratios is Total Assets = Debt + Non-Financial Liabilities + Shareholders Equity.

Country-Specific Variables

Independent Variables

FOREIGN DIRECT INVESTMENT RATIO (FRINVGDP)

Foreign direct investment ratio is measured as the net inflows of investment to acquire a lasting management interest (10% or more of voting stock) in an enterprise operating in an economy other than that of the investor scaled by GDP[8]. In particular, numerator measures a net inflow (new investment inflows less disinvestment) in the reporting economy from foreign investors. The investment inflow is the sum of equity capital, reinvestment of earnings, and other long-term and short-term capital as shown in the balance of payments.

SIZE OF HIGH-TECH SECTOR RATIO (HITECHNA)

The ratio is measured as a proportion of net assets associated with the high-tech sector in a given country in the total net assets of all public companies incorporated in the same country.

THE STRENGTH OF CREDITORS' LEGAL RIGHTS INDEX (CRSTR)

The index ranges from 0 to 10, with higher scores indicating that collateral and bankruptcy laws are better designed to expand access to credit (www.mcc.gov/who-we-fund/indicator/access-to-credit-indicator). This index was developed by the World Bank (www.doingbusiness.org). Presumably, better creditor rights protection creates a favorable environment for debt financing. Although creditor protection affects both banks and bondholders, taking into account the fact that bondholders are usually less specialized than banks, it makes sense to assert that bondholders benefit from this protection more than lending banks.[9]

BANK NET ASSETS TO CAPITAL RATIO (BNATNA)

This variable is measured as the ratio of bank funds available for lending to banks' total capital and reserves. Capital and reserves include funds contributed by owners, retained earnings, general and special reserves, provisions, and valuation adjustments. Capital includes tier 1 capital (paid-up shares and common stock), which is a common feature in all countries' banking systems, and total regulatory capital, which includes several specified types of subordinated debt instruments that need not be repaid if the funds are required to maintain minimum capital levels (these comprise tier 2 and tier 3 capital) (https://fred.stlouisfed.org/series/DDSI03USA156NWDB). Assets include all financial assets.

GDP GROWTH RATE AND *PUBLIC DEBT* (PUBDGDP)

Growth rate (GDPGR) is calculated as the GDP growth rate between two subsequent years, and PUBDGDP is calculated as the amount of public debt scaled by GDP (%).

Control Variables

COUNTRY RISK (CRISK)

To test the existing contextual diversities in various nations within which they operate I employ the countries' variability of the return on assets, defined as the standard deviation of the return on assets by country in a given year (Booth et al., 2001). Booth et al. (2001) show a differential effect of country risk (financial distress) on debt maturity across countries. Indeed, within the European Union, the economic and financial policy remains first and foremost a competence belonging to each Member State; there is nothing like an EU Treasury, a centralized EU economic policy institution, or a common EU financial services regulator. Although some economic coordination takes place at the EU level, notably under the framework of the Stability and Growth Pact, the unity of action is still dependent on agreement by the representatives of the member states who sit on the Economic and Financial Affairs Council (Gérard, 2008).

INFLATION (INFL)

The literature documents a positive relationship between leverage and expected inflation (Frank and Goyal, 2007). A positive relation can also arise if managers issue debt when expected inflation is higher than current interest rates.

MARKET CAPITALIZATION RATIO (MCAPCR)

To control for the importance of national financial markets I use the ratio of stock market capitalization to GDP as this ratio has been identified as a good approximation for the importance of equity market. It is expected that a well-developed stock market provides an alternative source of financing, thus becoming indicative of the difference in corporate leverage (Booth et al., 2001; Rajan and Zingales, 1995). With the integration of capital markets, the significance of national financial markets declines, however.

TAX SYSTEM (TXSYS)

The tax system and in particular tax treatment of interest and dividend payments have been identified as significant determinants of capital structure (Fan et al., 2012). Because the information on corporate income taxes has not been consistently disclosed by the European firms in the sample, it was not feasible to calculate a sophisticated tax variable to handle an effect of loss carry-forward or other tax incentives. Thus, in accord with Fan et al. (2012) I use three main categories of tax regimes to control for the impact of the tax system on leverage. The first category includes countries with classical tax systems (dividend payments are taxed on both the corporate and personal levels, and interest payments are tax-deductible corporate expenses). The second category includes countries with dividend relief tax systems (dividend payments are taxed at a reduced rate at the personal level). The third category is the dividend imputation system (corporate profit is taxed only once, i.e., firms deduct interest payments and domestic investors receive tax credit for the taxes paid by a firm).[10]

BUDGET DEFICIT TO GDP RATIO (BUDGET)

As an additional way to control for country-specific variations in the level of economic development during the pre- and post-2008 periods I use BUDGET computed as country budget deficit scaled by GDP (%).

Industry-Specific Variables

INDUSTRY RISK (IRISK)

I control for industry risk for two reasons. First, firm value, growth, risk, and cash flow problem may be either more or less severe in specific industries due to differences in competitive intensity and industry maturity (Demsetz and Lehn, 1985; Fama and French, 1997; Giroud and Mueller, 2007; Zeckhauser and Pound, 1990). Second, Frank and Goyal (2003) show that firms in certain industries tend to have higher leverage. To control for existing diversities in the various industrial sectors, I use the industrial sectors' variability of return on assets, defined as the standard deviation of the return on assets by sector in a given year (Booth et al., 2001) using two-digit SIC codes.

Firm-Specific Variables

Firm-Level Characteristics and Leverage

Consistent with previous research, I add a set of firm-level variables that capture factors influencing leverage (Titman and Wessels, 1988; Rajan and Zingales, 1995, 2003; Frank and Goyal, 2009). These variables include profitability (return on assets), performance/growth opportunities (market-to-book ratio), firm size (natural logarithm of total assets), asset tangibility (fixed assets over total assets ratio and long-term fixed assets over total assets ratio), and company risk (interest coverage ratio). Due to data limitations, I did not use research and development expenditure, selling expenses, and capital expenditures in the test, replacing them with the market-to-book ratio, which has been used to proxy for growth opportunities, the collateral value of assets by Fan et al. (2012).

FINANCING DEFICIT (FDSALE)

Financing deficit ratio is measured as Financing Deficit / Sale, where

Financing Deficit = Interest Payment + Change in Working Capital + Dividends – Operating Cash Flow / Annual Sale.

Lemmon and Zender (2004) introduced the idea of debt capacity as an important element in understanding firms' capital structure. They report that debt capacity constrained firms to face severe informational asymmetry and, thus, they should issue more equity than firms with no target debt ratio, which are mostly small and fast-growing. Unlike in the US,[11] as several surveys conducted by Brounen et al. in 2004, 2005, and 2006 evidence, more than 90% of European firms, small or large, fast-growing or not, predominantly have no target debt ratio of any kind. Thus, I think that with no constraint imposed by the target debt ratio, the financial deficit of European companies will show no significant bearing on debt utilization.

PROFITABILITY (ROA)

ROA is measured as Operating Income / Net Assets; where

Net Asset = Total Assets – Deposits – Marketable Securities – Accounts Payables – Deferred Revenue – Accrued Expenses – Pension Liabilities – Restructuring Liabilities

To operationalize a firm's profitability, I use ROA as defined in Nissim and Penman (2003). To the extent that leverage is associated with both the numerator and denominator of the profitability measure, I disentangle all components of the balance sheet and income statement that involve operating and financing activities to concentrate on the profitability of production assets mostly.

ROA is consistently used in the literature to test for the differences in capital structure (Myers, 2001). Numerous studies in the US support the conjecture that, as firms prefer internal finance over external funds, assuming fixed investments and dividends, more profitable and higher performing firms should become less leveraged over time (Frank and Goyal, 2007; Rajan and Zingales, 1995; Fama and French, 1998; Myers, 1984, 2001). Thus, they all evidence a negative association between ROA and leverage that contradicts Jensen's (1986) claims that more profitable firms should have more debt, because expected bankruptcy costs are lower, and interest tax shields are more relevant.

PERFORMANCE/GROWTH OPPORTUNITIES (MVBV)

Market value to book value of equity ratio is consistently used in the research to test the association between performance and leverage (Caskey et al., 2012). MVBV ratio is based on future return on shareholders' funds. Thus it is based on expected performance, growth in book value, and the cost of equity capital (Nissim and Penman, 2003). Ergo, a reasonable conjecture is that a firm with higher MVBV ratio is willing to take on more financing debt because it has lower bankruptcy costs and faces a lower risk of the difference between profitability and borrowing rate turning unfavorable. Interestingly, MVBV is also commonly used as a proxy for growth opportunities to control for the idea that, taking agency concerns into consideration, all else equal, a firm with higher current or expected future growth opportunities must be more leveraged (Harris and Raviv, 1991).

TANGIBILITY OF ASSETS (TATA AND LATA)

To operationalize a firm's assets tangibility, I use two variables: TATA is a ratio of tangible assets to total assets, and LATA is a ratio of fixed long-term assets to total assets. Both ratios have been used in the literature as a proxy for the liquidation value of the borrowing firm. A larger proportion of tangible assets and even more so a more significant portion of fixed long-term assets, whose market value can be measured more precisely and suffer a smaller loss in value when a firm goes into distress, are more perceptible to outside creditors and thus, act as collateral. Therefore, in the case of a default, creditors can measure the probability of recovering their debt more accurately (Titman and Wessels, 1988; Rajan and Zingales, 1995). Thus, complementary to the TATA test I also employ LATA, a ratio of fixed long-term assets to total assets, and expect to see positive significance coefficients for both ratios.

FIRM SIZE (SIZE)

Myer (2001) predicts that large firms will have more debt since they are more mature, more diversified, and have lower default risk. Thus, firms with an established reputation face lower agency costs of debt, but they also should be successful using the market. Thus, when choosing among sources of debt, larger firms supposedly issue public debt before using bank loans. Size is measured as the natural logarithm of total assets.

GROWTH (GROWTH)

The relation between leverage and growth is featured in many cross-sectional studies, including those by Long and Malitz (1985), Barclay et al. (2006), and Frank and Goyal (2007). Consensus has not been reached yet, as some studies report a negative relation between leverage and growth, while others suggest that firms with more investments should accumulate more debt over time, assuming performance is held constant, so growth and leverage are expected to be positively related. GROWTH is measured as a change in sale between two subsequent years (%).

INTEREST COVERAGE RATIO (ICR)

In line with Myers' (1977) predictions, leverage has been found to decrease with operating risk going up (Harris and Raviv, 1990; Bancel and Mittoo, 2004). I operationalize ICR as a ratio of earnings before interest, depreciation, and taxes divided by total interest payments (interest expense and capitalized interest).

Results

Descriptive Statistics

The initial exploratory data analysis identified outliers. After winsorizing, Table 4.2, Panel A reports a significant decrease (on 0.0001 level) in all three leverage ratios after 2008 (TLTA, BLTA, and FLTA, respectively). Consistent with procyclical tendencies in the time of crisis, companies display an acute change in risk-taking behavior by cutting down on their fixed obligations. This trend potentially has a significant implication for liquidity and risk.

The results also show a two-fold decrease in firms' sales growth (GROWTH), along with a significant decrease in profitability (ROA) after 2008. Not surprisingly, I also find that the market-to-book ratio (MVBV), assets tangibility measured as LATA, and operating risk (ICR) increased significantly after 2008. Both ratios, MVBV and LATA, are proxies for agency costs and costs of financial distress (Myer, 1977; Booth et al., 2001). In particular, the increase in MVBV (firms' growth opportunities) is associated with an increase in the agency costs of debt and a reduction

Table 4.2 Descriptive statistics

Panel A: Firm-level variables

Sample	*Total Sample*		*Pre-2008*		*Post-2008*		*ANOVA*
	Mean	*St. Dev.*	*Mean*	*St. Dev.*	*Mean*	*St. Dev.*	*F values*[1)]
Financial Leverage Ratios							
TLTA(%)	31.007	31.302	38.523	31.932	26.919	30.180	701.530****
BLTA(%)	13.884	17.546	17.470	19.150	11.934	16.282	503.800****
FLTA(%)	18.590	23.315	23.361	24.854	15.995	22.005	505.060****
Firm-Specific Variables							
FDSALE	15.622	356.877	15.458	403.900	15.711	328.499	0.000
ROA(%)	6.541	29.859	7.968	26.731	5.765	31.403	26.960****
MVBV	70.317	195.294	62.110	185.281	74.781	200.395	20.840****
TATA	0.835	0.190	0.849	0.176	0.827	0.197	67.960****
LATA	0.549	0.259	0.536	0.260	0.556	0.258	28.760****
GROWTH(%)	13.549	48.158	20.982	50.966	9.506	46.060	284.450****
SIZE [=LN(ASSETS)]	5.930	2.397	6.122	2.401	5.825	2.388	59.000****
ICR	133.734	1499.730	89.174	961.255	157.972	1722.930	10.080***
Sample size	21,671		7,635		14,036		

(See Appendix for variables definition.)

Table 4.2 (Continued)

Panel B: Pearson correlations

	BLTA	*FLTA*	*FDSALE*	*ROA*	*MVBV*	*TATA*	*LATA*	*GROWTH*	*LNASSET*	*ICR*
TLTA	0.779****	0.895****	–0.038****	0.041****	0.106****	0.005	0.283****	0.020***	0.257****	–0.068****
BLTA		0.491****	–0.031****	0.013****	0.020	0.045****	0.209****	0.028****	0.122****	–0.053****
FLTA			–0.030****	0.061****	0.137****	–0.006	0.281****	0.023***	0.285****	–0.056****
FDSALE				–0.021***	–0.015*	0.004	0.002	0.075****	–0.066****	0.163****
ROA					0.041****	0.051****	0.035****	0.017*	0.112****	–0.002
MVBV						–0.008	0.128****	–0.021***	0.406****	–0.013*
TATA							–0.083****	–0.036****	0.079****	0.025***
LATA								0.028****	0.386****	–0.003
GROWTH									–0.025***	0.011
SIZE										–0.048****

(See Appendix for variables definition.)

Panel C: Country-specific variables

	FRINVGDP		*HITECHNA*		*CRSTR*	*BNATNA*		*PUBDGDP*		*GDPGR*		*CRISK*		*INFL*		*BUDGET*		*MCAPCR*	
	Pre	*Post*	*Pre*	*Post*		*Pre*	*Post*	*Pre*	*Post*	*Pre*	*Post*	*Pre*	*Post*	*Pre*	*Post*	*Pre*	*Post*	*Pre*	*Post*
Austria	12.92	–2.20	25.60	24.91	7.00	14.24	15.09	64.54	68.85	2.69	0.63	8.92	14.95	3.11	1.72	–1.37	–3.03	41.60	12.73
Belgium	24.51	26.79	3.40	3.65	7.00	4.99	16.44	89.07	94.78	2.21	0.53	17.83	16.52	1.98	2.57	–0.73	–3.53	80.10	40.82
Bulgaria	40.72	6.36	16.18	12.26	8.00	–14.17	–9.88	25.10	15.23	5.72	–1.14	13.94	14.56	6.97	5.44	1.37	–1.95	71.10	22.67
Cyprus	14.32	3.45	2.99	2.70	9.00	1.07	3.59	65.37	60.13	4.40	–0.08	8.45	13.66	2.29	2.68	–0.03	–4.20	40.90	7.77
Czech Republic	6.94	4.77	10.14	8.75	6.40	0.18	0.27	27.22	35.85	6.01	–0.10	5.56	9.87	2.39	2.69	–2.10	–3.98	73.40	36.05
Denmark	3.28	1.78	3.82	3.49	8.90	1.45	1.86	31.55	40.85	2.09	–1.18	18.11	20.68	1.70	2.45	5.07	–0.95	1.86	1.45
Finland	6.01	2.08	41.03	35.93	8.00	1.99	2.83	37.89	43.84	3.95	–0.83	14.13	21.61	1.34	2.64	2.17	–0.93	156.00	51.61
France	4.77	2.14	10.41	10.61	6.40	0.75	1.01	64.86	78.98	2.02	0.07	41.99	37.53	1.70	1.82	4.07	–0.30	85.70	50.04
Germany	2.92	1.81	6.59	7.23	7.40	–1.73	–1.64	66.75	76.34	2.00	0.51	24.12	38.46	1.96	1.60	–2.63	–5.78	41.90	28.32
Hungary	48.95	–7.98	35.58	35.48	7.00	1.26	1.49	63.62	78.76	2.84	–1.30	11.82	10.07	4.49	4.76	–1.57	–2.15	49.40	21.60
Ireland	5.18	12.59	22.16	24.59	9.00	0.00	0.00	25.48	77.49	5.12	–2.24	16.53	21.17	3.34	0.30	–5.80	–11.20	34.80	7.31
Italy	2.67	1.48	8.62	7.78	3.00	0.93	1.16	106.20	115.10	1.15	–1.07	10.80	12.16	2.08	2.20	–7.47	–2.05	43.40	12.57
Latvia	13.14	7.38	8.91	10.56	10.00	0.00	0.00	9.95	36.24	8.83	–4.20	5.74	6.88	6.67	5.55	1.57	–16.40	16.40	5.86
Lithuania	8.13	4.31	2.61	2.00	5.00	–16.15	14.47	17.94	29.89	7.87	–2.51	7.69	13.08	3.00	5.19	–3.13	–4.15	61.70	17.51
Luxembourg	490.10	791.60	50.50	63.40	6.70	3.28	4.14	5.49	14.82	4.78	–0.35	14.10	24.97	2.70	2.36	–0.43	–6.43	4.14	3.28
Netherlands	1275.00	39.00	4.82	4.62	6.00	0.27	0.40	49.12	61.80	2.14	–0.34	28.88	18.14	1.57	1.83	1.70	0.18	59.70	31.80
Norway	1.27	2.14	21.69	11.80	7.00	1.32	1.61	47.35	42.31	3.15	0.18	21.87	23.32	1.35	2.41	–2.70	–3.70	91.60	55.62
Poland	8.56	4.56	17.77	14.36	8.40	0.72	2.65	45.93	50.58	5.01	3.29	13.02	16.42	1.93	3.78	0.13	–3.73	97.30	45.99
Portugal	4.43	4.13	35.76	28.65	3.00	–0.59	–0.47	65.82	88.96	1.29	–1.05	10.44	22.30	2.31	1.70	–3.20	–6.00	30.70	16.74
Romania	12.04	3.11	52.94	36.99	8.70	–10.36	0.07	19.25	26.68	5.00	–1.90	3.84	8.01	7.28	6.33	–4.73	–6.95	95.60	28.66
Spain	5.05	3.52	1.20	1.37	6.00	–17.02	6.28	4.20	6.06	3.29	–1.03	12.00	13.74	4.57	4.56	1.87	–8.38	59.00	33.25
Sweden	8.90	1.55	3.55	3.66	7.00	3.66	3.86	37.19	36.95	3.38	1.62	21.08	23.31	2.79	2.78	2.70	0.53	104.00	65.54
Switzerland	12.02	3.54	6.94	7.87	8.00	1.21	1.92	48.26	37.02	2.52	1.06	15.70	17.60	0.84	0.72	0.00	0.00	157.00	101.20
UK	9.21	2.81	9.00	8.29	10.00	–0.30	0.50	43.35	72.13	2.54	–0.47	23.02	34.94	2.04	3.39	–2.93	–8.75	82.10	51.73

(See Appendix for variables definition.)

Table 4.2 (Continued)

Panel D: Industry risk (IRISK) measured in terms of standard deviations of ROAs

SIC (First Digit)	*Industry Name*	*Pre-2008*	*Post-2008*
00~09	Agriculture, forestry, and fishing	16.214	54.245
10~19	Mining	19.288	32.889
20~29	Construction	17.973	28.608
30~39	Manufacturing	15.200	19.429
40~49	Transportation and communications	29.796	23.215
50~59	Trade	38.120	38.663
70~79	Service	20.058	22.502
80~89	Health Service	36.406	42.664
90~99	Public Administration	36.020	26.720

The pre-2008 time period is defined as 2005–2007. The post-2008 time period is defined as 2009–2011. See Appendix for variable definitions. *, **, ***, and **** indicate significance at the 10%, 5%, 1%, and < 1%, respectively.

in the agency costs of managerial discretion. So, the result is consistent with the theoretical prediction that while companies experience larger operating risk (ICR) they strive for a higher level of tangible assets as the latter provides greater ability to issue secured debt, yet less information related to the future profits will be revealed. In addition, a high proportion of hard long-term tangible assets increases debt capacity and reduces otherwise fast-growing distress and agency costs during the crisis. I also report that the variance of TATA increases, but the mean of TATA is getting smaller, suggesting that the current portion of tangible assets decreases significantly during the crisis.

Table 4.2, Panel B presents the Pearson correlations between the firm-specific variables. The total liabilities ratio (TLTA) significantly correlates ($r = .895$) with bond debt (FLTA) and bank loans ratios (BLTA, $r = .779$), whereas BLTA and FLTA correlation is only around .491. The strong correlation between the dependent variables might be due to the fact that they share a common accounting property. Not surprisingly, the market-to-book ratio (MVBV) is significantly positively correlated to the total debt ratio (TLTA) and the bond debt ratio (FLTA) but is not significantly associated with the bank loans (BLTA), as bank credit decisions are mostly based on accounting measures and covenants. All leverage ratios are significantly and inversely correlated with interest coverage ratio (ICR). It is worth noting that larger companies seem to use more debt, and have more long-term tangible assets and higher market-to-book ratio. They also have smaller financial deficit ratio (FDSALE) and interest coverage ratio (ICR).

Table 4.2, Panel C contains information on the state of national institutions suggesting the heterogeneity of economic environments, which might pose a severe test for capital decisions, even though macroeconomic variables supposedly play little role in most capital models. The highest index measuring the strength of creditors' rights (CRSTR) is reported in the UK, Latvia, Ireland, and Cyprus, followed by Denmark, Romania, Poland, and Finland. Austria, Belgium, and the Netherlands have approximately the same CRSTR (between 7.5 and 6) showing that all these countries have fairly mature collateral and bankruptcy laws. The lowest level of creditors' protection is reported in Portugal and Lithuania, indicating lack of strong collateral and bankruptcy laws there. According to the World Bank, those indexes did not materially change from the pre- to post-2008 period.

Foreign direct investment ratio (FRINVGDP) noticeably dropped from the pre- to post-2008 period for most European countries. Intuitively it makes sense that foreign investors, being more risk-averse than domestic, in the time of crisis significantly reduced their exposure to risk. I noticed here that while UK, Switzerland, Bulgaria, Cyprus, Hungary, and especially the Netherlands experienced a tremendous loss of foreign investors' confidence during the crisis, Luxembourg, Belgium, Ireland, and Norway enjoyed an even higher level of foreign investments than before 2008. I think it's because all those small economies have always been considered "safe" business heavens. The size of the high-tech sector (HITECHNA) remains almost the same before and after 2008 for every given country except for Romania, Norway, and Portugal, where it was significantly reduced. Across countries, the size of the high-tech sector varies, ranging from about 3.6 in Belgium and Sweden to mid-30 in Romania, Hungary, and Finland up to mid-60 in Luxembourg.

After 2008, the country risk (CRISK), the budget deficit (BUDGET), and public debt ratios (PUBDGDP) increased in every country included in the sample. While the escalation in the level of public debt ratio is rather noticeable in every European country, in countries like the Netherlands, Czech Republic, Denmark, UK, Luxembourg, Latvia, Lithuania, Ireland, and Romania, it soared immensely. The increase in the public debt ratio does not necessarily correspond with the increase in inflation rates (INFL), but after 2008 the largest increase in the inflation rates (INFL) is mostly observed in the countries with dramatic decrease in market capitalization ratio (MCAPCR) (for example, Belgium, Cyprus, Czech Republic, Denmark, France, Italy, Norway, Poland, and the UK). Overall, the importance of the stock market is down from the pre- to post-2008 period for every country in the sample, and across countries the level of the market capitalization ratio remains very different, varying from 1.45 in Denmark, 5.86 in Lithuania, and 7.31 in Ireland, up to 65.54 in Sweden and 101.22 in Switzerland. Consistent with expectations, all former Eastern bloc countries (Bulgaria, Czech Republic, Latvia, Lithuania, Poland, and Romania) display higher levels of inflation and very low levels of bank net assets during pre- and post-2008 periods, a noticeable increase in country risk, and a significant drop in market capitalization ratio and GDP growth after 2008. The size of the high-tech sector in all of these countries except Lithuania is somewhat average for all European countries.

Table 4.2, Panel D reports an increase in industry risk (IRISK) measure from the pre- to post-2008 period in all industries. However, IRISK did not rise uniformly throughout all industries. The agriculture, forestry, and fishing industries experienced a three-fold increase in IRISK, whereas in the manufacturing industry IRISK increased by only about four percentage points. The lowest increase in IRISK is reported in the service industry (by about two percentage points), and transportation and communications also report a decrease in industry risk after 2008.

Regression Analyses[12]

Table 4.3 presents the results of the regressions of leverage on the country- and firm-specific variables. The t-statistics are computed with clustering standard errors by both firm- and time-specific fixed effects together as I have two sources of dependence in the data. In Panel A the dependent variable is total leverage (TLTA) as measured by total liabilities scaled by total assets, while in Panels B and C I restrict the analysis to bank loans (BLTA) and bonds (FLTA) only. For each table, the first column reports the results for the overall sample, while in the second and third columns I separate the sample into pre- and post-2008 periods. Finally, the last column reports if the difference in the results between the two subsamples is statistically significant. A number of findings emerged from this analysis.

I draw several general conclusions from Table 4.3. First, the adjusted R^2-s look reasonable, with no significant variations among leverage ratios. Second, the adjusted R^2-s for the pre-2008 period are consistently higher than for the post-2008 period, mostly indicating the change in the significance of firm-specific variables, and suggesting possible structural changes in the firms due to the crisis. Third, the outcomes for TLTA, for the most part, are congruent with those for FLTA, as these two dependent variables are correlated with each other. Thus, I mostly concentrate the analysis on the results for BLTA and FLTA ratios. Finally, overall the outcome of the investigation supports the conjecture that during troubled periods the role of institutions in explaining firms' leverage is changing when debt is being measured as bank loans and bond debt ratios. And, finally, the impact of each independent variable is not completely uniform across the leverage ratios. For instance, while the index associated with

Table 4.3 Regression results

Panel A: TLTA regressions

	Total Sample	*Pre-2008*	*Post-2008*	*Difference*
INTERCEPT	17.448***	5.962***	17.786****	0.498
Country-Specific Variables				
FRINVGDP	0.021	0.000	-0.080**	0.055
HITECHNA	-0.230***	-0.068***	-0.195***	0.241***
CRSTR	-1.005***	-0.150***	-1.105***	0.956*
BNATNA	0.430****	0.228****	0.526****	-0.185
PUBDGDP	-0.157****	0.011****	-0.166****	0.194***
GDPGR	-0.595****	-0.303****	-1.355****	0.973***
CRISK	-0.076*	0.026*	0.147***	-0.030
IRISK	-0.116***	-0.085***	-0.009	-0.055
INFL*10^2	-2.072****	-0.934****	-1.464****	0.269
BUDGET*10	0.228*	0.464*	-0.064	0.714****
DBTGDP*10^2	5.375**	4.425**	3.810	-3.170
MCAPCR	6.052***	0.420***	-3.331	-1.871
TXSYS	10.212****	4.985****	2.956**	-2.266

(*Continued*)

Table 4.3 (Continued)

	Total Sample	*Pre-2008*	*Post-2008*	*Difference*
Firm-Specific Variables				
FDSALE	−0.156**	−0.026**	−0.200*	0.243
ROA	1.519	1.669	1.164	0.351
MVBV*10^{-2}	0.329**	−0.281**	1.036****	−1.413****
TATA	0.036*	−0.025*	0.056***	−0.125****
LATA	0.293****	0.355****	0.247****	0.105****
GROWTH	0.018***	0.014***	0.003	0.015
SIZE	1.594****	2.237****	1.325****	0.670***
ICR	−0.116*	−0.214*	−0.087	−0.174
F-value	35.23****	27.33****	40.4****	44.23****
Adjusted R square	14.91	17.33	14.50	18.00
Number of clusters	1,638	1,307	1,585	1,638

Panel B: BLTA regression results

	Total Sample	*Pre-2008*	*Post-2008*	*Difference*
INTERCEPT	12.946****	16.026***	11.067****	11.916**
Country-Specific Variables				
FRINVGDP	−0.003	−0.014	−0.068***	0.045**
HITECHNA	−0.150***	−0.091*	−0.128***	0.070*
CRSTR	−0.708****	−0.764***	−0.545***	−0.447
BNATNA	0.206****	0.060	0.261****	−0.176**
PUBDGDP	−0.076****	−0.041	−0.071****	0.031
GDPGR	−0.244****	−0.229	−0.625****	0.676***
CRISK	−0.157****	−0.141****	−0.058*	−0.069*
IRISK	−0.018	−0.001	0.031	−0.031
INFL*10^2	−0.997****	−0.958****	−0.653****	−0.796***
BUDGET*10	0.128*	0.191*	0.016	0.265**
DBTGDP*10^2	1.676	0.188	1.218	−2.097
MCAPCR	2.095**	−1.566	−1.724	−2.189*
TXSYS	6.735****	4.862****	3.284****	0.304
Firm-Specific Variables				
FDSALE	−0.111**	−0.059	−0.121*	0.096
ROA	0.078	0.400	−0.071	0.204
MVBV*10^{-2}	−0.149*	−0.410***	0.124	−0.492***
TATA	0.049****	0.036**	0.051****	−0.027*
LATA	13.884****	17.707****	10.817****	7.784****
GROWTH	0.012***	0.014**	0.002	0.016**
SIZE	0.052	0.130	0.075	−0.186
ICR	−0.053*	−0.101**	−0.039	−0.087
F-value	23.68****	15.24****	26.88****	33.36****
Adjusted R square	9.26	10.15	8.86	11.58
Number of clusters	1,638	1,307	1,585	1,638

Panel C: FLTA regression results

	Total Sample	*Pre-2008*	*Post-2008*	*Difference*
INTERCEPT	0.171	-13.300**	2.601	-8.465
Country-Specific Variables				
FRINVGDP	0.019	0.006	-0.020	0.004
HITECHNA	-0.087*	0.017	-0.073	0.201***
CRSTR	-0.257	0.554*	-0.464**	1.208***
BNATNA	0.248****	0.155	0.298****	-0.025
PUBDGDP	-0.093***	0.029	-0.098****	0.144***
GDPGR	-0.325****	-0.050	-0.775****	0.268
CRISK	0.059*	0.146***	0.197****	0.047
IRISK	-0.067**	-0.044	-0.017	0.013
INFL*10^2	-1.361****	-0.409*	-0.975****	0.742*
BUDGET*10	0.138	0.304**	-0.087	0.551****
DBTGDP*10^2	4.488***	5.267***	2.825*	-0.859
MCAPCR	4.169***	1.458	-1.850	-1.266
TXSYS	4.396****	1.030	-0.210	-2.720*
Firm-Specific Variables				
FDSALE	-0.055	0.030	-0.083	0.151
ROA	2.442**	3.063***	1.933	1.149
MVBV*10^{-2}	0.493***	0.126	0.970****	-0.972****
TATA	0.016	-0.027	0.033**	-0.097****
LATA	0.203****	0.245****	0.171****	0.070****
GROWTH	0.014***	0.012**	0.004	0.009
SIZE	1.551****	2.067****	1.294****	0.721***
ICR	-0.070**	-0.128**	-0.053*	-0.103
F-value	28.03****	24.66****	28.06****	27.47****
Adjusted R square	14.55	16.99	14.21	17.14
Number of clusters	1,638	1,307	1,585	1,638

1) ****,***,**, and * are significant at the levels of 0.0001, 0.01, 0.05, and 0.1 respectively.

(See Appendix for variables definition.)

the strength of creditors' protection (CRSTR) has a consistently strong negative association with the bank loans ratio throughout the whole period under investigation (Panel B), the association with the bond debt ratio becomes significant only after 2008 (Panel C). This might be explained by the fact that during economic downturns when fixed financial obligations become more strenuous, the bankruptcy laws act as a mediator of lending, preventing firms from enlarging their leverage. Consistent with the initial conjectures, the association between the bank loans ratio and (1) the foreign direct investment ratio (FRINVGDP), (2) the public debt ratio

(PUBDGDP), (3) the bank net assets ratio (BNATNA), and (4) the size of the high-tech sector ratio (HITECHNA) become significant only after 2008 and have expected signs. According to Demirgüç-Kunt et al. (1999), these results can also be interpreted as evidence that countries with larger high-tech sectors require a considerable amount of external capital, making equity financing of greater consequence. This effect seems to be amplified by the financial crisis as the impact of high-tech sector size on bank loans seems to grow during the troubled periods (Panel B).

The association between the bond debt ratio and the foreign direct investment ratio stays insignificant throughout the whole period under investigation, suggesting that foreign investors are not that sensitive when it comes to debt raised on the public market, probably because the public market to some extent assists in keeping the agency costs of managerial discretion under control (Panel C). The association between the bond debt ratio and the size of the high-tech sector remains insignificant throughout the whole period as well (Panel C).

From other country-level variables considered, the country risk impact on bond debt ratios is positive and significant, and this association is inverse and marginally significant when it comes to the bank loans. As Shyam-Sunder and Myers (1999) suggest, profitability is related to growth opportunities, so the negative association between CRISK and BLTA is a proxy for the obscurity in getting bank loans against intangible growth opportunities, especially in the time of elevated risk, so firms are turning to bonds.

From all firm-specific variables considered in testing the bond ratio, the tangibility of assets measured as LATA, the firm size (SIZE), and the interest coverage ratio (ICR) are significant always and have the expected signs. The association of assets tangibility (both LATA and TATA) with bank loans is exceptionally strong, which is consistent with the common rationale that amount of tangible assets (collateral) has a positive impact on the ability to issue secured debt. During the pre-2008 period the financing deficit (FDSALE) is negatively correlated with the total debt ratio only, which is inconsistent with the results reported by Lemmon and Zender (2004) for US firms, and the coefficient becomes insignificant in the post-2008 period for all three leverage ratios. The coefficient on the change in sales (GROWTH) is positive and significant for the pre-2008 period only, while the market-to-book ratio (MVBV) is positive for all three leverage ratios for the post-2008 period, but significant only for TLTA and FLTA. This result could be interpreted as a shift in firms' emphasis during troubled periods from current to expected conditions. In this regard, the MVBV could be inferred as a proxy for expected future growth opportunities (and less as performance), while GROWTH is a proxy for current growth conditions. Firm accounting performance (ROA) does not seem to play a role in explaining the leverage of European firms.

Another noticeable outcome is the change in the association between MVBV and BLTA from being significantly inverse for the pre-2008 period to becoming insignificant for the post-2008 period (Panel B). It is logical to assume that during the relatively stable economic period, firms with high market-to-book ratios can most likely successfully tap the equity market. During crisis periods, with equity markets highly perturbed, such firms have probably to turn to bond market rather than to bank loans, as the market better recognizes and rewards their outstanding performance. Positive and significant coefficients during the post-2008 period reported for MVBV and total liabilities in Panel A and for bonds' debt in Panel C are in line with this conjecture. Furthermore, the coefficient between FLTA and MVBV reported in Panel C of Table 4.3 changes from being insignificant during the pre-crisis period to becoming strongly significant (on 0.1% level) after 2008. Another notable result is that the coefficient of the size of a firm (SIZE) is insignificant in the case of bank loans.

Conclusions

Motivated by the recent economic crisis, this study seeks to investigate the determinants of using debt by European firms before and after 2008. To test the hypotheses, I employ clustered standard error estimates for the panel data set. A number of findings emerged from this analysis. First of all, I report a significant decrease in the use of debt from the pre- to post-2008 period consistent with the conjecture that the loss of investor confidence after financial shocks leads to increased risk aversion associated with reduced use of credit. Following the logic of the dynamic view of the capital structure, the pre-crisis level of leverage could not be immediately restored due to the transaction costs that may vary across the firms and tend to increase or decrease leverage, conditional on whether they were over- or under-levered before the crisis. Second, viewing the crisis in the light of agency conflict coupled with an elevated level of uncertainty, I provide important evidence that during economic instability the role of institutional environments in explaining firms' leverage is changing. Along with the notable decrease in foreign direct investment after 2008, I report a strong inverse association between direct foreign investment ratio and total debt and bank loans utilization, which I interpret as the result of strong risk-averse behavior on the part of foreign investors in a time of crisis. National variations in high-tech sector size, bank net assets, and public debt ratios all have a strong association with leverage after 2008. The only unexpected result is the inverse association between index measuring the strength of creditors' rights and leverage, which I explain by the mediating role of collateral and bankruptcy laws, protecting firms from over-levering.

Third, I evidence that leverage measured as bank loan ratio is less sensitive to the crisis and, thus, the difference in use of bank credit between pre- and post-2008 periods are much less pronounced. Finally, I also provide evidence that during troubled periods firm-specific variables that capture current conditions (i.e., accounting performance or growth) do not explain the firms' utilization of bonds anymore as the focus is shifting on future conditions and expected growth measured by a proxy as the market-to-book ratio. The prominent outcome is that the national level of market capitalization plays no role in debt utilization as Euronext provides the equity capital for all firms regardless of their country of incorporation.

Appendix

Definition of Variables

Variables	*Definition*
Dependent Variables	
TLTA	Total liabilities scaled by total assets
BLTA	Bank loans payable scaled by total assets
FLTA	Financial debt scaled by total assets
Country-Specific Variables	
CRISK	Country risk (standard deviation of ROA by country in a given year)
IRISK	Industry risk (standard deviation of ROA by sector in a given year)
FRINVGDP	Foreign direct investment scaled by GDP
HITECHNA	High-tech industries' net assets scaled by all industries' net assets
CRSTR	The strength of creditors' legal right index
BNATNA	Banking industries' net assets scaled by all industries' net assets
INFL	Inflation rate
BUDGET	Country budget deficit scaled by GDP
PUBDGDP	Public debt scaled by GDP
GDPGR	The growth rate of the GDP computed for two subsequent years
MCAPCR	Total equity capital-market value scaled by total public credit
TAXSYS	capital by country in a given year
Firm-specific variables	
FDSALE	Financing deficit (Interest Payment + Change in Working Capital + Dividends – Operating Cash Flow) / Sales
ROA	Operating income scaled by net assets
MVBV	Market value of equity to book value of equity ratio
TATA	Tangible assets scaled by total assets
LATA	Fixed long-term assets scaled by total assets
GROWTH	Percentage change in sales between two subsequent years
SIZE	The logarithm of total assets
ICR	Interest coverage ratio (earnings before interest, depreciation, and taxes divided by interest paid)

Table 4.4 reports the estimates from the regression with standardized coefficients to aid in the interpretability of the results. The pre-2008 time period is defined as 2005–2007. The post-2008 time period is defined as 2009–2011. See Appendix for variable definitions. *, **, ***, and **** indicate significance at the 10%, 5%, 1%, and < 1%, respectively.

Notes

1. Certainly, these factors do not influence the personal vs. corporate leverage decisions that is at the heart of the Modigliani and Miller (1958) capital structure framework.
2. Economic sentiment is a combination of consumer and business confidence reported by European Commission only for the Euro area.
3. In Europe, the relationship with banks is a much broader concept than just an emphasis on the special nature of the business relationship between banks and industrial clients. It is generally defined as the connection between a bank and a customer that goes beyond the execution of anonymous financial transactions, where banks play an important intermediary role during financial distress and bankruptcy.
4. According to Bienz and Walz (2008), the amount of *ex ante* bargaining power is increasing through the expanded use of covenants, which were rarely observed in the contracts of firms before 2005. Secondly, there has been a recent trend for capital rules to shift from primarily balance-sheet-based measurements towards the increased use of profit and loss accounts and cash flow statement information. In making this switch it appears that the relationship of net assets to capital that lies at the center of the traditional legal capital rules in CE is gradually losing its significance as creditors increasingly rely on financial ratios to assess contractual terms.
5. The International Monetary Fund estimated that large US and European banks lost about $1 trillion on toxic assets and from bad loans during 2008.
6. Pagano and von Thadden (2004) report the issuance of corporate bonds on an unprecedented scale in the wake of Europe's monetary unification.
7. I name bonds liability as FL to avoid any confusion with an acronym used for banks loans.
8. http://article.sciencepublishinggroup.com/pdf/10.11648.j.jbed.20170204.16.pdf.
9. The ownership structure of public debt is usually widely dispersed and bondholders cannot easily meet in order to undertake collective action. The enforcement of the law should help these weaker creditors and, in turn, favor public debt relative to private debt.
10. http://documents.worldbank.org/curated/en/650351468766824277/115515322_20041117162031/additional/multi0page.pdf.
11. Graham and Harvey (2001), after summarizing the responses of 392 American CFOs, indicated that 81% of them report either target debt ratio or range.
12. Because of the differences between Anglo-Saxon and Continental European business environments, the same analysis has been executed using only the data for Continental European firms (not tabulated here). There seems to be no significant difference in the results.

References

Armthe, J., 2000. Share Capital and Creditor Protection: Efficient Rules for a Modern Company Law. *Modern Law Review*, Vol. 63, 355, 374–375.

Bancel, F., and U. R. Mittoo, 2004. Cross-Country Determinants of Capital Structure Choice: A Survey of European Firms. *Financial Management*, Vol. 33, 103–132.

Barclay, M. J., E. Morellec, and Jr. C. W. Smith, 2006. On the Debt Capacity of Growth Options. *Journal of Business*, Vol. 79, 37–59.

Barth, M. E., J. Gomez-Biscarri, and G. Lopez-Espinoza, 2012. Fair Value Accounting and Firm Valuation. Working paper. Stanford University.

Beck, T., A. Demirguc-Kunt, and V. Maksimovic, 2008. Financing Patterns around the World: The Role of Institutions. *Journal of Financial Economics*, 467–487.

Bevan, A., and J. Danbolt, 2001. On the Determinants and Dynamics of UK Capital Structure. EFMA 2001 Lugano Meetings. Available at SSRN: http://ssrn.com/abstract=269732 or doi:10.2139/ssrn.269732

Bienz, C., and U. Walz, 2008. Venture Capital Exit Rights. Presentation at the ESSEC Private Equity Conference. Available at www.essec-private-equity.com.

Booth, L., V. Aivazian, A. Demirguc-Kunt, and V. Maksimovic, 2001. Capital Structures in Developing Countries. *Journal of Finance*, Vol. 56, No. 1, 87–130.

Brounen, D., A. de Jong, and K. Koedijk, 2004. Corporate Finance in Europe: Confronting Theory with Practice. *Financial Management*, Vol. 33, No. 7, 1–101.

Brounen, D., A. de Jong, and K. Koedijk, 2005. Capital Structure Policies in Europe: Survey Evidence. ERIM Report Series reference Continental Europe number, ERS-2005-005-F&A.

Brounen, D., A. de Jong, and K. Koedijk, 2006. Capital Structure Policies in Europe: Survey Evidence. *Journal of Banking and Finance*, Vol. 30, No. 5, 1409–1442.

Caskey, J., J. Hughes, and J. Liu, 2012. Leverage, Excess Leverage, and Future Returns. *Review of Accounting Studies*. Published online: 30 November 2011.

Dahlquist, M., and G. Robertson, 2001. Direct Foreign Ownership, Institutional Investors, and Firm Characteristics. *Journal of Financial Economics*, Vol. 59, 413–440.

Day, J., P. Ormerod, and P. Taylor, 2004. Implications for Lending Decision and Debt Contracting of the Adoption of International Financial Reporting Standards. *Journal of International Banking Law and Regulation*, Vol. 19, 475–486.

Demirgüç-Kunt, A., and V. Maksimovic, 1999. Institutions, Financial Markets, and Firm Debt Maturity. *Journal of Financial Economics*, Vol. 54, No. 3, 295–336.

Demirguc-Kunt, A., and H. Huizinga, 1999. Determinants of Commercial Bank Interest Margins and Profitability: Some International Evidence (English). *The World Bank economic review*, Vol. 13, No. 2 (May 1999), 379–408. http://documents.worldbank.org/curated/en/432491468175436769/Determinants-of-commercial-bank-interest-margins-and-profitability-some-international-evidence

De Jong, A., R. Kabir, and T. T. Nguyen, 2008. Capital Structure around the World: The Roles of Firm—and Country—Specific Determinants. *Journal of Banking & Finance*, Vol. 32, 1954–1969.

Demsetz, H., and K. Lehn, 1985. The Structure of Corporate Ownership: Causes and Consequences. *Journal of Political Economy*, Vol. 96, No. 6, 1155–1177.

Faccio, M., L. P. H. Lang, and L. Young, 2010. Pyramiding vs. Leverage in Corporate Groups: International Evidence. *Journal of International Business Studies*, Vol. 41, 88–104.

Fama, E., and K. R. French, 1997. Industry Costs of Equity. *Journal of Financial Economics*, Vol. 43, 153–193.

Fama, E., and K. R. French, 1998. Taxes, Financing Decisions, and Firm Value. *The Journal of Finance*, Vol. 53, No. 3, 819–843.

Fan, J. P. H, S. Titman, and G. Twite, 2012. An International Comparison of Capital Structure and Debt Maturity Choices. *Journal of Financial and Quantitative Analysis*, Vol. 47, No. 1, 23–56.

Frank, M. Z., and V. K. Goyal, 2003. Testing the Pecking Order Theory of Capital Structure. *Journal of Financial Economics*, Vol. 67, 217–248.

Frank, M. Z., and K. V. Goyal, 2007. Trade-Off and Pecking Order Theories of Debt. *Handbook of Corporate Finance: Empirical Corporate Finance*, Vol. 2, 1–82.

Frank, M. Z., and K. V. Goyal, 2009. Capital Structure Decisions: Which Factors Are Reliably Important? *Financial Management*, Vol. 38, No. 1, 1–37.

Frydenberg, S., 2011. Theory of Capital Structure: A Review. *Freedom and Plurality-Honorary Thesis for Odd.* G. Arntzen, L. Fallan, and O. Gustafsson, eds., Trondheim, Norway: Tapir Academic Press, NO-7005. Available at SSRN: http://ssrn.com/abstract=556631

Gaud, P., M. Hoesli, and A. Bender, 2007. Debt-Equity Choice in Europe. *International Review of Financial Analysis*, Vol. 16, No. 3, 201–222.

Gérard, D., 2008. Managing the Financial Crisis in Europe: Why Competition Law is Part of the Solution and not the Problem. Available at: www. abstract=1330326

Giroud, X., and H. M Mueller, 2007. Does Corporate Governance Matter in Competitive Industries? ECGI—Finance Working Paper No. 185/2007. 2nd Annual Conference on Empirical Legal Studies Paper. Available at SSRN: http://ssrn.com/abstract=1006118

Gorton, G., 2010. *Slapped by the Invisible Hand: The Panic of 2007*. Oxford: Oxford University Press.

Gorton, G., and A. Metrick, 2010. Regulating the Shadow Banking System, Brookings Paper. Available at: www.brookings.edu/~/media/Files/Programs/ES/BPEA/2010_

Graham, J. R., and C. Harvey, 2001. The Theory and Practice of Corporate Finance: Evidence from the Field. *Journal of Financial Economics*, Vol. 60, Nos. 2–3, 187–243.

Harris, M., and A. Raviv. 1990. Capital Structure and the Informational Role of Debt. *The Journal of Finance*, Vol. 45, No. 2, 321–349.

Harris, M., and A. Raviv. 1991. The Theory of Capital Structure. *The Journal of Finance*, Vol. 46, No. 1, 297–355.

International Monetary Fund. 2012. Global Financial Stability Report. Available at: www.imf.org/External/Pubs/FT/GFSR/2012/02/

Jensen, M. C., 1986. Agency Costs of Free Cash Flow, Corporate Finance, and Take-Overs. *American Economic Review*, Vol. 76, No. 2.

Knight, F. H., 1921. *Risk, Continental Europertainty, and Profit.* Boston, MA: Hart, Schaffner & Marx; Houghton Mifflin Co.

Kubler, F., 2004. A Comparative Approach to Capital Maintenance: Germany. *European Business Law Review*, Vol. 15, 1031–1036.

Lemmon, M. L., and J. F. Zender, 2004. Debt Capacity and Tests of Capital Structure Theories. Working paper, University of Utah and the University of Colorado at Boulder.

Long, M. S., and I. B. Malitz, 1985. The Investment-Financing Nexus: Some Empirical Evidence. *Midland Corporate Finance Journal*, Vol. 3, 53–59.

Miguel, de A., and J. Pindado, 2001. Determinants of Capital Structure: New Evidence from Spanish Panel Data. *Journal of Corporate Finance*, Vol. 7, 77–99.

Miller, E. M. 1977. Risk, Uncertainty, and Divergence of Opinion. *The Journal of Finance*, Vol. 32, No. 4, 1151–1168.

Myers, S. C., 1977. Determinants of Corporate Borrowing. *Journal of Financial Economics*, Vol. 5, 147–175.

Myers, S. C., 1984. The Capital Structure Puzzle. *Journal of Finance*, Vol. 39, 575–592.

Myers, S. C., 2001. Capital Structure. *The Journal of Economic Perspectives*, Vol. 15, No. 2. (Spring), 81–102.

Nissim, D., and S. H. Penman, 2003. Financial Statement Analysis of Leverage and How It Informs about Profitability and Price-to-Book Ratios. *Review of Accounting Studies*, Vol. 8, 531–560.

Paananen, M., and N. Parmar, 2008. The Adoption of IFRS in the UK. AAA 2009 Mid-Year International Accounting Section (IAS) Meeting. Available at SSRN: http://ssrn.com/abstract=1275805

Pagano, M., and E. L. von Thadden, 2004. The European Bond Markets under EMU, *Oxford Review of Economic Policy*, Vol. 20, 531–554.

Petersen, M. 2008. Estimating Standard Errors in Finance Panel Dataset: Comparing Approaches. *The Review of Financial Studies*, Vol. 22, No. 1, 435–480.

Rajan, R. G., and L. Zingales, 1995. What Do We Know about Capital Structure? Some Evidence Form International Data. *Journal of Finance*, Vol. 50, No. 5 (December), 1421–1460.

Rajan, R. G., and L. Zingales, 2003. The Great Reversals: The Politics of Financial Development in the Twentieth Century. *Journal of Financial Economics*, Vol. 69, 5–50.

Schoen, T., 2004. The Future of Legal Capital. *European Business Organization Law Review*, Vol. 5, 429, 438–442.

Shambaugh, J. 2012. The Euro's Three Crises. *Brookings Papers on Economic Activity. 2012*, No. 1, 157–231.

Shyam-Sunder, L., and S. C. Myers, 1999. Testing Static Tradeoff Against Pecking Order Models of Capital Structure. *Journal of Financial Economics*, Vol. 51, 219–244.

Thompson, S., 2011. Simple Formulas for Standard Errors That Cluster by Both Firm and Time. *Journal of Financial Economics*, Vol. 99, No. 1, 1–10.

Titman, S., 2002. The Modigliani and Miller Theorem and the Integration of Financial Markets. *Financial Management*, Vol. 31, 101–115.

Titman, S., and R. Wessels, 1988. The Determinants of Capital Structure Choice. *The Journal of Finance*, Vol. 43, No. 1, 1–19.

Tweedie, D., 2008. Bringing Transparency to Financial Reporting: Towards an Improved Accounting Framework in the Aftermath of the Credit Crisis. *Financial Stability Review*, Vol. 12, 115–120.

Zeckhauser, R. J., and J. Pound, 1990. Are Large Shareholders Effective Monitors?: An Investigation of Share Ownership and Corporate Performance. *Asymmetric Information, Corporate Finance, and Investment*. Chicago: University of Chicago Press, 149–180.

Part 2

5 Consolidation of Investees Under IFRS

Paul Munter

Background

Coming out of the financial crisis, there were concerns among some that the previous consolidation and disclosure standards failed to adequately portray the risks that investors in certain entities were exposed to. This concern was further exasperated by the fact that investee entities were described in a variety of different ways, including special purpose entities in IFRS, variable interest entities in US GAAP, and also special purpose vehicles and structured entities in practice.

IFRS 10, *Consolidated Financial Statements*, replaced IAS 27 (2008), *Consolidated and Separate Financial Statements*, and SIC 12, *Consolidation—Special Purpose Entities*, and applies to all investees unless the investee is an investment entity. In that circumstance, the investor accounts for its investment in the investee at fair value through profit or loss.

Adding to the challenge described was the fact that IFRS previously had two different consolidation models: one for special purpose entities (a risk and rewards model) and another for all other investees (a control model). This, of course, made the judgment around whether the investee was or was not a special purpose entity an especially important judgment area.

In its revised consolidation standard, IFRS 10, the IASB stated that its objective was to develop a single consolidation model applicable to all investees. Under the IFRS 10 control model, an investor has control and therefore consolidates an investee when it has (1) power, (2) exposure to variability in returns, and (3) linkage between the two.

While IFRS 10 articulates a single control model, there nevertheless is a gating question because IFRS 10 provides guidance for evaluating investees in which voting and potential voting rights are important to the determination of power vs. situations in which factors other than voting rights are important to the determination of power over an investee. While this may sound similar to the previous distinction of whether the investee is a special purpose entity, it is a different concept (although most investees that previously were classified as special purpose entities would be entities for which factors other than voting rights are important). Likewise, this concept is different from the US GAAP concept of a variable interest entity investee. As a consequence, it is clear that IFRS 10 is a different approach from that which previously existed under IFRS and it is also a different approach than that which currently exists under US GAAP.

Exposure to variability in returns is a broader concept than ownership benefits or risks and rewards. Returns can include not only ownership benefits such as dividends and changes in the value of the investment, but also fees, remuneration, tax benefits, economies of scale, cost savings, and other economic synergies.

The IASB also explicitly included the concepts of principal vs. agent in the linkage component of control. Further, IFRS 10 specifically addresses *de facto* control wherein an investor may have control over an investee for which voting rights are important even with less than a majority of the current voting rights. The principal/agent analysis is particularly important for industries such as funds, asset management, and real estate but can also be important in other situations. The explicit inclusion of *de facto* control introduced changes from previous practice since most entities had applied the previous standard, IAS 27, on the basis of legal rather than *de facto* control.

Lastly, while the consolidation project was, at one time, a joint project between the IASB and the FASB, the FASB decided not to pursue completion of consolidation as a joint project. Accordingly, while the FASB has made a number of changes to its consolidation model over many years, US GAAP continues to have a separate model for variable interest entities vs. that for voting interest entities. As a consequence, there are a number of circumstances for which the consolidation answer under US GAAP will differ from that under IFRS.

Overview of the IFRS 10 Model

Under the IFRS 10 control model, an investor has control and therefore consolidates an investee when it has (1) power, (2) exposure to variability in returns, and (3) linkage between the two. Control is assessed on a continuous basis. This means that control is reassessed as facts and circumstances change. However, a change in market conditions does not trigger a reassessment of the control conclusion unless it changes one or more of the elements of control, e.g., whether potential voting rights are substantive.

In making the control assessment, the investor considers the purpose and design of the investee. This is important in the identification of the investee's relevant activities, in how decisions about those activities are made, in who has the current ability to direct those activities, and in who receives returns. To have power, it is necessary for the investor to have *existing rights* that give it the *current* ability to direct the activities that significantly affect the investee's returns. An investor can have power over an investee even if other parties have existing rights to participate in the direction of the relevant activities.

The definition of power is based on *ability* rather than exercise of power. Therefore, power does not need to be exercised for an investor to have control over the investee. Conversely, evidence that the investor has been directing the relevant activities is not in itself conclusive in determining that the investor has power over the investee. Also, in the absence of other rights, economic dependence of an investee on the investor does not automatically result in the investor controlling the investee. For example, a franchisee may be heavily dependent upon the activities and support of the franchisor, but that does not mean that a franchisor controls its franchisees.

In many cases the assessment of control is straightforward: the investee is clearly controlled by means of equity instruments and the investor holding a majority of the voting rights controls the investee. In other cases, the assessment is more complex and a number of factors will need to be considered.

The investor also needs to consider the nature of its relationships with other parties when assessing control. The assessment of control is performed on a continuous basis and the investor reassesses whether it controls an investee if facts and circumstances indicate that there are changes to one or more of the elements of control:

- Power, e.g., substantive rights held by other parties lapse
- Returns, e.g., the investor ceases to receive returns
- Linkage between power and returns, e.g., the investor no longer acts as an agent or vice versa because of a change in the investor's economic interest in the investee

Determining how decisions about the relevant activities are made is also assessed on a continuous basis.

A change in market conditions does not trigger a reassessment of the control conclusion unless it changes one or more of the three elements of control or the overall relationship between a principal and an agent, such as a change in the expected returns used in evaluating the investor's economic interest in the investee. A change in market conditions alone normally will not cause potential voting rights to become substantive or cease to be substantive. This is because determining whether potential voting rights are substantive is a holistic analysis that takes into account a variety of factors, including market conditions.

Consideration of Purpose and Design

The investor considers the purpose and design of the investee at various steps of the analysis. First it is considered so as to identify:

- The relevant activities
- How decisions about such activities are made
- Who has the current ability to direct those activities
- Who receives returns

The purpose and design of the investee is of high-level consideration in the analysis, but is also important in determining how decisions over the relevant activities are made.

The purpose and design of the investee is also considered in the context of an investor holding potential voting rights. This consideration includes an assessment of the terms and conditions of the rights as well as the reasons for agreeing to them. Purpose and design are also considered when rights other than voting rights are relevant in assessing whether an investor controls an investee. This includes consideration of involvement in the investee's design, decisions, contractual arrangements made at the investee's inception, investees with predetermined activities, and situations in which an investor has a commitment to ensure that the investee continues to operate as designed. Finally, purpose and design of the investee is considered when assessing whether a decision maker is a principal or an agent. This is particularly relevant when assessing the scope of the decision-making authority.

Identify the Investee

The term "investee" is not defined in IFRS 10. However, it is used throughout IFRS 10 as an entity or a deemed entity that is or may be a subsidiary of the investor. Control by an investor generally is assessed at the level of the legal entity. However, in some cases an investor has power over only specified assets and liabilities of an entity and treats that portion of the entity as a deemed separate entity (i.e., a "silo"). A silo is assessed for consolidation purposes only if:

- In substance, the assets, liabilities, and equity of the silo are separate from the overall entity such that none of those assets can be used to pay other obligations of the entity and those assets are the only source of payment for specified liabilities of the silo
- Parties other than those with the specified liability have no rights or obligations related to the specified assets or to residual cash flows from those assets

In practice, very few structures meet these requirements. As a consequence, in the vast majority of circumstances the consolidation analysis is performed at the legal entity level.

Identify the Relevant Activities of the Investee

Relevant activities of the investee are the activities of the investee that *significantly* affect the investee's returns. There may be investees:

- With a range of operating and financing activities significantly affecting their returns
- For which several investors each direct different relevant activities
- For which relevant activities occur only when particular circumstances or events occur

A Range of Operating and Financing Activities Significantly Affect Returns

In many investees, a range of operating and financing activities significantly affect returns: sales of goods or provision of services, management of financial assets, acquisitions and disposals of operating assets, management of research and development activities, and determination of the funding structure. In these cases, the decisions affecting the returns will typically be associated with decisions such as establishing operating and capital decisions, e.g., budgets, and appointing, remunerating, and terminating key management personnel or other service providers.

Different Investors Direct Different Relevant Activities

There can be investees in which different investors have the ability to direct different relevant activities. In such cases, the investor that has the *current* ability to direct the activities that *most significantly* affect the returns of the investee has power. This principle also applies if different relevant activities occur at different times.

For example, A and B (unrelated entities) create a separate legal entity C. C's purpose and design is to conduct research and development on a biotechnology initiative. If the research and development is successful, C will then commercialize and sell the biotech product. A has the power over the research and development activities—i.e., A has exclusive decision-making authority over all aspects of the research and development phase. If the research and development is successful, B then has all the decision-making authority over the commercialization and sale of the subsequent product. The initial question is: which is the most significant activity of C? If it is the research and development activity, then A will have power. Conversely, if it is the commercialization and sale of the product, the B will have power. This will often require significant judgment and could be heavily dependent on the risk of the research and development undertaking. If the research and development is "early stage," it is likely that the research and development will be the relevant activity and A will have power (although if successful, a reassessment likely will be required at that point). Conversely, if the research and development is in the latter stages at the time that C is created, it is likely that the commercialization will be the relevant activity and B will have power.

Relevant Activities Occur Only When Particular Events Occur

There can also be investees for which relevant activities occur only when particular circumstances arise or events occur, as the direction of activities is predetermined until this date. In this case, only the decisions when those events occur can affect the returns significantly and therefore be relevant activities.

For example, entity A holds mortgages that have been sold to the structure by a variety of unrelated mortgage originators. Entity B is the servicer for A. B manages the collection of the mortgage payments and the distribution of the cash to the investors in accordance with the predetermined waterfall. However, in the event of default, C has the authority to make the decision about the mortgage (i.e., pursue foreclosure, modify the terms of the mortgage, etc.). Because defaults are what changes the returns to the investors, even when there have been no defaults to date, C has power over the relevant activities of A.

Identify How Decisions About the Relevant Activities Are Made

Determining how decisions about the relevant activities are made is key in the IFRS 10 approach and represents a "gating" question in the control analysis. This gating question seeks to determine whether voting rights are relevant in assessing whether the investor has power over the investee, i.e., whether the investee is controlled by means of voting instruments; or if voting rights are not relevant in assessing whether the investor has power over the investee, i.e., the investee is controlled by means of other rights. Depending on the answer to this gating question, a different analysis will be performed to assess which investor has power over the investee.

Investee Controlled by Means of Voting Rights

When the investee is controlled by means of equity instruments, with associated voting rights, the assessment of power focuses on which investor, if any, has voting rights sufficient to direct the investee's relevant activities, absent any additional arrangements that alter the decision-making. In straightforward cases, the investor holding the majority of the voting rights has power over (and controls) the investee.

More Complex Cases

For more complex cases, a number of factors are relevant for (1) assessing what is determinative in assessing control, i.e., voting or other rights; and then (2) identifying the controlling party. This will involve an analysis of:

- What the purpose and design of the investee is
- What the relevant activities are
- How decisions about the relevant activities are made
- Whether the investor is exposed or has rights to variable returns from its involvement with the investee
- Whether the investor has the ability to use its power over the investee to affect the amount of the investor's returns

Investees Designed So That Voting Rights Are Not Relevant

Some investees are designed so that voting rights are not relevant to the determination of power, but instead other rights are relevant. These entities generally are referred to as structured entities. In these structures, consideration of the purpose and design of the investee includes consideration of:

- The risks that the investee was designed to create
- The risks that the investee was designed to pass on to the parties involved in the transaction
- Whether the investor is exposed to some or all of these risks

The consideration of risks includes both downside risk and the potential for upside return.

The Gating Question Is Subject to Continuous Assessment

Determining how decisions about the relevant activities are made is assessed on a continuous basis: changes in the decision-making rights can, for example, imply that the relevant activities are no longer controlled by means of equity instruments but by means of contractual rights.

Structured vs. Nonstructured Entities

Although there is no distinction between different types of entities in determining whether one entity controls another, as noted earlier there is a "gating" question in the analysis that distinguishes between entities for which:

- Voting rights are the dominant factor in assessing whether the investor has power over the investee, i.e., the investee is controlled by voting instruments.
- Voting rights are not the dominant factor in assessing whether the investor has power over the investee, i.e., the investee is controlled by means of other rights.

This chapter refers to entities for which voting rights are relevant as "nonstructured entities" and those for which voting rights are not relevant as "structured entities."

Nonstructured Entities

An investor "controls" an investee if the investor is exposed to (has rights to) variable returns from its involvement with the investee, and has the ability to affect those returns through its power over the investee. "Control" involves power, exposure to variability of returns, and a link between the two.

If the investee is controlled by equity instruments, with associated voting rights, then the assessment of power focuses on which investor, if any, has sufficient voting rights to direct the investee's relevant activities. This assessment would be relevant when there is an absence of any additional arrangements that alter the decision-making. In the most straightforward cases, the investor holding the majority of the voting rights has power over and likely controls the investee.

An investor considers both substantive rights that it holds and substantive rights held by others. To be "substantive," rights need to be exercisable when decisions about the relevant activities are required to be made, and the holder needs to have a practical ability to exercise those rights. Protective rights are related to fundamental changes in the activities of an investee, or are rights that apply only in exceptional circumstances. As such, they cannot give the holder power or prevent other parties from having power and therefore control over an investee.

In assessing control, an investor considers its potential voting rights—e.g., a call option over shares of the investee—as well as potential voting rights held by other parties to the extent those rights are substantive, to determine whether it has power. Potential voting rights are considered only if they are substantive. Determining whether rights are substantive requires judgement taking into account all available facts and circumstances. Factors to consider include:

- Whether there are barriers that prevent the holder from exercising the rights, such as:
  - Financial penalties or incentives

  - A conversion or exercise price that creates a financial barrier for the holder
  - Terms and conditions that make it unlikely that the rights will be exercised (e.g., if the holder exercises it must dispose of a significant portion of its existing operations)
  - The absence of a mechanism by which the holder can exercise the rights
  - The inability of the rights holder to obtain the information necessary to exercise its rights
  - Operational barriers/incentives that would prevent the holder from exercising its rights
- Whether several parties need to agree for the rights to become exercisable or operational:
  - The more parties that are required to agree to exercise the rights, the less likely it is that those rights are substantive
  - Removal rights exercisable by a governing body are more likely to be substantive than if the rights are exercisable individually by a large number of investors who must come together to agree to exercise the rights
- Whether the party that holds the rights would benefit from their exercise:
  - The rights are more likely to be substantive when the potential voting rights are in the money or when the investor can realize other benefits (including economic synergies) with the investee by exercising the potential voting rights

Box 5.1 Example—Exercise of Voting Rights in Relation to Relevant Activities

Investee X, whose activities are controlled through voting rights, has annual shareholder meetings at which decisions to direct the relevant activities are made. The next shareholder meeting is scheduled in eight months' time. However, shareholders can call a special meeting to change the existing policies over relevant activities, but there is a requirement to give a 30-day notice to the other shareholders before a meeting can be held.

Scenario 1

Investor A holds a majority of the voting rights in X. A's voting rights are substantive because A is able to make decisions about the relevant activities when they need to be made. The fact that it takes 30 days before A can exercise its voting rights does not prevent A from having power.

Scenario 2

Investor B holds an option to acquire the majority of the shares in X that is exercisable in 25 days and that is deeply in the money. B has rights that are essentially equivalent to the majority shareholder in scenario 1 because B as the holder of the option can make decisions about the direction of the relevant activities when they need to be made because the rights are exercisable before a special meeting would be held.

It takes longer for B to call a special meeting than for an ordinary shareholder (25 days + 30 days). However, as it takes 30 days for the meeting to be held, if any other shareholder calls a special meeting, the potential voting rights held by B can become voting rights by the time the meeting is held, since the option is exercisable in 25 days. This, coupled with the fact that the option is deeply in the money and no other barriers to exercise exist, is the reason why these rights are considered substantive currently.

Scenario 3

Investor C is party to a forward contract to acquire the majority of the shares in X. The forward contract's settlement date is in six months' time. In contrast to the previous scenarios, C does not have a substantive right *currently* because C does not have the current ability to direct the relevant activities of X. C does not have this ability because the settlement of the forward contract is in six months' time; therefore, the existing shareholders have the ability to direct the relevant activities. However, because the assessment is a continuous one, as the forward contract gets closer to the settlement date, C may conclude that it has control prior to settlement, e.g., once settlement is less than 30 days.

Box 5.2 Example—Protective Rights

Bank A is the primary lender to Borrower X. Borrower X's activities include a wide variety of operating and financing activities and as such power over the relevant activities is exercised through voting rights. Investor B owns all of the voting rights of X. The lending agreement states that in the event of default, any significant changes in the business (e.g., decisions to sell assets, restructure operations, capital expenditures) must be approved by Bank A.

Scenario 1

X is currently in compliance with the covenant provisions on its loans. As a consequence, the rights held by Bank A are deemed to be protective rights and therefore do not give it power over X. Accordingly, B has power over X.

Scenario 2

X has experienced significant operating losses and has fallen into default of its lending arrangements with Bank A. Bank A has not yet exercised its rights to approve significant changes in the business, choosing to allow management of X to develop a restructuring plan and work its way out of its current financial difficulties. In this scenario, the rights that previously were deemed to be protective have now become substantive by virtue of X being in default. Notwithstanding the fact that Bank A has chosen to allow management to continue to make the ongoing relevant decisions, Bank A has power because it has the current ability to exercise those decisions. The fact that it has chosen not to is not relevant. Because the assessment is continuous, when X went into default, Bank A would reassess its relationship with X and would conclude that it has power over its relevant decisions.

An investor can have power over an investee when the investee's relevant activities are directed through voting rights in the following situations:

- The investor holds the majority of the voting rights; or
- The investor holds less than a majority of the voting rights but:
  - Has an agreement with other vote holders
  - Holds rights arising from other contractual arrangements
  - Holds potential voting rights that are exercisable when the decisions about significant activities of the investee will be made (see example above)
  - Holds voting rights sufficient to unilaterally direct the relevant activities of the investee
  - Holds a combination of these rights

If the activities of the investee can be directed by a vote of the investor or the majority of the members of the governing body of the investee can be appointed by a vote of the investor, then the investor has power, unless:

- The voting rights are not substantive (see previous example with respect to protective rights that become substantive)
- The voting rights do not provide the investor with the current ability to direct the relevant activities
- Another party has existing rights to direct the relevant activities of the investee and that party is not an agent of the investor

For example, an investor does not control an investee whose relevant activities are directed by a liquidator or regulator because in that situation the liquidator or regulator is acting in the best interests of parties other than the equity holders.

The investor can have power without a majority of the voting rights of an investee, for example, when an agreement with other vote holders gives the investor the right to exercise voting rights or to direct enough other vote holders on how to vote, sufficient to give it power.

De Facto Power Over the Investee

In assessing whether the investor's current voting rights are sufficient to give it power even though it has less than half of the voting rights, IFRS 10 sets up a two-step approach:

- Step 1—investor considers relevant facts and circumstances, including:
  - Size of investor's holding of voting rights relative to the size and dispersion of the holders of other vote holders
  - Potential voting rights held by the investor, other vote holders or other parties
  - Other contractual arrangements
  - Assessment outcomes:
    - Sufficient evidence exists to conclude that investor has power (stop at Step 1)
    - Sufficient evidence exists to conclude that investor does not have power (stop at Step 1) or
    - Analysis is inconclusive (go to Step 2)
- Step 2—investor considers additional facts and circumstances, including:
  - Voting patterns at previous shareholders' meetings
  - Evidence of power
  - Special relationships with investee
  - Level of investor's exposure to variability in returns (i.e., disproportionality between legal ownership interest and economic participation in investee's returns)
  - Assessment outcomes:
    - Additional analysis is sufficient to conclude the investor has power
    - Additional analysis is sufficient to conclude the investor does not have power
    - Additional analysis is inconclusive—in which case investor does not have *de facto* power

Thus, even without potential voting rights or other contractual rights, when the investor holds significantly more voting rights than any other vote holder or organized group of vote holders, it may be sufficient evidence of power. In other situations, these factors may provide sufficient evidence that the investor does not have power. In some cases, these factors may not be conclusive and the investor will need to proceed to the second step. The smaller the size of the investor's holding of voting rights and the less the dispersion of the holding of other vote holders, the more reliance is placed on the additional factors, with a greater weighting on the evidence of power.

The meaning of "voting patterns at previous shareholders' meetings" is explained in the implementation guidance to IFRS 10. It requires consideration of the number of shareholders that typically come to the meetings to vote, i.e., the usual quorum in shareholders' meetings, and not how the other shareholders vote, i.e., whether they usually vote the same way as the investor.

Box 5.3 Example—*De Facto* Power

Scenario 1

Company A holds 48% of the voting rights of Company X, with the rest of the voting rights held by thousands of shareholders, none of whom individually hold more than 1% of the voting rights in X. None of the shareholders has any arrangements to consult each other or make collective decisions, and coordination between other shareholders would not be easy. In this case, on the basis of the size of its holding and the relative size of the other shareholdings, it is likely that A has a sufficiently dominant voting interest to meet the power criterion without the need to consider any other evidence of power.	The first step is sufficient to conclude that A has power.

Scenario 2

Company A holds 45% of the voting rights of Company X. Two other investors unrelated to A each hold 26% of the voting rights in X. The remaining 3% of the voting rights are dispersed. There are no other arrangements that affect decision-making. In this case, considering the size of A's voting interest and its relative size to the other shareholdings, it is likely that A would conclude that it does not have power as only two other investors would need to cooperate to be able to prevent A from controlling X.	The first step is sufficient to conclude that A does not have power.

Scenario 3

Company A holds 35% of the voting rights in Company X and three other investors each hold 8% of the voting rights in X.	The first step is not conclusive, and the second step evaluation needs to be conducted.

The remaining 41% is widely dispersed, with no other shareholder holding as much as 1%. There are no other arrangements that affect decision-making. In this case, considering the size of A's holding and the relative size of the other shareholdings alone is not conclusive to determine whether A has rights sufficient to give it power. So far, A has been directing the relevant activities of X as a sufficient number of other shareholders voted in the same way as A. Decisions about relevant activities of X require the approval of a majority of votes cast at relevant shareholders' meetings. At recent relevant shareholders' meetings, 75% of the voting rights have been cast. That is, A holds 47% (35/75) of the "active" voting rights in X.	In the second step, the active participation of the other shareholders at recent relevant shareholders' meetings indicates that A does not have the practical ability to direct the relevant activities unilaterally.

Structured Entities

IFRS has no concept of variable interest entities. Instead, "structured entities" are entities designed such that voting or similar rights are not the dominant factor in assessing control. When voting rights are not relevant to the analysis, the investor considers the purpose and design of the investee and the following factors:

- Evidence of practical ability to direct the relevant activities
- Indications of special relationships with the investee
- Whether the investor has a large exposure to variability in returns

When these three factors are considered, greater weight is given to the first factor.

The assessment of the purpose and design of the investee includes consideration of the risks that the investee was designed to create and to pass on to the parties involved in the transaction, and whether the investor is exposed to some or all of those risks. Other items to consider include:

- Involvement and decisions made at the investee's inception.
    - Does the involvement provide the investor with rights that are sufficient to give it power?
    - Does involvement in design of investee indicate that the investor had the opportunity to obtain rights sufficient to give it power?
- Contractual arrangements such as call rights, put rights, or liquidation rights established at the investee's inception.
    - Do the decision-making rights embedded in contractual arrangements that are closely related to the investee give the investor power?

- Circumstances in which the relevant activities occur only when particular circumstances arise or events occur.
    - Are the decisions when those events occur the decisions that can affect the returns of the investee significantly (e.g., decision-making in the event of default in a mortgage securitization structure)?
- The investor's commitment to ensuring that the investee continues to operate as designed.
    - Does this commitment increase the investor's exposure to the variability of returns (particularly losses) increase the likelihood that it has power?

In some circumstances it may be difficult to determine whether an investor's rights are sufficient to give it power over an investee. In those circumstances an investor considers any evidence that it has the practical ability to direct the relevant activities. Examples of these circumstances are when the investor can appoint or approve the investee's key management personnel who have the ability to direct the relevant activities or when the investor can direct the investee to enter into a significant transaction for the benefit of the investor.

In some situations, the nature of the relationship that the investor has with the investee may suggest that the investor has more than a passive interest in the investee (i.e. "special relationships"). This could mean that the investor has other rights or provide evidence of existing power over the investee. The investor should consider situations when:

- The investee's key management personnel who direct the relevant activities are current or previous employees of the investor.
- The investee's operations are dependent on the investor, e.g., for funding, critical technology, or intellectual property.
- A significant portion of the investee's activities either involve or are conducted on behalf of the investor.
- The investor's exposure, or rights, to the returns from its involvement with the investee is disproportionately greater than its voting rights.

The IASB also considered reputational risk during its deliberations on the project but concluded that reputational risk is *not* an indicator of power in its own right. However, it may be a factor to consider together with other facts and circumstances. It may create an incentive for the investor to secure its rights in the investee, which may give it power over the investee.

When assessing whether an investor has power over an investee, the investor determines whether it is exposed or has rights to variable returns from its involvement with the investee. A large exposure to variability of returns is likely to mean that the investor has power over the investee; however, a large exposure to variability of returns is not, on its own, determinative.

Exposure to Variability in Returns

In addition to power over the relevant activities of the investee, to have control, an investor needs to be exposed to or have rights to variable returns from its involvement with the investee. Returns might be only positive, only negative, or either positive or negative. Sources of returns include:

- Dividends or other economic benefits, such as interest from debt securities and changes in the value of the investor's investment in the investee.
- Remuneration for servicing an investee's assets or liabilities, fees, and exposure to loss from providing credit or liquidity support.
- Tax benefits.
- Residual interests in the investee's assets and liabilities on liquidation.
- Returns that are not available to other interest holders, such as the investor's ability to use the investee's assets in combination with its own to achieve economies of scale, cost savings, or other synergies.

There is no specific guidance on fees paid to a decision maker in determining the variability of returns. However, this is a consideration in determining whether there is linkage between power and returns.

Link Between Power and Returns

To have control, in addition to power and exposure to variable returns from its involvement with the investee, an investor needs the ability to use its power over the investee to affect its returns. If the investor is an agent, then this linkage element is missing.

If the decision maker has the power to direct the activities of the investee that it manages to generate returns for itself, then it is a principal. If the decision maker is engaged to act on behalf of and for the benefit of another party or parties, then it is an agent and does not control the investee when exercising its decision-making authority. However, a decision maker is not an agent simply because other parties can benefit from the decisions that it makes.

This analysis is often particularly relevant for fund managers. In applying the guidance, two tests are determinative:

- If a single party holds substantive kick-out rights (i.e., the decision maker can be removed without cause), then the decision maker is an agent. In that case, the linkage test is failed and the decision

maker does not consolidate the investee. This is regardless of the level of remuneration.
- If the decision maker's remuneration is not commensurate with the services provided, or the terms and conditions are not on an arm's-length basis, then the decision maker is the principal. In that case, the linkage test is met and the decision maker consolidates the investee.

Unless a single party holds substantive rights to remove the decision maker without cause, the decision maker considers the overall relationship between itself and other parties, and all of the following factors, to determine whether it is an agent (and does not consolidate the investee) or a principal (and consolidates the investee):

- The scope of its decision-making authority over the investee.
- The rights held by other parties, including substantive removal rights not held by a single party.
- Its remuneration (level of linkage with the investee's performance).
- Its exposure to variability of returns because of other interests that it holds in the investee.

The last two factors, i.e., remuneration and other interests held sometimes are considered in aggregate in IFRS 10 and referred to as the decision maker's "economic interests" in the investee. The greater the magnitude of and variability associated with its economic interests, the more likely the decision maker is a principal.

When assessing the scope of its decision-making authority, the investor considers the following:

- The activities that are permitted according to the decision-making agreement(s) and specified by law.
- Its level of discretion.

The investor considers the purpose and design of the investee as explained previously. If the investor was involved in the design of the investee, then this may indicate that it had the opportunity and incentive to obtain power over the investee.

When a single party holds substantive rights to remove the decision maker without cause, this is sufficient to conclude that the decision maker is an agent. However, if more than one party needs to act together to remove the decision maker, then this fact alone is not sufficient to conclude that the decision maker is a principal or that the removal rights are not substantive. Such rights are considered in the overall evaluation of whether the decision maker is acting as a principal.

Rights that restrict the decision maker's discretion are considered in a similar manner to removal rights. Consequently, if the decision maker needs to obtain approval from a small number of parties to make its decisions, then generally it is an agent. Consideration of the rights held by other parties includes rights exercisable by the investee's board of directors or other governing body and their effect on the decision-making authority. The greater the number of parties required to act together to exercise removal or similar rights, and the greater the magnitude and variability associated with the decision maker's economic interests, the less weighting is placed on this factor.

For the decision maker to be an agent, its remuneration needs to:

- Be commensurate with the services provided.
- Include only terms, conditions, or amounts customarily present in arrangements for similar services and level of skill negotiated on an arm's-length basis.

If the remuneration does not meet both of these two criteria, then the decision maker is a principal. If the remuneration meets these two criteria, then the decision maker can be, but is not necessarily, an agent, as the other factors also would need to be considered.

If the decision maker holds other interests in an investee, then this may indicate that it is a principal. Other interests can be investments in the investee or guarantees provided with respect to the performance of the investee. The decision maker considers whether its exposure to variability of returns is different from that of the other investors, and if so, whether this might influence its actions.

Box 5.4 Example—Fund Management

Fund Manager A establishes, markets, and manages a fund that provides investment opportunities to a number of investors. A makes decisions in the best interests of all investors and in accordance with the fund's governing agreements, but it has wide decision-making discretion.

A receives a market-based fee equal to 1% of assets under management and 20% of all of the fund's profits above a "hurdle rate" if a specified profit level is achieved.

	Principal/Agent Analysis
Scenario 1	
A has a 2% investment in the fund. The investors can remove the fund manager by a simple majority vote in the event of breach of contract (i.e., for cause only).	A is likely to be an *agent* because: the 2% investment increases exposure to variability of returns but the exposure is not sufficient to indicate that A is acting as principal (i.e., A's economic interest is not significant relative to other investors); and A's remuneration is at market.

Scenario 2	
A has a more substantial investment in the fund (40%). The investors can remove the fund manager by a simple majority vote in the event of breach of contract (i.e., for cause only).	A is likely to be a *principal* because: the removal rights are not considered substantive as they are exercisable only in case of breach of contract; and the combination of A's remuneration together with its investment (its overall economic interest) could create exposure to variability of returns from the activities of the fund that is of such significance that it indicates that A is principal.
Scenario 3	
A has a 20% investment in the fund. The fund has a board of directors, the members of which are independent from A and are appointed by other investors. The board of directors appoints A annually. The services performed by A can be performed by other fund managers in the industry.	A is likely an *agent* because the board of directors provides other investors with a mechanism to ensure that they can remove the fund manager, i.e., there are substantive removal rights. The substantive removal rights receive greater emphasis in the analysis, which outweighs the fact that A has significant exposure to variability of returns due to its combined remuneration and 20% interest in the fund.

When assessing control over an investee, the investor considers the nature of its relationships with other parties and whether those other parties act on the investor's behalf. This determination requires judgment in assessing the consequence of how those parties interact with each other and with the investor. The investor treats the decision-making rights delegated to its agent as held by the investor directly.

A contractual arrangement is not required in a principal-agent relationship. A party is a *de facto* agent if the investor or those who control the investor have the ability to direct that party to act on the investor's behalf. IFRS 10 provides a list of examples of parties that, by the nature of their relationship, might act as *de facto* agents for the investor:

- Related parties of the investor.
- A party received its interest in the investee as a contribution or loan from the investor.
- A party that has agreed not to sell, transfer, or encumber its interest in the investee without the investor's prior approval.
- A party that cannot finance its operations without subordinated support from the investor.

- A party for which a majority of the members of the governing body or key management personnel is the same as that of the investor.
- A party that has a close business relationship with the investor.

Disclosures

During the financial crisis there was a perception held by some that there was a lack of transparency about the risks to which some reporting entities were exposed due to their involvement with entities commonly referred to as "special purpose vehicles." The IASB addressed this issue by requiring specific disclosures about interests in structured entities.

The objective of IFRS 12, *Disclosure of Interests in Other Entities*, is to require disclosure that helps users of financial statements evaluate:

- The nature of, and risks associated with, an entity's interests in other entities.
- The effects of those interests on the entity's financial position, financial performance, and cash flows.

In this context, *interests in other entities* include both contractual and non-contractual involvement that exposes an entity to variability of returns from the performance of the other entity. These interests may, for example, take the form of equity or debt instruments, but also can comprise other forms of involvement, such as the provision of funding, liquidity support, credit enhancement, and/or guarantees. However, IFRS 12 confirms that an interest in another entity does not exist solely as a result of a typical customer-supplier relationship.

Interests in another entity are the basis for many of the disclosures in IFRS 12. The standard notes that understanding the purpose and design of the other entity may assist in identifying such interests. Consistent with IFRS 10, the entity considers the risks that the other entity was designed to create and the risks the other entity was designed to pass on to the reporting entity and other parties.

How Does US GAAP Compare?

The FASB developed an alternative consolidation model to the voting model in 2003 when it developed the original variable interest entity model in response to the criticisms of US GAAP standards on accounting for special purpose entities coming out of the Enron scandal. While that model has been revised several times in the years since, US GAAP retains a dual consolidation model: one for variable interest entities and another for voting interest entities.

At one point during the Boards' convergence efforts, the FASB and IASB were working with the hope of achieving a converged consolidation model. Ultimately, however, the FASB decided to retain its approach that distinguishes between variable interest entities (VIEs) and non-VIEs (i.e., voting interest entities). Importantly, this distinction between VIEs and non-VIEs is not the same as the distinction between structured entities and nonstructured entities under IFRS. This will obviously result in a number of potential differences in the consolidation conclusion between IFRS and US GAAP. Even in situations where a non-VIE entity is also a nonstructured entity under IFRS, there will be differences in the consolidation conclusion (e.g., consideration of *de facto* power and consideration of potential voting rights under IFRS). Likewise, when a VIE entity is also a structured entity under IFRS, there will be differences in the consolidation conclusion, in particular because fees are evaluated to determine whether they are variable interests under US GAAP, whereas they are evaluated for linkage (i.e., principal/agent analysis) under IFRS.

Non-VIEs

Like IFRS, if the investee (that is a non-VIE under US GAAP and a nonstructured entity under IFRS) is controlled by means of equity instruments, with voting rights, then the assessment of power focuses on which investor, if any, has sufficient voting rights to direct the investee's relevant activities, unless there are other arrangements that alter the decision-making. Like IFRS, in straightforward situations the investor holding the majority of the voting rights has power over (and controls) the investee.

An investor considers "substantive" kick-out rights held by others. However, this concept is narrower than under IFRS because it is limited to kick-out rights that are exercisable by a simple majority of the investors.

Unlike IFRS, the control model for non-VIEs does include the assessment of potential voting rights. The non-VIE control model also does not include the concept of *de facto* power.

VIEs

Under US GAAP, an investor "controls" a VIE if the variable interest holder has both (1) the power to direct the activities that *most significantly* impact the VIE's economic performance and (2) the obligation to absorb losses of the VIE, or the right to receive benefits from the VIE that could potentially be significant to the VIE. While the decision-making power is similar to IFRS, the threshold in the second criterion ("could potentially be significant") is generally a lower threshold than is used in evaluating the decision maker's economic interest in applying the linkage analysis under IFRS.

Reporting entities need to explicitly determine whether an entity is a VIE and to reconsider whether it is a VIE when changes in facts and circumstances occur. Furthermore, unlike IFRS, which uses the same model regardless of the form of the investee, under US GAAP the determination of whether an investee is a VIE is different for a corporate investee vs. an investee that is a partnership or similar entity. This often leads to significant differences in the consolidation analysis for investments in partnership entities since non-consolidation is often the outcome under US GAAP.

To be a primary beneficiary of a VIE investee (i.e., parent), the investor must have a variable interest in the VIE. An investor considers substantive kick-out rights held by others, which is narrower than the guidance under IFRS. Unlike IFRS, kick-out rights that are not exercisable by a single investor or related party group (unilateral kick-out rights) are not considered substantive.

An investor that is the general partner in a limited partnership or similar entity considers the following, which often result in a difference from IFRS:

- A limited partnership or similar entity is not a VIE only when substantive kick-out rights are exercisable by either a single limited partner or a simple majority of all limited partner voting interests (excluding those held by the general partner, entities under common control with the general partner, and other parties acting on behalf of the general partner). In that case, the limited partnership or similar entity is assessed for consolidation under the non-VIE model.
- Other entities that have a decision maker whose fee is a variable interest may qualify to be assessed for consolidation under the non-VIE model even if substantive kick-out rights are not exercisable by either a single limited partner or a simple majority of all limited partner voting interests (excluding those held by the general partner, entities under common control with the general partner, and other parties acting on behalf of the general partner).

Fees paid to a decision maker or service provider are not variable interests (and therefore the decision maker or service provider will not consolidate the VIE investee) if:

- They are commensurate with the level of effort required to provide the services.
- The decision maker or service provider does not hold other interests that would absorb (receive) more than an insignificant amount of the VIE's expected losses (returns).
- The service arrangement has terms and conditions consistent with an arm's-length arrangement.

As a consequence, there are a variety of reasons why the consolidation conclusion under IFRS would differ from that under US GAAP, including (but not limited to):

- The investee is a non-VIE under US GAAP (and hence the analysis focuses on voting power) and is a structured entity under IFRS (and hence the analysis focuses on other factors) or vice versa (the entity is a VIE under US GAAP and a nonstructured entity under IFRS). This can occur in a variety of different structures but is particularly likely when the investee is a partnership or similar entity.
- The investee is a non-VIE under US GAAP and a nonstructured entity under IFRS but power is conveyed through potential voting rights under IFRS.
- The investee is a non-VIE under US GAAP and a nonstructured entity under IFRS but the investor has *de facto* power.
- The investee is a VIE under US GAAP and a structured entity under IFRS but the decision maker's fees are not a variable interest under US GAAP.
- The investee is a VIE under US GAAP and a structured entity under IFRS and the decision maker could absorb losses that are potentially significant but under IFRS the economic interest of the decision maker results in a conclusion that linkage does not exist.

How Does This Analysis Affect Business Combination Accounting?

One of the earlier and more successful convergence projects of the Boards was the accounting for business combinations. To have a business combination under both US GAAP and IFRS, the acquirer must:

- Obtain control.
- Over a business.

While that is true under both US GAAP and IFRS, each of those requirements can result in a difference between IFRS and US GAAP.

With respect to whether the acquired set is a business, the FASB revised its definition of a business and in particular added a step 1 "screen" test which does not exist currently under IFRS. The screen test says that if substantially all of the fair value of the acquired set is concentrated in a single asset or a group of similar assets (e.g., all the assets acquired are residential properties held for rental purposes), then the set is not a business. While in most transactions the conclusion about whether the acquired set is or is not a business will be the same under both GAAPs, there certainly are circumstances where this conclusion could differ. If so, the transaction could be the acquisition of a group of assets under one GAAP and the acquisition of a business under the other GAAP.

The other potential for a significant difference as to whether or not a business combination has occurred derives from the conclusion of whether the acquirer has obtained control over the acquiree. Since both GAAPs refer to their respective consolidation guidance to determine whether control is obtained, the various differences in the consolidation analysis as described previously can result in a difference in whether (or when) a business combination has occurred. To illustrate how these differences might arise, consider the scenarios in Box 5.5.

Box 5.5 Example—Has a Business Combination Occurred?

	Business Combination Analysis
Scenario 1	
Entity A is a business. A is a non-VIE under US GAAP and a nonstructured entity under IFRS. On June 1, 20X1, B acquires a 45% voting interest in A. The remaining 55% voting interest is extremely widely held with no single investee owning as much as a 1% voting interest.	**IFRS analysis:** B concludes that it has obtained *de facto* power and therefore control over A on June 1, 20X1. Therefore, B has entered into a business combination of A as of that date. **US GAAP analysis:** Because A is a non-VIE and B has less than a majority of the voting interest in A, B does not have control over A. Accordingly, B would account for its investment in A using the equity method.
Scenario 2	
Assume the same facts as in Scenario 1. On December 1, 20X2, B acquires an additional 12% of the voting interest in A.	**IFRS analysis:** Because B obtained control of A on June 1, 20X1, this transaction is an equity transaction (i.e., the acquisition of noncontrolling interest) and there is no remeasurement of the existing assets and liabilities of A. **US GAAP analysis:** The acquisition of the additional 12% interest on December 1, 20X2 gives B control over A. As a consequence, a business combination occurs on that date. This will result in measuring all assets and liabilities at their fair value on December 1, 20X2 and the previously held interest (45%) is remeasured to fair value with a gain recognized in net income on that date.

Scenario 3	
X owns a 40% voting interest in Y. Y is a non-VIE under US GAAP and a nonstructured entity under IFRS. On April 1, 20X3, X acquires a call option that is exercisable at any time over the next three years which gives X the right to acquire an additional 15% voting interest in Y. There are no barriers to exercise the call option. On July 1, 20X4, X exercises the call option and acquires the additional 15% voting interest in Y.	**IFRS analysis:** On April 1, 20X3, X has entered into a business combination because the call option together with its existing voting rights gives X control over Y. Accordingly, X would measure all the assets and liabilities of Y at their fair value on that date. The consideration paid would be the fair value of the 40% previously held interest (with a gain recognized in net income for the remeasurement to fair value) plus the fair value of the call option. On July 1, 20X4, when the call option is exercised, X accounts for the transaction as an equity transaction (i.e., the acquisition of noncontrolling interest). Existing assets and liabilities are not remeasured on that date. **US GAAP analysis:** On April 1, 20X3, X has not obtained control. It continues to account for the 40% interest using the equity method and it accounts for the call option in accordance with other GAAP (if the call option meets the definition of a derivative and is in the scope of Topic 815, it is accounted for as a derivative, otherwise it likely is accounted for on a cost basis). On July 1, 20X4, when the call option is exercised, X has a business combination because it has obtained control over Y. On that date it would remeasure its previously held 40% interest and apply acquisition accounting to the assets and liabilities of Y.

Business Combination Under Common Control

US GAAP has explicit guidance on the accounting for a business combination under common control. Under US GAAP, such a transaction is accounted for on a carryover basis (i.e., "as if pooling"). Because business combinations under common control are scoped out of the business combinations standard under IFRS and there is no guidance elsewhere in IFRS, there is significant diversity in practice in the accounting for such transactions. The IASB has begun work on a project to provide guidance to such transactions, but the project is in its early stages and it is unclear what direction the IASB is likely to take on this project.

In practice, under IFRS, one of three approaches can be seen:

- Book value accounting—while this is consistent with US GAAP in terms of the measurement model, there is further diversity in practice under IFRS as to whether or not the comparative periods are recast as if the transaction had occurred as of the earliest period presented (assuming common control existed for all comparative periods). Under US GAAP, comparative periods are required to be recast, consistent with the as if pooling approach.

- Fair value accounting—while the transaction is scoped out of the business combination standard, some entities believe that this is nonetheless the most relevant guidance and therefore apply business combination accounting to the transaction.
- Transaction price accounting—some entities will account for the transaction based upon the price paid (which cannot be presumed to be fair value since the entities are under common control).

Joint Arrangements

As part of its "consolidation suite" of standards, the IASB also issued guidance on the accounting for joint arrangements. Importantly, US GAAP does not have explicit guidance on the accounting for joint arrangements. The only guidance in US GAAP is that applicable to investments in corporate joint ventures to which the equity method is applied under US GAAP. As a consequence, differences often arise in the accounting for joint arrangements under IFRS vs. US GAAP.

Under IFRS, joint arrangements are defined as arrangements over which there is joint control of the arrangement between two or more parties. Joint arrangements are identified as either:

- *Joint operations*, whereby the parties with joint control have rights to the assets and obligations for the liabilities, relating to the arrangement.
- *Joint ventures*, whereby the parties with joint control have rights to the net assets of the arrangement.

A *joint arrangement* is an arrangement in which two or more parties have *joint control* of the arrangement. For joint control to exist there must be a contractually agreed sharing of control such that there must be unanimous agreement required for decisions about the relevant activities.

An entity that jointly controls a joint arrangement determines the type of joint arrangement by considering:

- The structure.
- The legal form.
- The contractual arrangement.
- Other facts and circumstances.

Specifically, the entity performs the following analysis:

- Structure: is the arrangement structured through a vehicle (i.e., a legal entity) that is separate from the parties to the arrangement? If yes, the arrangement is a joint operation. If no, consider legal form.
- Legal form: does the legal form of the separate vehicle give the parties rights to the assets and obligations for the liabilities of the arrangement? If yes, the arrangement is a joint operation. If no, consider contractual arrangement.
- Contractual arrangement: do the contractual arrangements give the parties rights to the assets and obligations for the liabilities of the arrangement? If yes, the arrangement is a joint operation. If no, consider other facts and circumstances.
- Other facts and circumstances: do the parties have rights to substantially all of the economic benefits of the assets of the arrangement and does the arrangement depend on the parties on a continuous basis for settling its liabilities? If yes, the arrangement is a joint operation. If no, the arrangement is a joint venture.

The most challenging criterion and where significant differences between IFRS and US GAAP often arise is with respect to the other facts and circumstance test. In arrangements where the parties to the arrangement have contractually agreed to take substantially all of the output from the arrangement (e.g., a corporate entity that extracts natural gas and is contractually required to sell all of its output to the parties), the arrangement will be a joint operation under IFRS. However, that same arrangement under US GAAP would be accounted for under the equity method because it is conducted within a corporate entity.

Joint Operation Accounting

A joint operator recognizes its assets, liabilities, and transactions, including its share of those incurred jointly. These assets, liabilities, and transactions are accounted for in accordance with the relevant IFRSs. To the extent that the arrangement is carried out within a legal entity and the arrangement is a joint operation because of the other facts and circumstances test, this accounting will look very much like the outcome when proportionate consolidation is applied. Because proportionate consolidation is generally not permitted under US GAAP (with the exception of a very limited set of industry-specific circumstances), this will yield a significantly different outcome from US GAAP.

Joint Venture Accounting

The parties that participate in a joint arrangement that is deemed to be a joint venture account for their interest in the arrangement using the equity method.

Conclusions

Because control is the starting point for determining which investees are included in the consolidated financial statements and because IFRS and US GAAP approach this from very different perspectives, we see, in practice, many significant differences in the accounting under IFRS and US GAAP. Further, because of the interaction of the concept of control with a business combination, this can also result in differences in terms of whether, and if so, when a business combination has occurred, creating further differences between the accounting under IFRS and US GAAP.

Accordingly, a financial statement user who is attempting to compare a company reporting under IFRS with another company reporting under US GAAP will need to very carefully understand the types of investees held by each entity, how those investees are evaluated for consolidation purposes, and what differences can arise between those entities. This will often mean that the financial statement user will need to carefully consider the disclosures provided by the respective entities about their investees. However, because only summarized quantitative information and high-level qualitative information will be provided in the notes, financial statement users will need to make some significant assumptions when trying to make the comparison between the two. This, of course, means that there is, by definition, some degree of information uncertainty (and depending on the types of entities being evaluated, there could be a significant degree of information uncertainty) that the user will ultimately need to price into the analysis.

6 The Impact of IFRS 9 on Banks Across the EU and Implementation Challenges

Samuel Da-Rocha-Lopes[1]

Introduction

In 2016, the European Union adopted[2] the IFRS[3] 9 after the respective IASB publication in 2014. Banks under IFRS were required to apply IFRS 9 as of the starting date of the bank's first financial year beginning on or after January 1, 2018. The benefits of the new accounting regime are several. The incentives to improve the credit appraisal processes, the monitoring of under-performing exposures and credit impairments, as well as the capital and business planning were improved. Transparency and the enhancement of market disclosures to the stakeholders were also promoted. A key aspect to embrace the benefits of the new accounting regime is the high-quality implementation of the process.

A key concern for the banking sector was that the application of IFRS 9 could lead to a sudden and material increase in expected credit loss (ECL) provisions. As an immediate consequence, this would cause an abrupt significant decrease in Common Equity Tier 1 (CET1) capital and ratios for many banks. We should bear in mind that the significant improvement of the CET1 ratios after the financial crisis was an important achievement for the EU banking sector. The implementation of the IFRS 9 could challenge such a positive evolution and destabilize the banking sector, so the concerns were understandable. At the same time, while discussions proceed on the longer-term regulatory treatment of provisions, transitional arrangements were introduced in order to smooth the implementation of the IFRS 9 in the EU. These transitional arrangements for five years (between 2018 and December 2022) allow banks to mitigate the potential significant negative impact on CET1 arising from ECL accounting.

In the meantime, EU banks have made further progress[4] on the implementation of IFRS 9. In 2017, as expected, smaller banks were still lagging behind in their preparation compared with larger banks. Various data, processes, and models are used to estimate expected credit losses. Similarly to the IRB models in the calculation of capital requirements, the variability of approaches will affect comparability among banks and, therefore, disclosures are key. It is crucial that stakeholders have sufficient and comparable information to understand and evaluate the impact of the application of IFRS 9. For this reason, uniform disclosure of IFRS 9 transitional arrangements is an important element. This ensures that banks' Pillar 3 disclosures on capital and leverage ratios are consistent across the EU during the transitional period of five years. In addition, the uniform disclosure of IFRS 9 transitional arrangements reduces the complexity of the analysis and assessments, taking into account the technical implementation of a dynamic approach (e.g., for deferred tax assets).

The estimated impacts of IFRS 9 were mainly driven by IFRS 9 impairment requirements. The estimated increases of provisions were on average higher compared to the levels of provisions under IAS 39. As a consequence, the CET1 ratios were expected to decrease. Smaller banks (mainly using the Standardized Approach [SA] for measuring credit risk) estimated a larger impact on own funds ratios than larger banks.

Discussions at the EU and international levels will continue to be necessary in order to further explore if any changes to the current regulatory framework may be necessary. The variation in provisions across banks will be influenced not only by underlying risks but also by modelling assumptions. Banking supervisors and market participants need to be able to disentangle both. The main concern is to ensure a proper interaction of the capital framework with the expected credit loss model in accounting.

Transitional Arrangements of Five Years

In May 2017, the EU adopted[5] a five-year transitional period for mitigating the impact on own funds of the implementation of IFRS 9. A new Article 473a of the CRR (EU Capital Requirements Regulation) was proposed, with provisions on the introduction of IFRS 9 and ECL models transitional arrangements. These created the conditions for a phase-in of the impact of IFRS 9 impairment requirements on capital and leverage ratios. If a bank's balance sheet, as of the first application of IFRS 9, reflects a decrease in CET1 capital due to increased ECL provisions (compared to the balance sheet on the previous day), the bank is allowed to include in its CET1 a certain defined portion of the increased ECL provisions during the transitional period (i.e., between 2018 and 2022). In practical terms, this will offset the impact of extra provisioning on capital. This is more important for banks under SA instead of a forward-looking loan loss model.

Banks can decide whether to apply the transitional arrangements and should inform the banking supervisors accordingly. When applying transitional arrangements, banks cause adjustments in the calculation of supervisory regulatory items, directly affected by ECL provisions, in which case banking supervisors need to ensure that banks do not receive

Table 6.1 Evolution of "excess" provisioning included in CET1 capital between 2018 and 2022

	2018 (Year 1)	*2019 (Year 2)*	*2020 (Year 3)*	*2021 (Year 4)*	*2022 (Year 5)*	*2023 (not in force)*
Total provisions in CET1	95%	85%	70%	50%	25%	0%
Year reduction of provisions in CET1	-5%	-10%	-15%	-20%	-25%	-25%

Source: EU (European Parliament and Council).[6]

inappropriate regulatory capital relief. The banking supervisors need to ensure that a bank would not benefit from both an increase in its CET1 capital due to transitional arrangements, as well as a reduced exposure value. These will be more difficult to monitor in case of a dynamic transitional arrangement.

The transitional period is of five years from the first day of application of IFRS 9. The portion of ECL provisions included in CET1 capital decreases over time with full implementation due by the end of 2022. The proportion that can be included in CET1 capital is not linear throughout the five years, allowing a higher proportion in the first years and a quicker reduction at the end of the transition period.

For the banks that decide to apply IFRS 9 transitional arrangements, the disclosure of such effects on own funds, risk-based-capital, and leverage ratios is required. Since the banking supervisors are concerned with the disclosure and transparency of the process, a uniform format for the banks' disclosure requirements of IFRS 9 and analogous ECLs transitional arrangements was developed. This will allow a consistent and comparable disclosure among banks during the transitional period of five years. Regarding the additional disclosure costs, banks are already required to disclose the information on the transitional value of the parameters (included in the disclosure format), so the marginal cost and impact of the implementation is expected to be negligible. At the same time, the improvement of the information available to market participants will ensure consistency and comparability, further fostering market discipline.

Impact Assessment

In 2017, the average estimated impact of IFRS 9 on CET1 ratio for the EU was a 45 basis points (bps) decrease (and the average estimated impact on the total capital ratio was a 35 bps decrease), without taking into consideration any possible transitional arrangements.[7] In effect, the EU Global Systemically Important Banks (G-SIBs)[8] decreased their end-point weighted CET1 ratio to 13% in 1Q 2018, from 13.3% in 4Q 2017.[9] The implementation of IFRS 9 in 1Q 2018 had a weighted average impact of around 29 bps on CET1 ratio. In recent years, the EU CET1 ratios in general (i.e., not only for EU G-SIBs) have always decreased in the first quarter, but on average only about 10–20 bps. In Q1 2018, most of the EU G-SIBs showed a decrease higher than 25 bps, ranging from +50 bps to –100 bps. The weighted average impact of around –29 bps on CET1 ratio for EU G-SIBs is lower than estimated in 2017 (–45 bps). Interestingly, the implementation of IFRS 9 fully offset, on average and almost in the same proportion, the positive contribution from 1Q 2018 retained earnings (+24 bps). This impact is calculated also assuming full adoption of the IFRS 9 (notwithstanding that some banks have adopted transitional measures).

The total estimated impact of IFRS 9 on banks' own funds is driven mainly by the impairment requirements. This is different from how it would be under IAS 39 (i.e., this would be a "continuous impact"). The main impact seems to be driven by the estimation of lifetime ECL for stage 2 exposures (i.e., exposures that have experienced a significant increase in credit risk but are not defaulted).[10] The main instruments and portfolios for the impacts are loans and advances to households and nonfinancial corporations. In comparison with the levels of provisions under IAS 39, the estimated increase in provisions of IFRS 9 was 13% on average. For EU member states, in which the coverage ratio increases, the capital ratios have accordingly decreased. The coverage ratio increases are driven by banks and countries with significant NPL ratios. However, the decrease in capital ratios is also impacted by other effects (e.g., dividend distribution).

The impacts are different between G-SIBs and smaller banks (for example, with total financial assets below €100 billion and which tend to use the SA for measuring credit risk). Smaller banks estimated a larger impact on own funds ratios than larger banks (with higher use of the internal ratings-based IRB approach). The difference between IRB banks and SA banks is significant in several aspects. In contrast to IRB banks, the SA banks are not able to recognize any excess in IFRS 9 provisions over regulatory expected loss (EL) in Tier 2 capital. A similar situation exists for IRB banks, but only when they exceed[11] the regulatory capital for recognizing any excess in accounting provisions over regulatory EL in Tier 2. In such cases, these IRB banks will not have any capital relief either.

Regarding the change in classification and measurement requirements, the impact would be limited for most banks. However, the operationalization of the classification and measurement requirements means resources are needed. In this context, banks should not underestimate the challenges of implementing those classification and measurement requirements. To recall, the same topics and challenges were seen in the EU during the asset quality review in 2014, with several material misclassifications of exposures due to different capital requirements (SMEs and large firms, public sector entities, etc.). Moreover, several banks anticipated that IFRS 9 impairment requirements would increase volatility in profit or loss.

This is mainly due to the expected "cliff effect," from moving exposures from stage 1 to stage 2 (i.e., from 12-month ECL to lifetime ECL) and the practical use of forward-looking information. In contrast, the ECL model under IFRS 9, if properly implemented, also leads to more gradual and timely recognition of losses compared with IAS 39 (based on an incurred loss model). In principle, this reduces the surprises and delays in the recognition of losses. From an economic analysis perspective, IFRS 9 may have an impact on the lending practices of banks and portfolio composition. In relation to long-term investments in equity instruments (also a means of financing the economy), it has been observed that these instruments represent a minor part of the banks' balance sheets. These aspects need to continue to be assessed in the longer term.

Robust Validation Process and Governance Framework for the ECL Measurement

In the implementation of the IFRS 9, banks are using, some of them for the first time, various processes, data, systems, and models in order to provide sound estimations of expected credit losses. These estimations are complex and require the intensive use of internally generated data and credible assumptions. The approaches on ECL measurement vary significantly across banks and depend mainly on factors such as the type of exposure (e.g., retail or wholesale); materiality; stage at which the exposure is classified under IFRS 9 (i.e., stage 1, 2, and 3); whether a collective or individual assessment is performed; and classification in the SA or IRB portfolio. There are several factors to take into account and some elements are not always available. For this reason, when processes, data, systems, and models are not available, banks need to use simplifications, proxies, and practical solutions to estimate ECL. For banking supervisors, it is very important that banks apply a sound and consistent methodology and governance process when making use of simplifications and approximations to meet the objectives of IFRS 9. This will avoid material bias in ECL measurement. It is fundamental for banking supervisors that banks ensure, on an ongoing basis, that the use of approximations remains appropriate. This is particularly relevant if circumstances change, forcing the need for a change in the use of such approximations. For this reason, banking supervisors are very interested in achieving a detailed understanding of how the differences in the several factors mentioned as drivers of the approaches followed by banks may interact and affect the measurement of ECL.

Factors such as data quality, availability of historical data, and the assessment of "significant increase in credit risk" (as required under IFRS 9), are the most significant challenges for EU banks. For the latter, banks are using various indicators for assessing significant increase in credit risk, together with IFRS 9 practical expedients and expert judgement.

The assessment of significant increase in credit risk under inexistent, poor and/or deficiently employed internal policies leads to a disarticulation between the assessment criteria and process, thus becoming unreliable and leading necessarily to a miscalculation of risks. Therefore, a robust validation process for ECL measurement is paramount and needs to be well defined and implemented in order to ensure a regular monitoring of the key elements of the ECL models. The soundness and consistency of the methodology and governance process are even more important when making simplifications (expected in the absence of available data) and when assessing significant increase in credit risk. In addition, it is also necessary that banks implement robust governance frameworks of processes and controls on an ongoing basis.

A particular concern to banking supervisors is the expected reduced parallel runs of IFRS 9 and IAS 39 decided by banks during the implementation phase, and in some cases the absence of parallel runs. For EU banks that decide to apply IFRS 9 transitional arrangements, the parallel runs should be a requirement. From a banking supervisory perspective, the parallel runs allow a better assessment and testing of banks' IFRS 9 processes and approaches. This is particularly evident in the implementation of the impairment requirements. In comparison, the IRB implementation also requested a parallel calculation in order to compare the capital requirements for the same exposures for both calculations, IRB and standardized approaches. And more recently, during the reassessment of the IRBs and respective variability of RWs, the parallel calculations for comparison with the SA were important requirements. In addition, it allows the consideration of other means, if necessary, to ensure the quality of implementation of IFRS 9.

Furthermore, the governance framework is key, especially after the financial crisis. Key stakeholders, such as the board of directors and the audit committees, need to be sufficiently involved in the IFRS 9 implementation. The absence of adequate governance and lack of accountability, namely of the senior management to the management body, has been seen to withdraw the incentives of quality assurance throughout the implementation process. The same applies to IRB and stress testing exercises.[12] The lack of involvement leads to insufficient allocation of resources to the implementation of IFRS 9 and insufficient focus by the EU banks. An insufficient involvement of the board of directors and audit committees will also create more challenges for the other stakeholders in exercising their duties effectively.

Financial Stability Implications

There is a long debate on the use of fair value or historical cost for the measurement of financial assets and the suitability of these methods for different bank assets. From an EU perspective,[13] the classification of financial assets under IFRS 9 is clearer and sounder than under IAS 39. In addition, it should not generally lead to a significant increase in the use of fair value by EU banks, at least at the aggregate level.

In particular, it is expected that a sound and strict implementation will increase transparency and facilitate the earlier and more comprehensive recognition of impairment losses, which has been found to have positive effects on financial stability. In retrospect, before the financial crisis there were strong evidences of tardy recognition of losses which also contributed to the build-up of risks in the banking sector. However, it is prudent to be aware of potential developments whereby the interaction of the new standard with the reaction of the various actors involved, regulation, and the evolution of the aggregate economy may have detrimental effects on financial stability.

There are five primary areas identified as deserving special attention from the perspective of financial stability: (1) usage of fair value accounting; (2) modeling risk; (3) lending behavior; (4) procyclicality; and (5) standardized approach (SA) and less sophisticated banks. Among these, there are two fundamental challenges for micro- and macro-supervisors: the modelling risk and the possible procyclicality implications.

Firstly, the modelling risk for IFRS 9 resembles the discussions on the IRB implementation. On the one hand, the current implementation of the IRB models has led to substantial divergences across banks and a lack of comparability in terms of model outcomes, where not all differences appear to be justified by risk-based drivers. On the other hand, the monitoring of the internal credit risk models only through backtesting results does not allow for a full comparison of the identified differences in the models' outputs in order to explain and justify the differences from risk profiles. In addition, the process of authorization of IRB models is also substantially different from the process of consequent ongoing monitoring.

In general, banking supervisors have a very in-depth assessment when authorizing IRB models but then relax significantly the procedures and requirements during the ongoing monitoring of the same IRB models. This seems to be influenced not only by different supervisory practices and different levels of trust in banks' capacity to maintain the quality of the models, but also by possible lack of enough resources at the technical level and IT systems to closely follow such evolutions, a similar bank problem. Implementation of the internal models framework requires a substantial resource commitment on the part of both banks and banking supervisors (BCBS, 2004). The same happens with the implementation of IFRS 9.[14] The skills of existing staff need to be constantly upgraded. As potential main areas for possible improvements in the medium term, a stronger oversight role on internal model validation has been necessary.[15]

For these reasons, the importance of the development of benchmarking exercises[16] conducted by banking supervisors (EBA, BIS, and national authorities) for internal models used for capital requirements and also the industry should be underlined. Benchmarking exercises mean that banking models are measured in comparison with a benchmark. Ideally, this benchmark should represent the true value of the risk for a given perimeter. This is an impossible achievement because risk does not have a true value, as its definition is "the possibility of incurring misfortune or loss,"[17] so the benchmark should only be considered as shedding light on some aspects of, for instance, IRB or ECL approaches and respective assumptions. For IRB models, the benchmarking exercises become compulsory at the European level and are useful for the assessment of internal models and reliability of RWA.[18] These benchmarking exercises may also help to ensure the quality of IFRS 9 implementation and the regular monitoring of the key elements of the ECL models. A proper disclosure of such ECL benchmarks would also be useful, as is happening with the IRB approaches, from a market participant perspective.

Secondly, the possible procyclical implications of the ECL approach are an important aspect to consider. A more timely and forward-looking recognition of credit losses addresses the criticism of the "too little, too late" provisioning resulting from the incurred loss approach; therefore, by expediting loss recognition, IFRS 9 may improve financial stability. In fact, the "too little, too late" provisioning resulting from the incurred loss approach seems more procyclical (because it helps to reinforce the cycle) than expediting loss recognition and reducing the build-up of losses before a tardy recognition (lower level of reinforcement of the economic cycle). It is important to remember that procyclicality stems from inappropriate responses by financial system participants to changes in risk over time.[19] Assuming that the downturn or its implications can be identified sufficiently early on may, in fact, reduce the severity of procyclicality and the credit contraction in a downturn.

Banks need to estimate ECL using probability-weighted multiple future economic scenarios, and ECL provisions will start to rise as quick as a bank considers a negative economic scenario as a possibility. Moreover, in the unfolding of a crisis, previous acknowledged behavior of early loss recognition reduces market concerns regarding capital adequacy of the banks. In addition, early loss recognition is typically regarded as a positive element to enhance confidence, transparency, and the effectiveness of market discipline. It is now expected that the market participants get used to a new behavior based on earlier loss recognitions. The ECL approach implies reacting immediately to new and forward-looking information as it is received. This means that impairment allowances may increase suddenly and significantly in case of aggregate economic indicators deterioration. It is a normal consequence of a more timely reaction instead of a too-late provisioning, therefore, something that needs to be assimilated. This is not procyclicality if it does not reinforce the economic cycle but only provides timely information. If recognized in a timely manner, the cyclical sensitivity of the credit risk parameters used for the estimation of ECLs and from the shifts of exposures between stages will not reinforce the economic cycle, quite the opposite, thus helping to reduce existent procyclicality under IAS 39 and limit the development and consequences of serious financial imbalances.

Conclusion and Areas of Further Work

The EU banking regulators are contributing to a sound implementation of the IFRS 9. The EBA opinion on transitional arrangements and credit risk adjustments to mitigate the effect of the accounting standard IFRS 9 on prudential ratios, as well as the guidelines on ECL, provide useful information and important guidance for banks on the requirements for a robust implementation of IFRS 9. In addition, the new methodology[20] of the 2018 EU-wide stress test exercise also takes into account the implementation of IFRS 9.

Banking supervisors should continue the dialogue with banks and auditors on the implementation challenges and encourage banks to continue their efforts towards the high-quality implementation of IFRS 9 across banks. At the same time, it is expected that banks continue improving elements of the implementation of IFRS 9 after its initial application in 2018. From an economic analysis perspective, it is important to have a better understanding of how the differences in the implementation of IFRS 9 may affect the measurement of expected credit losses. Therefore, comparisons and benchmarks will be a very useful and powerful supervisory tool.

Furthermore, the possible impact on lending behavior needs to be assessed and there are several aspects to take into account from an economic analysis perspective. The repricing of loans may be one of the aspects to assess in detail. Banks may adjust the interest rates charged on loans to compensate for the new impairment allowances (and respective capital cost). From an efficiency point of view, the possible repricing may allow a more adequate pricing of risk, thus being a prudent action and advantage of the IFRS 9. The mispricing was another relevant aspect before the financial crisis. However, it may also alter the composition of credit portfolios in banks' balance sheets and the respective evolution throughout the business cycle. There is a risk that such a response would create a potential to shift credit risk to entities not subject to IFRS 9 (depending on the degree of competition in certain loan markets), including beyond the regulatory perimeter. Banking supervisors need to pay attention to such possible moves from the regulatory perimeter.

Furthermore, banks worried about and more affected by the cliff effects associated with loans that move from stage 1 to stage 2 may reduce the maturity of their loans or prefer borrowers with activities and within sectors less sensitive to the business cycle. Another example is the fact that some contracts (e.g., embedded derivatives) will no longer qualify to have the non-derivative component measured at amortized cost. This fact may result in a decline in the prevalence of certain forms of optionality. There are several topics that will need further analysis: How will IFRS 9 continue to influence banks' capital ratios? How will banks respond to IFRS 9 changes in capital requirements? Will banks alter capital, lending, asset mix, and balance sheet size? The combined impact of all these possible changes is difficult to determine in advance taking into account micro- and macro-prudential concerns. Consequently, these issues, among other topics, will need to be part of the post-implementation review of IFRS 9, for which academic researchers will contribute.

In addition, EU banking regulators and supervisors consider it important to obtain more details and a better understanding of the various IFRS 9 implementation practices. In this regard, a future transversal review of the implementation of the ECL across banks would provide useful insights. An analysis of the impact of the use of different inputs, models, and methodologies on ECL measurement is a fundamental task in the future. The areas for further work will provide insightful information for the discussions at the EU and international levels (i.e., with the Basel Committee on Banking Supervision [BCBS]). It is important to explore in detail if any changes to the current regulatory framework on the treatment of accounting provisions may be necessary in future. This will provide meaningful analysis to ensure the proper interaction of the capital framework with the ECL model for accounting and possible supervisory policy implications from such interaction.

Notes

1. Any views expressed are only those of the author and should not be attributed to the European Banking Authority (EBA), Nova School of Business and Economics (Nova SBE) and Aarhus University. I would like to thank the anonymous reviewers for their suggestions. To the memory of Samuel's beloved mother, Filomena Da-Rocha.
2. The European Commission adopted it through Commission Regulation (EC) No 2016/20673.
3. International Financial Reporting Standard 9—Financial Instruments.
4. EBA Report on results from the second EBA impact assessment of IFRS 9, July 2017.
5. Proposal for a Regulation of the European Parliament and of the EU Council amending the CRR (Capital Requirements Regulation—575/2013).
6. "Regulation (EU) 2017/2395 of the European Parliament and of the Council of 12 December 2017 amending Regulation (EU) No 575/2013 as regards transitional arrangements for mitigating the impact of the introduction of IFRS 9 on own funds and for the large exposures treatment of certain public sector exposures denominated in the domestic currency of any Member State."
7. EBA Report on Results From the Second EBA Impact Assessment of IFRS 9, July 2017. The figures are based on banks' estimations as of December 31, 2016.

8. Identified as G-SIBs by the FSB and BCBS and as G-SIIs (Global Systemically Important Institutions) by the EU. FSB, 2017. 2017 list of global systemically important banks (G-SIBs), November 2017.
9. Public financial statements and author's own calculations.
10. There are also differences on other aspects, namely: hedge accounting (improved the relationship between the accounting treatment and risk treatment of the assets, as the risk treatment will be better reflected in the financial statements of the banks); classification and measurements (IFRS 9 is principle-based therefore it only uses a single classification and measurement approach for financial assets which depend on the institutions' business model and the type of the contractual cash flows); own credit risk treatment (IFRS 9 uses another comprehensive income - OCI - treatment when there is a change in the fair value of the issuer's credit risk for liabilities designated as fair value through P&L; the problem with the previous standard (IAS 39) was that when an institution was more likely to default, it would recognize a gain in FVPL).
11. In accordance with Article 62(d) of the CRR (EU Capital Requirements Regulation—575/2013).
12. EBA Guidelines on Institutions' Stress Testing (EBA/CP/2017/17).
13. ESRB Report: Financial Stability Implications of IFRS 9, July 2017.
14. A similar topic is being discussed in the US: The impact of the current expected credit loss standard (CECL) on the timing and comparability of reserves. Sarah Chae, Robert F. Sarama, Cindy M. Vojtech, and James Wang, Federal Reserve Board of Governors.
15. European Commission, 2014. Report from the Commission to the European Parliament and the Council on the Operation of the European Supervisory Authorities (ESAs) and the European System of Financial Supervision (ESFS).
16. Paolo Bisio, Samuel Da-Rocha-Lopes, and Aurore Schilte. *Europe's New Supervisory Toolkit* (2015: Risk Books).
17. Collins, 2015. *The English Dictionary.*
18. EBA, 2017. EBA Report—Results From the 2016 High Default Portfolios (HDP) Exercise (EBA BS 2017 027).
19. BIS, 2001. Claudio Borio, Craig Furfine, and Philip Lowe. Procyclicality of the Financial System and Financial Stability: Issues and Policy Options.
20. EBA, 2017. 2018 EU-Wide Stress Test—Methodological Note.

7 Analysis of Changing Regulatory Conditions, New Accounting Policies, and the Global Financial Crisis

The Case of Swedish Banks

Henrik Andersson and Niclas Hellman

Historical Background

At the time of the global financial crisis (GFC), fair value accounting had been introduced in Sweden as in many other countries, and the Swedish banking system was very much an oligopoly, with four large banks covering 75% of the market (Riksbanken, 2008b). It had not always been like this. In fact, this was a far cry from the historical state of affairs.

Looking back at the development of Swedish accounting during the twentieth century, there was initially a long period of German influence (Monsen & Wallace, 1995) with an emphasis on creditor protection. This was reflected in conservative accounting practices, but also in terms of legally prescribed dividend restrictions and mandatory retention of profits. From the 1950s the impact of tax accounting considerations increased as the government introduced tax-related incentives for companies while at the same time having strong links between tax accounting and financial accounting (Davidson & Kohlmeier, 1966; Zeff & Johansson, 1984). The tax accounting link reinforced conservative accounting practices and the creation of hidden valuation reserves. In the accounting system classification made by Nobes (1983), Sweden constituted a group of its own positioned at one end of the spectrum, characterized as government-driven and tax-oriented.

Another feature of Sweden is the disproportionally high number of multinational companies (Cooke, 1989) which, arguably, relates to the Swedish model of corporate governance (cf. the brotherhood model; Collin, 1993) and the cooperation between major ownership spheres and the political sector (Randøy & Nielsen, 2002; Henrekson & Jacobsson, 2003). During the 1950s and 1960s, these governance practices were well aligned with the conservative and tax-related accounting practices, i.e., the conservative accounting regime made it easy for companies to retain profits in order to finance growth while the extensive use of hidden reserves gave insider shareholders (the ownership spheres) informational advantages (Hellman, 2011a). The idea of wealthy companies where owners let the companies grow instead of withdrawing dividends corresponded well with the political goals of the governing party.

Focusing more specifically on financial firms, Sweden has an oligopolistic banking sector. In the past, there were many small and local savings banks and some bigger banks serving the multinational companies and linked to particular ownership spheres; however, consolidation gradually took place from the 1970s and onwards.

In the first years of the 1990s, there was a domestic real estate crisis that turned into a major financial crisis for the country. The culprit was really the speed of the liberalization and reforms of the financial markets during the 1980s. When credit restrictions were lifted in 1985, the extent to which real estate property was mortgaged doubled or even tripled up to 1990 (Wohlin, 1998). Although it began from a very low level in comparison to other countries, the high indebtedness led to problems as real estate prices first increased dramatically, then leveled off, and eventually started to decline. The banks were not immediately affected, as there was no direct link. However, the banks had financed the credit institutes that in turn had financed the highly levered real estate companies that were now insolvent.

In the end, this led to a substantial restructuring of the Swedish banking system and four large players eventually emerged (Nordea, Handelsbanken, SEB, and Swedbank). Many small and local savings banks were merged into larger units and the fifth largest bank, GOTA, was forced into Nordbanken (later Nordea) that was majority-owned by the Swedish state. The M&A history that eventually led to the oligopoly situation is depicted in Figure 7.1.

Although severe, the Swedish real estate and financial crisis in the beginning of the 1990s soon faded out. The major reason was probably that is was a domestic crisis and the international boom period helped Sweden get out of the recession that came as an effect of the crisis. Also the handling of the crisis has received some accolades. Non-performing loans were lifted from the banks into separate entities so that the financial system soon could function as intended. This is also interesting in comparison to Japan. There is a view that non-performing loans, dating back to the real estate crash of 1988, continued to plague the Japanese banks long after. Therefore it also hampered the function of the financial system, contributing to the rather weak economic development during the decade after the crisis of 1988 (Lincoln, 1998).

Soon enough, the Swedish banks were back to business as usual, although the structure had changed due to consolidation. Now came the next phase of development in the banking sector, expansion into the Nordic and Baltic markets (dashed boxes in Figure 7.1). The most conservative of the banks, Handelsbanken, had actually started this process of expansion into neighboring countries right after the crisis in the beginning of the 1990s,

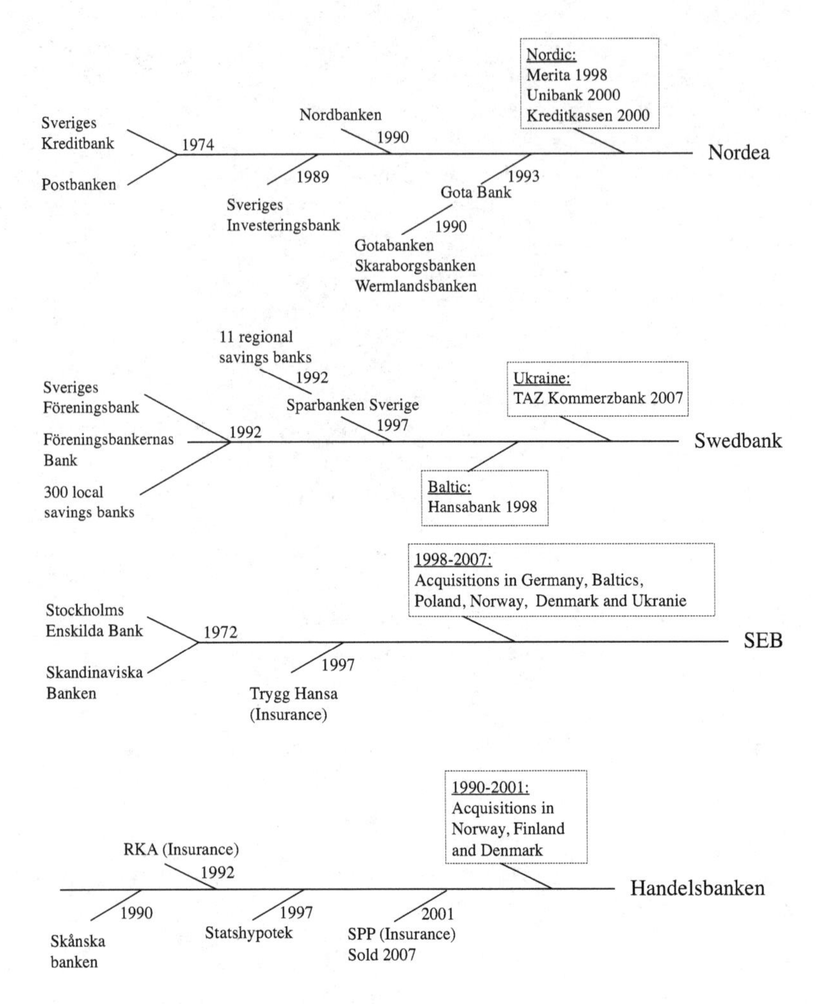

Figure 7.1 The structural transformation of the Swedish banking sector into four large players

Sources: Annual reports and various public sources.

as its relative position had been strengthened by the crisis. The expansion was supported by a period of economic growth that continued up to the crash of the IT bubble around 2001.

We are now closer to the time of the GFC in 2008. In addition to the Swedish banking system being an oligopoly, and that the banks had now expanded into neighboring countries, two other characteristics were also apparent at the time of the GFC: the banks were well capitalized and they had recently come under a new accounting regime (adoption of International Financial Reporting Standards, IFRS, which led to the use of fair value accounting and the incurred loss model for credit losses).

Changes in the Accounting Regime Before the Introduction of Fair Value Accounting

Sweden could be seen as gradually moving away from the emphasis on conservativism and the use of hidden reserves and provisions towards the Anglo-Saxon ideal of the financial statements providing a "true and fair" view of the entity's business activities, and later on, even the use of fair value accounting. The starting point for this change can be traced back to the 1980s, and the de-regulation and liberalization of the capital markets referred to earlier. A number of Swedish multinationals took part in the international M&A boom and became more dependent on foreign capital markets, for example by cross-listing the shares as American Depository Receipts. In turn, foreign investors requested listed companies' financial accounting to follow "best practice" (i.e., US GAAP or UK GAAP). The Swedish practice of reporting seemingly incomprehensible "appropriations to untaxed reserves" in the consolidated income statements and allowing for a very flexible view on goodwill accounting, was not in line with capital-market requirements.

In 1989, a new body was formed (the Swedish Financial Accounting Standards Council, SFASC) that issued recommendations based on the International Accounting Standards (IAS). SFASC's first recommendation introduced deferred tax accounting and set new requirements with regard to goodwill accounting. During the period 1990–2004, the SFASC translated and issued recommendations corresponding to all existing IASs except for IAS 39 (Financial Instruments: Recognition and Measurement), IAS 40 (Investment Property), and IAS 41 (Biological Assets). Although Swedish accounting became increasingly capital-markets-oriented during this period, the change in accounting regime pertained primarily to the consolidated financial statements whereas the traditional conservative view remained at the legal entity level where the accounting regime was still heavily tax-influenced (Hellman, 2011b). Furthermore, Sweden-specific legal restrictions against fair value accounting were difficult to change and were therefore an obstacle against SFASC adoption of the three fair value standards (IAS 39, IAS 40, and IAS 41). Thus, when fair value accounting was introduced through EU regulation 1606/2002 on January 1, 2005, this represented a new accounting regime in Sweden with regard to the financial instruments, investment property, and biological assets. However, this change only pertained to the consolidated financial statements while the traditional conservative accounting practices still applied to legal entities' financial statements.

Capital Adequacy in Swedish Banks Before the Crisis

The Basel Accord of 1988, later amended several times, brought minimum capital requirements on the banks. As the financial system is important for the functioning of the real economy, the consequence of letting major banks fail can be substantial. Governments therefore often bail out big banks in times of crisis in order to lessen the effect on the real economy. Naturally, in a Modigliani-Miller (MM) world with no taxes and no cost of bankruptcy, the capital structure does not matter. Operating with much equity is not a cost for the bank. Introducing the tax advantages of debt and also bankruptcy risk does not alter the situation dramatically. The traditional tax advantage of debt has also been challenged lately. Van Binsbergen, Graham and Yang (2010) show that the costs of operating with too much debt far outweigh the tax benefit. There is more to lose than to gain by playing with the capital structure.

However, if governments bail out the banks in times of crisis, the playing field changes. Now the governments have in effect issued a put option on the bank, free of charge. The way to maximize option values is to maximize risk and therefore operate with little equity. The response by the authorities has been to gradually tighten the capital requirements of Basel I in 1988 to the present Basel III. There has also been an academic debate whether the MM capital structure irrelevance propositions are applicable to banks. Credits created in the banking system are part of the money supply and proving the irrelevance propositions is therefore not purely a portfolio allocation problem. Fama (1980) makes the argument that the irrelevance propositions hold provided that banking is competitive. Gersbach, Haller and Müller (2015) further make the argument that minimum capital requirements actually help to restore the irrelevance propositions by guaranteeing a single equilibrium.

Reading newspapers and business magazines, one might easily get the impression that many banks, most of the time, complain about the rules of capital adequacy. They claim that it increases costs, and in the end these costs are carried by the customers. Whether these worries are real, or just bank lobbying rhetoric, is difficult to judge. Anyway, the Swedish banks up to the time of the GFC were a noteworthy exception to these complaints. There is not much to complain about if you have adopted a capitalization policy of exceeding the minimum capital requirements by a fair amount.

There may be several reasons behind this behavior. First of all, the experience of being hit very hard during the financial crisis in the beginning of the 1990s most likely made both the banks and the Swedish authorities more cautious during the decades that followed. Secondly, there was a widespread and long-standing tradition of banks being run as savings banks, including also the lower level of risk that such banks often prefer to operate with. This, in combination with a conservative accounting regime (e.g., allowances for expected credit losses), may have contributed to high levels of capital adequacy. Thirdly, the banks may have kept capital adequacy levels high in order to be able to finance further acquisition-based growth outside of the Nordic region and the Baltic States. Operating with very little equity, close to the Basel-rule minimum requirements, makes it more difficult to act quickly when there is a business opportunity, whereas being financially strong may provide opportunities during the aftermath of a crisis, as shown by the Handelsbanken example during the 1990s crisis. Some entries into Ukraine, Germany, and the UK were also made by the Swedish banks in the 2000s, before the GFC, but only on a smaller scale. As a fourth alternative, the banks may also have believed that a little bit of financial theory, as accounted for above, actually made sense: higher levels of equity do not come at a cost but at a lower level of risk.

Whatever the reasons were, one of the banks, SEB, states in their annual report of 1998 (and it is later repeated) that: "The group strives to achieve long-term growth based upon a capital base for the financial group of undertakings that must not be inferior to a core capital ratio of 7 per cent in the long run." The actual Basel I requirement was 4%. For the total capital ratio their internal policy was to maintain a minimum of 10.5% as a comparison to the required 8%. The slightly smaller difference in the total capital ratio as compared to the core capital ratio reveals that SEB planned to achieve this rather high level of adequacy through the use of equity, rather than other instruments such as preferred stocks, perpetual subordinated bonds, etc. It is perhaps also of interest to note that the first coco-bond, a contingent convertible bond where the issuer can force conversion into equity if a capital ratio is below a certain threshold, was issued in Sweden in the 1990s. This kind of financing was therefore also available at the time of the GFC.

Other banks had similar targets. Nordea states that it aims at a core capital ratio "well above" 6.5% in order to attain "high rating and cost effective financing" (Merita-Nordbanken's Annual Report 1998). Swedbank, who experienced problems during the GFC, actually lowers the objective over time. Created by a merger of many local savings banks it reports an objective of 7.5% in 1997, 7% in 2004 and 6.5% in 2006. Still much larger than the 4% required by Basel I.

The core capital ratios of the four major banks are shown in Figure 7.2. The traditionally most conservative of the banks, Handelsbanken, does

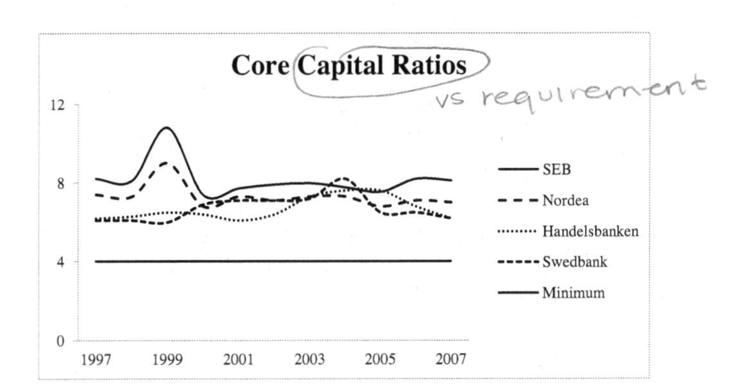

Figure 7.2 Core (Tier 1) capital ratios for the four major Swedish banks during 1997–2007 compared to the minimum Basel I level of 4%

Sources: Annual reports from SEB, Nordea, Handelsbanken, and Swedbank.

not report any objectives. Neither does their core ratio stand out. Actually, it dropped from 10% to 6% in 1997 due to a major acquisition, and thereafter on average stays at this level.

The Behavior of Swedish Banks and Government Authorities During the Crisis

As all the major banks had capitalizations far above the minimum requirements, they entered the crisis year of 2008 in relatively good shape. At the onset, they were not much affected either. They had generally abstained from entering into deals with structured products and most notably collateralized debt obligations (CDOs), thereby avoiding losses. CDOs have infamously been blamed for being the vehicle that lead to the GFC. There is actually a story, told by the chairman of Nordea, Hans Dalborg, where he phones the CEO, Christian Clausen, asking: "These CDOs, have we bought any?" "No," Clausen replies, "to be honest I never understood these instruments and therefore we didn't buy any." "We were damned lucky then," Dalborg replies. "Yes," Clausen says, "it's funny, the more I practice, the more luck I have." Of course, this is just prudent housekeeping. Know your business and stick to areas where you have an edge.

Apart from limited exposure to loss-providing instruments, the counterparty risk exposure against non-Swedish banks was also fairly low. This was before the days of central clearing and transaction registers for OTC deals, so it is doubtful whether the banks could account for the counterparty risk in any detail, but it was nevertheless not a major concern. Something that did exist was CLS (continuously linked settlement) services, where foreign exchange transactions were settled on a payment vs. payment basis. This lowers counterparty risks, for example timing differences, since transactions are done simultaneously.

What did become the biggest issue at the onset of the financial crisis was instead the financing. In traditional savings banking, deposits made by households through bank accounts are transformed into lending, for example to industrial companies who need to finance their plants and machinery. More generally, savings banking facilitates the separation of savings from borrowings, investments from consumption, i.e., facilitates the primary purpose of the capital market. Many banks have higher levels of lending than deposits. A large part of the funding needed is therefore borrowed on the capital markets, and this is especially true for the Swedish banks. As short rates normally are lower than long-term rates, short-term borrowing is tempting. However, borrowing with short maturity constantly needs to be replenished.

The balance sheets also reveal that most of the long-term borrowing is through covered bonds, where these bonds are backed by mortgages. The market for issuing covered bonds or long-term corporate bonds in general disappeared at the outset of the GFC. No one was interested in purchasing these at *any* reasonable price. Banks increasingly then had to rely on short-term financing to the extent available. As long as the banks can service their debt and do not make any credit losses, this is of no immediate concern. The banks will survive, but possibly operate on a smaller scale. The cost for the society is greater. If banks cannot, or do not want to, lend money to the public, then investments and consumption go down and therefore the GDP declines. We have entered the situation of a credit crunch. Reading reports from this period, most notably the Swedish central bank's semi-annual report on financial stability, the fear of a credit crunch and its effect on the real economy is the stated reason for the central bank's willingness to provide the banks with debt financing, in relation to GDP more so than in most other countries (Elmér, Guibourg, Kjellberg & Nessén, 2012). However, this is probably also a consequence of the banks' decision to hold more capital than the minimum requirements, i.e., being in good shape. With very small losses from financial instruments forecasted, and credit losses as a function of the possible downturn in the GDP, preventive action from the central bank seems a rather easy decision.

An alternative explanation of the Swedish central bank's high willingness to support the financial system is the fear built-up during the course of the crisis that at least one of the major banks would falter. Here it is rather the lack of evidence that points in this direction. The term "bank run" (the severe implication of when the public starts to withdraw their deposits en masse) is not mentioned at all in official documents from the central bank. One cannot help wondering if this was deliberately so in an attempt to calm the public. Not even when there is an account of the state deposit insurance being doubled in October 2008 are bank runs mentioned. If this was a preventive action and nothing acute, one would expect a more thorough account of the reason for it.

Credit Losses: Occurrence and Accounting Treatment

As the crisis unfolded in late 2008 and early 2009, credit losses likely to result from a weakening in the real economy became the greatest worry. However, it was not expected Swedish credit losses that were the greatest concern. It was instead in the banks' Baltic operations that the credit losses mounted. The Baltic countries had been hit much harder than the Swedish economy by the crisis. In the end, the economies in these countries were saved by the rather short crisis and a substantial so-called internal devaluation where wages and costs were cut. The Swedish central bank also helped out in a small way by extending swap facilities. The funding problem, which for the Swedish banks really started at the onset of the crisis, was never really problematic in the Swedish krona (SEK). In US dollars, it was much more acute, as this was where the liquidity dried up the most during the crisis (Riksbanken, 2009a). As half the banks' businesses pertain to foreign currencies, the dependency on foreign currencies is very strong. The Swedish central bank assisted to the extent possible, but it was only through a swap arrangement with the Federal Reserve that enough US dollars could be obtained. Now, the central bank could extend that courtesy to the Baltic central banks where the Swedish krona was in demand.

Lending volumes in the Baltic states were substantial, 500 billion SEK, but how bad was the crisis in the Baltics for the Swedish banks? It is difficult to tell because when reading the official documents produced during the crisis some years after the GFC, it seems like risks in general, and especially that of a bank run, were deliberately played down rather than discussed. It is probably fair to say that given the severity of the GFC, it was surprisingly short-lived and that at some point in time when markets were in free fall, future expected credit losses were much larger than final outcome. This also brings us to a core area in bank accounting: whether to account for the incurred or the expected credit losses.

Bank-issued credits will result in assets on the balance sheet referred to as *loans and receivables*, i.e., non-derivative financial assets that are not quoted in an active market. There are two commonly applied measurement bases for financial assets: fair value and amortized cost. Given the characteristics of loans and receivables, amortized cost has traditionally been used, where interest income is allocated to the relevant period by using the effective interest rate, i.e., the rate that exactly discounts estimated future cash receipts through the expected life of the financial instrument. If the expected receipts are lowered during this period, this will cause asset impairment (credit losses). Camfferman (2015) points at three different considerations standard-setters dealing with credit losses must make: (1) the relative weight assigned to recoverable amount vs. loss-event criteria; (2) whether the effective interest rate should be based on expected payments or contractual payments excluding future credit losses; and (3) to what extent collective provisioning for credit losses should be used.

Based on these considerations, two basic perspectives on accounting for credit losses have evolved over time: the expected loss model (ELM) and the incurred loss model (ILM). Before the era of having specific standards on financial instruments, the two models were not formalized and named (ibid.). Conventional accounting would prescribe an expected loss approach with prudent treatment of receivables, i.e., measurement on the basis of expected cash flows taking all available evidence into account, however, also allowing for considerable flexibility with regard to setting the expectations. This perspective dominated in Sweden at the time of the bank crisis in the early 1990s. Although loss-event criteria were considered, judgment of expected receipts seemed to play a major role.

Figure 7.3 shows the loan loss levels for three major Swedish banks during the bank crisis in 1990–1994. Nordbanken (today part of the bank

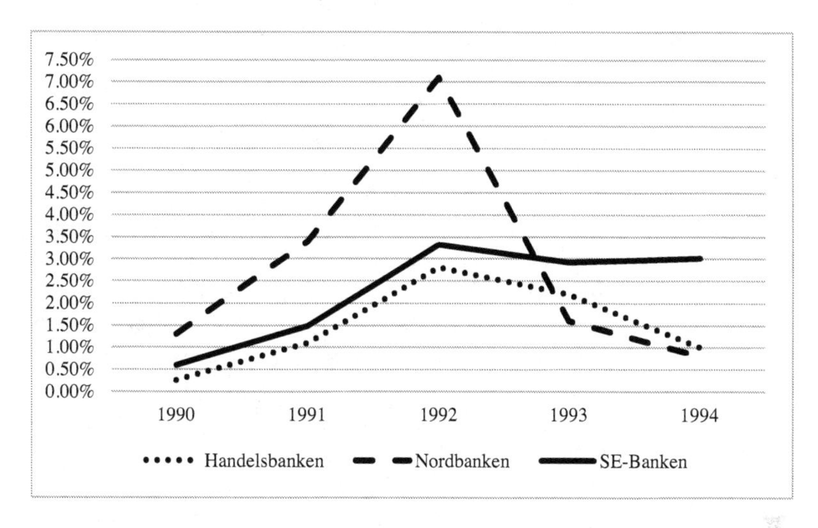

Figure 7.3 Loan loss ratio for three major Swedish banks during the bank crisis in 1990–1994, measured as loan-related impairment losses as a percentage of the opening balance of loans for the period

Sources: Annual reports from Handelsbanken, Nordbanken, and SE-Banken.

Nordea) had the biggest total losses and was taken over by the Swedish government in 1992, who made capital injections and initiated a process for recovering the value of impaired assets. The process was successful and already in 1995 the government sold 65.5% of the shares in Nordbanken in connection with an initial public offering on the Stockholm Stock Exchange. SE-Banken is a bank controlled by the Wallenberg family sphere and had a different profile for recognizing impairment losses. It wanted to avoid being taken over by the government but was unable to make a new issue of shares until the autumn 1993. It appears SE-Banken made a less negative judgment of expected losses than Nordbanken in 1992, which seems to have caused a delay compared to Nordbanken with regard to the recognition of impairment losses. Handelsbanken is the bank with the smallest total losses.

Thus, as illustrated by the difference in timing of loss recognition between Nordbanken and SE-Banken, the accounting regime during these early days could be said to prescribe an expected loss model but with a relatively high level of flexibility. In 1998, the International Accounting Standards Committee (IASC) issued IAS 39, which at the time, was considered an interim standard produced under time pressure to meet the deadline agreed on with the International Organization of Securities Commissions (IOSCO) of having this financial instruments standard as a part of IAS. The IAS 39 (1998) treatment of credit losses was a pragmatic solution much in line with the approach described for Swedish banks in the 1990s. It was based on expected cash flows but mentioned both recoverable amount and loss-event criteria, however, without specifying the relationship between the concepts (Camfferman, 2015, p. 10).

In the years following 1998, a revision of IAS 39 took place which involved a change in favor of ILM. During this process, the distinction between the two models (ILM and ELM) was also made clearer. Important inputs behind this change came from the US. Already during the savings and loans crisis of the late 1980s, application of the recoverable-amount criterion to expected receipts was criticized for being flexible and misused to delay recognition of losses (ibid., p. 7; cf. SE-Banken in Figure 7.3). Some years later, in 1998, Securities and Exchange Commission (SEC) Chairman Arthur Levitt argued that banks were abusing the expected loss approach by making excessive loan loss provisions in order to manage earnings (ibid., p. 8; cf. Nordbanken in Figure 7.3). Accordingly, the revised version of IAS 39, issued in 2003, prescribed the ILM in that the loss-event criterion clearly dominates and the effective interest rate is based on contractual payments explicitly excluding future credit losses (ibid., p. 10). The ILM is worded as follows in this version of the standard (p. 63, emphasis added):

> If there is *objective evidence* that an impairment loss on loans and receivables . . . has been *incurred*, the amount of the loss is measured as the difference between the asset's carrying amount and the present value of estimated future cash flows (*excluding future credit losses that have not been incurred*) discounted at the financial asset's original effective interest rate.

IAS 39 Basis for Conclusions (BC) for the revised standard also emphasizes that for a loss to be incurred, an event that provides objective evidence of impairment must have occurred *after* the initial recognition of loans and receivables (BC 110). The implementation guidance has an example that illustrates this (IG E4.2):

> For example, if Entity A lends CU1,000 to Customer B, can it recognize an immediate impairment loss of CU10 if Entity A, based on historical experience, expects that 1 per cent of the principal amount of loans given will not be collected?
>
> No. IAS 39.43 requires a financial asset to be initially measured at fair value. For a loan asset, the fair value is the amount of cash lent adjusted for any fees and cost. . . . In addition, IAS 39.58 requires that an impairment loss is recognized only if there is objective evidence of impairment as a result of a past event that occurred after the initial recognition. Accordingly, it is inconsistent with IAS 39.43 and IAS 39.58 to reduce the carrying amount of a loan asset on initial recognition through the recognition of an immediate impairment loss.

Listed banks within the European Union, including Sweden, adopted IFRS in 2005 (earlier voluntary adoption was allowed in some countries), and thus had to apply ILM. As previously described, this was a change compared to prior accounting practice in Sweden, and the GFC in 2008–2009 became a test of the new model.

Figure 7.4 shows that impairment losses were still low in 2008, despite the high uncertainty and peak of the crisis in the fourth quarter of 2008, following the Lehman Brothers bankruptcy. Objective evidence of the loss-event criteria does not appear to have been available until 2009. It should also be noted that the peak year is the same (2009) for all banks, which indicates a lower level of flexibility with regard to timing. This is in line with Leventis, Dimitripoulos and Anandarajan (2011) who studied 91 EU-listed commercial banks before and after IFRS adoption and found that earnings management using loan loss provisions was significantly reduced after implementation of IFRS. Similarly, Gebhardt and Novotny-Farkas (2011) found that the restriction to report only incurred losses under IAS 39 significantly reduced income smoothing in their sample of banks in 12 EU countries.

The Swedish bank with the highest level of credit losses during the GFC was Swedbank. In the end, credit losses were of the same magnitude as the two new issues of equity in 2008 and 2009, amounting to 27 billion SEK altogether (Riksbanken, 2009b). Most of the losses stemmed from the Baltics and Ukraine. The expansion into these countries took place very rapidly with a significant increase in lending during 2006 and 2007.

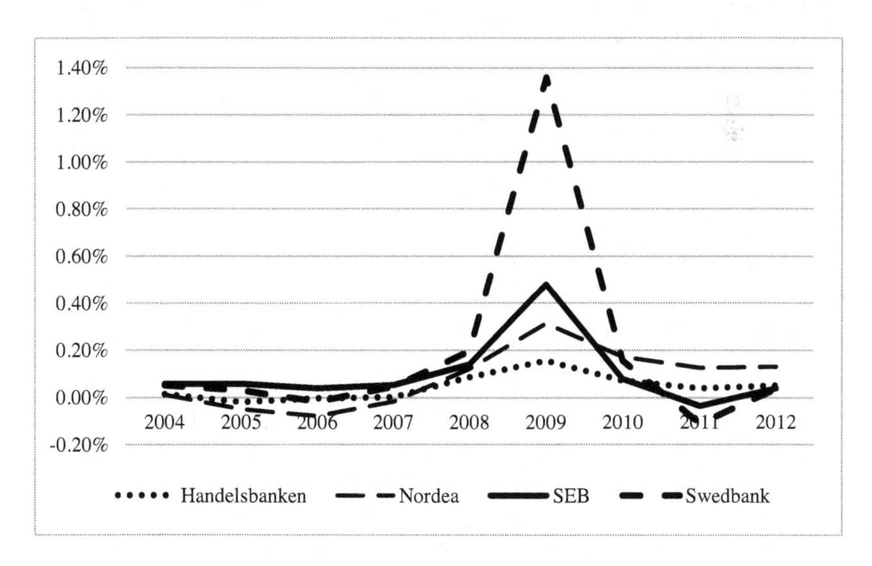

Figure 7.4 Credit losses as a percentage of the opening balance total assets for the four major Swedish banks during the financial crisis in 2008–2009

Sources: Annual reports from Handelsbanken, Nordea, SEB, and Swedbank.

Swedbank was also the bank most reliant on short-term financing which is problematic when liquidity dries up (Riksbanken, 2008a).

Going through the balance sheets for the crisis years, it is quite clear that the banks applied the ILM when accounting for credit losses. None of the banks report any major losses for 2008. In expectation, these losses were substantial. The non-negligible probability alone of one or more of the Baltic countries devaluing their currency would require a substantial allowance. Although the accounting, in line with ILM, did not take into account such expected events, the market reacted strongly. The market capitalization of Swedbank was only 60% of book equity in November 2008, and this was after the new issue of shares. In the end of 2009, when the acute crisis was over, the Swedish central bank estimated expected credit losses to 155 billion SEK for the period 2009–2011 (Riksbanken, 2009b). Reported credit losses for 2009 were only 45 billion SEK.

Swedbank was the Swedish bank reporting the biggest credit losses during the GFC. However, in 2011, when the crisis was over, Swedbank was reporting the lowest level of credit losses (a net reversal) among the banks, indicating that some flexibility still prevailed under ILM regarding the size of loan loss provisions.

Although there are advantages of the ILM in terms of less management discretion, there is also a major disadvantage in terms of delayed loss recognition. Based on a comprehensive literature review, Beatty and Liao (2014, p. 340) conclude that "no consensus about the best model has emerged." An important study by Bushman and Williams (2012) illustrates the unintended effects that may follow from allowing for increased discretion into loan provisioning. Still, in response to the GFC, the International Accounting Standards Board (IASB) decided to reconsider its use of ILM and proposed, as part of the replacement of IAS 39 by IFRS 9, a shift towards an expected loss model. Following additional exposure drafts in the 2011 and 2013, the shift to ELM was confirmed with the issuance of a revised version of IFRS 9 in 2014. The new situation is well described by Novotny-Farkas (2016, p. 197):

> Compared to the incurred loss model of IAS 39, the IFRS 9 ECL [expected credit loss model] incorporates earlier and larger impairment allowances and is more closely aligned with regulatory expected loss. The earlier recognition of credit losses will reduce the build-up of loss overhangs and the overstatement of regulatory capital. In addition, extended disclosure requirements are likely to contribute to more effective market discipline. . . . However, due to the reliance on point-in-time estimates of the main input parameters (probability of default and loss given default) IFRS 9 ECLs will increase the volatility of regulatory capital for some banks. Furthermore, the ECL model provides significant room for managerial discretion.

Thus, in a sense, the adoption of an expected loss model brings us back to the model used before ILM in IAS 39, however in a more sophisticated form, focusing more exclusively on the probability of future receipts.

Effects of Fair Value Accounting

The other major accounting challenge with regard to financial instruments is fair value accounting. As described earlier, for loans and receivables, the financial crisis led to changes in IFRS Standards that implied a return to the ELM for credit losses. With regard to fair value accounting, the crisis led to some important immediate changes of IAS 39 in 2008. After the crisis, IFRS 9 was developed over a number of years before a final version was issued in 2014 (mandatory in the EU countries from 2018), including some changes regarding the classification of financial instruments. In addition, IFRS 13 (Fair Value Measurement) was issued in 2011 (mandatory in the EU from 2013) in order to deal more consistently with the measurement of assets and liabilities at fair value, including financial instruments. Finally, the standard IFRS 7 (Financial Instruments: Disclosures) should be acknowledged. It was created before the GFC, in 2005, and was applied from 2007 within the EU. The standard focuses exclusively on disclosures, and this becomes particularly important when fair value measurement is based on the application of valuation models rather than mark-to-market values.

During the 1990s and early 2000s, Sweden had gradually adopted international accounting standards for consolidated financial statements of listed companies, while maintaining the more conservative accounting regime for individual companies (legal entities). However, fair value accounting (IAS 39, IAS 40, IAS 41) had not been adopted in Sweden before 2005 and therefore this was new to Swedish-listed companies and also represented a clash compared to the traditional accounting regime. Fair value accounting generally implies a need to recognize gains and losses over profit or loss as the fair value of the financial instrument changes. During the GFC, this pertained particularly to trading portfolios held by banks. In contrast to some of the large European banks, the four Swedish big banks did not own significant trading portfolios and were not significantly exposed to American subprime loans. This is confirmed by Figure 7.5, which shows the net gains and losses earned by the four major Swedish banks on balance sheet items measured at fair value during 2003–2012, expressed as percentages of total assets. The figure shows that positive results were earned by almost all banks all years, also during the GFC.

However, there were two smaller Swedish banks that had significant trading portfolios. We will describe these two cases below as they illustrate the way fair value accounting was applied in Sweden during these first years after adoption.

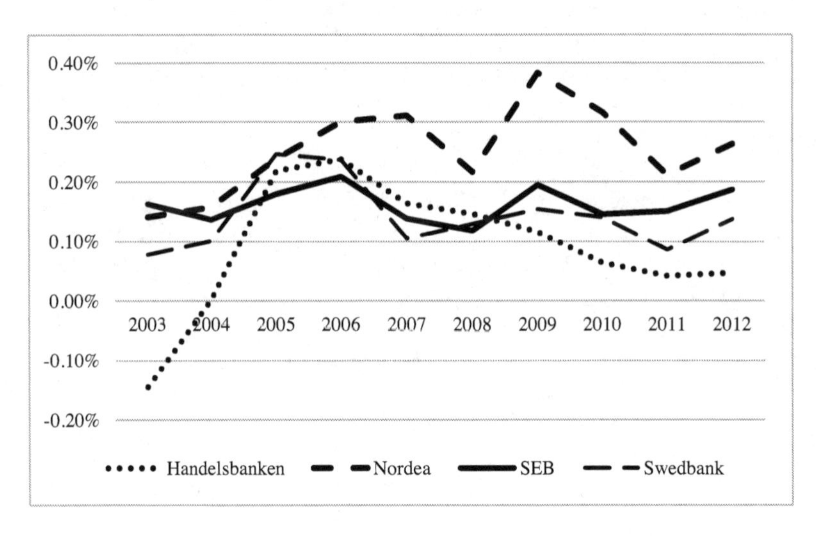

Figure 7.5 Net gains and losses on items measured at fair value (% of total assets), 2003–2012

Sources: Annual reports from Handelsbanken, Nordea, SEB, and Swedbank.

The Carnegie Case

In the early 2000s, Carnegie was a well-reputed Swedish-listed investment bank within equity capital-market services (M&A, new issues, IPOs), asset management, private banking, brokerage, and trading. During the period 2003–2006, Carnegie's return on equity increased every year from 16% in 2003 to 52% in 2006. The increased profitability was generated by positive developments in the trading business. The net gains from items measured at fair value (i.e., the trading portfolio) increased from 244 million SEK in 2003 to 714 million SEK in 2006. During the same period, the net income for the Carnegie group increased every year from 211 million SEK in 2003 to 1,013 million SEK in 2006.

In May 2007, Carnegie announced that the company's profit had been overstated by 630 million during 2005–2007 and by an additional 370 million during the first part of 2007. The Swedish Financial Supervisory Authority, Finansinspektionen, initiated an investigation and later the same year decided on a number of sanctions, including significant fines and requiring the election of a new board of directors.

The reason behind the overstated profits was that three employees (traders) had made manipulations to increase their bonuses. On December 31, 2006, Carnegie had 845 option contracts in the trading portfolio, whereof 595 had observable market prices and 250 did not (Finansinspektionen, 2007). The contracts without observable market prices were valued by using a theoretical model, i.e., the Black-Scholes model. The contracts with observable market prices were normally valued at the quoted price on the closing date, however, if this price was considered misleading the contract would be reclassified into mark-to-model valuation. In order to cause a reclassification, the three traders placed orders on the closing date in order to generate an option price that deviated substantially from the Black-Scholes value, and this was subsequently used as a reason for reclassification. For example, on December 29, 2006 (the last trading day in 2006), eight minutes before closing on the Frankfurt Eurex Exchange, they placed a buy order at 0.05 euro and a sell order at 2.98, causing the daily mid-price for the option to increase from 0.08 to 1.52 (Carnegie, 2007). On December 31, 2006, 125 of the 595 contracts with observable market prices were reclassified to being valued using the Black-Scholes model (Finansinspektionen, 2007).

Valuation according to the Black-Scholes model is heavily influenced by expected volatility. Carnegie used the preceding month's volatility as a proxy for expected volatility and the three traders made market transactions during this month in order to increase the volatility. In the example from the Frankfurt Eurex Exchange, the volatility had been increased so that the Black-Scholes value of the option was 0.53, whereas the daily quoted price of the option during the month (December 2006) varied between 0.10 and 0.16 (Carnegie, 2007). As Carnegie, in accordance with the IAS 39 requirements, measured derivatives at "fair value through profit or loss," overstating the option values led to the recognition of profits in the income statement, which in turn constituted the basis for the bonus calculation.

The Carnegie case shows the risk of manipulation whenever fair value measurement is not based on quoted prices, i.e., what is referred to as Level 1 in IFRS 13. Please note that the options were measured using a valuation technique (the Black-Scholes model) with *observable* inputs (e.g., the volatility), i.e., corresponding to Level 2 in IFRS 13, however, these observable inputs had been manipulated through real trading activities. Many assets measured at fair value under IFRS Standards will be using unobservable inputs, i.e., Level 3 in IFRS 13, which will involve further risks of manipulation. Although this was a case of fraud, there were anecdotal stories during the GFC a few years later of how banks refrained from making market transactions in financial instruments in order to avoid the occurrence of observable market prices so that valuation techniques at Level 3 or at least Level 2 would be used instead of quoted prices. Such behavior may have contributed to the low liquidity in many financial instruments during the GFC. Finally, it may be noted that the Carnegie fraud was not discovered by internal controls in Carnegie or by the external auditor, but it was market surveillance at the OMX Nordic Exchange Stockholm that first discovered possible market manipulations by Carnegie traders at the end of 2006 (Carnegie's annual report 2007).

The HQ Case

HQ was founded in 1990 by Sven Hagströmer and Mats Qviberg, two well-known, successful financial entrepreneurs in Sweden. The company was listed in 1992, and grew by creating the HQ Trading business in 1994 followed by investments in a private banking business and a mutual funds business. The company was successful and development of return on equity and dividends (including redemption of shares) as a percentage of equity are shown in Figure 7.6.

Figure 7.6 shows that HQ ran a profitable business for many years in the early 2000s. Year 2007 was the best year ever for HQ, with good performance for all businesses except for "Trading" who reported a small loss. HQ maintained a generous dividend policy and 94% of the net profit in 2007 was paid in dividends. The loss for "Trading" was attributed to the financial turbulence on the markets and it was stated in the annual report for 2007 that a decision had been taken to discontinue the trading business in its current form. This was the first year with a loss since the trading business was founded in 1994 and it did not say explicitly that the trading portfolio would be phased out. In the notes of the annual report for 2007, it shows that the trading portfolio consists of significant positions in equities and derivatives, accounted for according to the IAS 39 classification "fair value through profit or loss." It also says that the fair values of the derivatives had predominantly been determined by using valuation techniques, i.e., not quoted prices. In the annual report, HQ

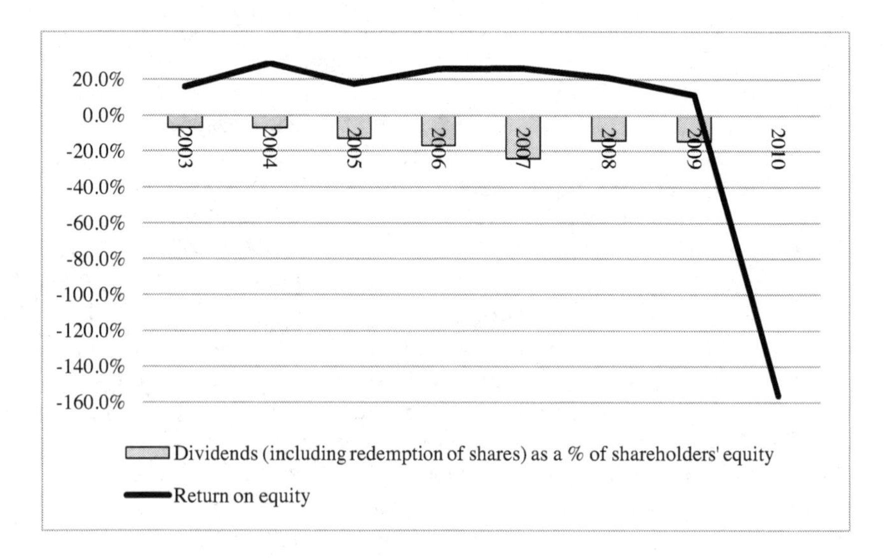

Figure 7.6 Return on equity and dividends (including redemption of shares) as a percentage of equity, 2003–2010

Sources: HQ annual reports.

also refers to using the Black-Scholes model and to use both observable and unobservable inputs. With regard to volatility, HQ refers to the use of historical volatility and implicit volatility in comparable instruments.

During 2008, the losses for "Trading" increase and correspond to about 4% of HQ's shareholders' equity, but the company as a whole is still quite profitable. However, the size of trading portfolio has increased and this business has not been discontinued. There is also a new paragraph in the accounting policies describing the use of "mean reversion" when valuing options, which here means that it is assumed that all options' volatility will revert towards their historical volatility averages. In addition, there is a new accounting note showing that 96% of the derivatives value was measured at Level 3 (unobservable inputs) in 2008 as compared to 57% in 2007. In 2009, there is again a loss in the trading business, but smaller than in 2008 and the company as a whole is still profitable. The trading portfolio continues to grow with most of the derivatives value (70%) measured at Level 3.

In May 2010, HQ announced a forced closing of the trading portfolio, which turned out to result in realized losses of about 1 billion SEK, while HQ's shareholders' equity amounted to about 1.2 billion SEK before the realization of these losses. HQ sold assets and initiated new issues of shares and preference shares, but in September the Swedish Financial Supervisory Authority cancelled HQ's banking license and filed for liquidation of HQ. According to the Financial Supervisory Authority, HQ had overstated the value of its trading portfolio during a long period of time, which had led to public misreporting of its financial position and a capital adequacy level below the legal minimum requirements since December 2008. The Financial Supervisory Authority argued that HQ had violated both the capital adequacy regulation (Basel Accord) and the accounting regulation (IFRS Standards).

The HQ events resulted in two major court cases; in one, a group of HQ shareholders sued the Board of HQ, the auditor, and the audit firm (KPMG) for 3.2 billion SEK in damages plus interest (about 5 billion SEK at the time the verdict was reached in December 2017). The verdict is a document with 2,605 pages and contains the Swedish court's (Stockholms tingsrätt, the Stockholm District Court) opinion on the correct interpretation of IAS 39 with regard to how to measure HQ's trading portfolio. Some of the court's observations and interpretations are of general interest (Stockholms tingsrätt, 2017):

- Special competence in the applied accounting legislation (IFRS Standards) was missing in the bank. In practice, the bank relied on KPMG and their accounting experts.

  (p. 2202)

- Even in cases where a market is not active (a requirement for the use of quoted prices), IAS 39 has a clear preference for the use of price information. Only when transaction prices did not reflect how the market could be expected to set prices, would the use of own assumptions be allowed.

(p. 2203)

- The bank's instructions were unclear with regard to how available price information should be used for fair value measurement purposes. The volatilities, and thereby the valuations, could be determined with the purpose to find a level in line with the plausible theoretical value, without any clear connection to the values indicated by price information on the options market at the time of the valuation.

(pp. 2203–2204)

- The same volatility was used for all options with the same underlying asset and expiration month. This assumption does not comply with IAS 39.

(p. 2205)

- The bank used an assumption of "mean reversion," i.e. that options' volatility will revert towards a historical average. In addition, the bank had made its own interpretation of the going concern principle, according to which the value could be determined by assuming a future point in time when the market price would better reflect the price level perceived to be correct according to the "mean reversion" assumption. Option prices that indicated a volatility level that deviated from the historical average were treated as mispriced.

(p. 2204)

As indicated before, the court rejected HQ's accounting for the trading portfolio and agreed with the Financial Supervisory Authority that it had been overvalued, however, the Board and the auditor and audit firm still won the court case because the plaintiff did not succeed in showing causality with the damages caused by the accounting misstatements and other circumstances.

Some Implications of the HQ Case

Going Concern

As mentioned earlier, the use of fair value accounting represented a new accounting regime in Sweden, and the HQ case shows some clear signs of this. First, the final bullet point regarding "going concern" suggests that HQ thought that the current market transactions did not reflect the true value and as the company believed it would survive many periods, i.e., be a going concern, it was not considered necessary to reflect the current market transactions in the valuation. This shows some similarities with the flexibility built into the prudence principle in the traditional Swedish accounting, cf. SE-Banken's delayed recognition of credit losses in 1993 and 1994 earlier in this chapter. However, from a theoretical point of view, the IAS 39 view on going concern in connection with fair value measurement should also be evaluated (IAS 39, AG69):

> Underlying the definition of fair value is a presumption that an entity is a going concern without any intention or need to liquidate, to curtail materially the scale of its operations or to undertake a transaction on adverse terms. Fair value is not, therefore, the amount that an entity would receive or pay in a forced transaction, involuntary liquidation or distress sale.

In the real world, companies will experience forced transactions and distress sales, especially during financial crises, and therefore stakeholders will be concerned if valuations are maintained with reference to this argument of going concern. The cited IAS 39 paragraph reminds us that fair value is not an entity-specific concept, i.e., does not capture the problems specific entities may experience, but relies instead on the market's view. However, during a financial crisis, when the market liquidity has dried up and only those who are forced to sell will sell, how should "going concern" be interpreted? What is the market's view in such a situation?

Business Model

The going concern argument for postponing value decreases even under fair value measurement is closely related to the business model argument, i.e., that banks did not have the intention to sell financial instruments in their trading portfolios during the GFC, even though they were classified as held for trading (measured at fair value through profit or loss). In comparison with the going concern argument, i.e., that we will consider the need to wait for a normal market situation in the valuation of the instrument (no forced sale price), the business model argument concerns the classification of the instrument into a different accounting category. During the crisis, some of the banks wished to reclassify the trading portfolio instruments from "held for trading" to the "available for sale" or "held to maturity" categories. The banks, together with certain politicians, were successful in their efforts and in October 2008, there was an EU-initiated change of IAS 39, where banks were given the option to reclassify financial instruments. Again, reflecting on the economic reality, some banks had decided to invest in American subprime loan assets and now they did not wish to report the fair value outcome of these investments in their income statements. André et al. (2008, p. 22) made the following critical comment on this:

> In our view, 2008 was a very unfortunate year for the international accounting standard-setting institution. Fair-value financial statements were telling banks they had made disastrous investment decisions, but the banks, some governments and the regulators preferred to believe the numbers were wrong ("shooting the messenger") rather than the investment decisions.

Fiechter (2011) investigated how many banks per country in Europe chose to use these new options in IAS 39 in 2008. He found that 35% of the European banks applying IFRS were "reclassifiers." Somewhat surprisingly, 60% of the Swedish banks were found to use the option, even though they were not much exposed to the subprime crisis. However, this may be a complementary reason why the effects on net gains and losses from items measured at fair value were so small in Figure 7.5.

Historical Numbers

The bullet points from the verdict also pointed at some wish for HQ to relate to historical numbers, in particular that the volatility would revert to a historical mean. The traditional accounting regime relied strongly on historical cost accounting and the realization principle, where only realized profits count and can be paid out as dividends. Although historical volatility is not comparable to a historical cost amount, some of the arguments made during the trial seemed to rely on the traditionally strong position of historical outcomes.

Uncertainty in Fair Value Measurement

As in the Carnegie case, the HQ case shows lack of reliability of values determined by using valuation techniques at Level 2 or Level 3. In the HQ case, the low reliability came from relying on very uncertain input information. It is also interesting to note the suggested lack of preparer knowledge of the accounting standard and the high reliance on the audit firm.

Changes in the Swedish Financial Market in Response to the GFC

Crises come at a high price, but may also prompt and enhance improvements that would otherwise have taken a longer time to materialize. They cause technological progress as well as societal evolvements as a response to what has occurred. In addition to international developments such as increased capital requirements and the introduction of liquidity coverage, more elaborate pillar 3 risk reporting, and central clearing and transaction registers of OTC deals, a number of other possible consequences can be seen in the behavior of Swedish companies and institutions on the financial market. These are most probably not confined to Sweden, but developed simultaneously in other countries as well.

- Liquidity coverage: The most acute liquidity problem for the banks during the GFC was in US dollars and the Swedish Financial Supervisory Authority (Finansinspektionen) therefore now requires liquidity coverage in single currencies in addition to the EU directive.
- Bond maturity: A couple of Swedish multinational companies had large bond issues maturing during the GFC. Due to their size and reputation they had no major problem in refinancing these, but it came at a substantial cost. Smaller companies had problems refinancing at all. Managing the maturities of bonds and liabilities has since become a concern. The idea is to avoid major issues maturing at the same time, and instead have an even spread of maturities. The traditional wisdom of placing short, in order to be ready for new business deals, and borrow long in order to not have any immediate surprises, has therefore been slightly improved upon.
- Revival of preferred stock: Preferred stock made a strong comeback in the aftermath of the GFC. It has always been used in private equity deals, but when it comes to listed Swedish companies preferred stock had not been used since the early 1990s. However, it got a public revival during the GFC due to the TARP program, where the US government supported troubled financial institutions partly by means of issuing preferred stock. This was a politically motivated decision. The US taxpayers should get their money back before the ordinary shareholders. In Sweden, Swedbank made a preferred stock issue in the autumn of 2008. The reason was probably a fear that an ordinary seasoned equity offering would not have been fully subscribed in the market that prevailed. Anyway, now awareness of preferred stocks was revived. After the crisis had faded away, many real estate companies issued preferred stock for a slightly different purpose. Although preferred stock is equity in legal sense, it can be given properties making it more like a subordinated bond in an economic sense, i.e., prioritized dividends, a nominal value in case of bankruptcy, no voting power, etc. As the market for corporate bonds in Sweden (and in many other countries) is rather undeveloped compared to the stock market, preferred stocks have been used as a way of having a slightly disguised market for subordinated bonds and perhaps finding an unsaturated investor demand, in order to reduce financing costs.

- Junk bond revival: There has recently been a high demand for junk bond placements from investors seeking returns as the yield of investment grade bonds has declined. It is actually quite possible that this trend started before the yields went down to unprecedented levels. The market for corporate bonds collapsed in the autumn of 2008, with no liquidity at all. A few fire-sale deals were done, but prices were arguably not representative of a market view, as there was no liquid market. When prices started to normalize in 2009, this was reported in newspapers, business press and savings magazines as gigantic returns (for 2009). Arguably, this spurred an interest in corporate bonds in general and even more so in junk bonds as these nowadays are called high-yield bonds (even the name suggests promises of high returns). The demand was so strong that some of the Swedish banks issued certificates to the public where the bonds of individual companies were mimicked. Since then, these certificates have been subsumed by the general increase in structured product offerings.
- Alternative investments: Possibly as a response to the major stock market decline during the GFC, alternative investments came very much into fashion during 2010. Investments with different return characteristics compared to the stock market, i.e., low market risk, were strongly marketed by financial institutions. Primary examples are real estate, commodity, and hedge fund investments. This even turned into speculations whether there was a bubble in the stock prices of real estate companies at the Stockholm Stock Exchange. The aggregate market capitalization of these companies is rather small and it is therefore possible that a sudden surge in demand can drive prices.

Conclusions

Sweden has historically had a German-influenced accounting tradition emphasizing creditor protection and conservatism, including the use of hidden reserves and provisions. Over time, taxation became influential and Nobes (1983) even classified Sweden at an extreme end of the accounting system spectrum, being government-driven and tax-oriented. However, at the time of the GFC, the Swedish accounting system gradually been transformed in order to meet the requirements of the financial markets. The final step was taken in 2005, when fair value accounting was introduced for the first time for listed companies' consolidated financial statements.

Having abstained from purchasing or issuing any of the most troubled instruments, most notably CDOs, the banks' major worry at the start of the GFC was financing. Public savings constituted a somewhat smaller part of the balance sheet liabilities and short-term market financing a somewhat larger part in relation to many foreign banks. Market financing became increasingly troublesome, but instead the Swedish central bank intervened and provided much of the financing needed in order to thwart a credit crunch.

As the crisis evolved, credit losses stemming from the loans in the Baltic States became the main issue. The accounting was done in accordance with the ILM (IAS 39, 2003 version), where only incurred losses are recognized, and as a consequence the credit losses occurred rather late and were perhaps smaller than if an expected loss approach had been applied. Criticism of the ILM for recognizing credit losses "too little, too late" led to a change from ILM to ELM after the crisis, however, the use of expected losses instead of more objective incurred loss criteria is likely to increase variability across banks.

The adoption of fair value accounting in 2005 had somewhat dramatic consequences for two of the small listed Swedish banks, Carnegie and HQ. The Carnegie case shows how the use of fair values open up for manipulation by combining market transactions with the use of valuation techniques (Level 2 and Level 3 measurement). The HQ case shows an example of how fair value accounting failed to fully reflect market prices during the GFC. The company was criticized by the court with regard to its handling of uncertainty regarding inputs in valuation models at Levels 2 and 3, suggesting insufficient use of price information. However, the court verdict also acknowledged the fact that IAS 39 prescribes a going concern reasoning where fair value will not reflect forced transactions even though they may occur frequently during a crisis.

However, what really stands out is that the Swedish banks were well capitalized at the onset of the crisis with equity levels far above the minimum requirements. With the exception of the two small banks with trading portfolios (Carnegie and HQ), they also managed to survive the financial crisis with only scratches. Perhaps it is just that simple.

References

André, P., A. Cazavan-Jeny, W. Dick, C. Richard, & P. Walton. 2008. Fair value accounting in the banking crisis in 2008: Shooting the messenger. *Accounting in Europe*, 6(1): 3–24.

Beatty, A., & S. Liao. 2014. Financial accounting in the banking industry: A review of the empirical literature. *Journal of Accounting and Economics*, 58: 339–383.

Bushman, R. M., & C. D. Williams. 2012. Accounting discretion, loan loss provisioning, and discipline of banks' risk-taking. *Journal of Accounting and Economics*, 54: 1–18.

Camfferman, K. 2015. The emergence of the 'incurred-loss' model for credit losses in IAS 39. *Accounting in Europe*, 12(1): 1–35.

Carnegie. 2007. Carnegie Investment Bank AB: s kompletterande överklagande angående Finansinspektionens beslut, 2007–11–15, mål nr. 22514–07 [in Swedish]. Appeal in court by Carnegie in response to the Swedish Financial Supervisory Authority's decision regarding Carnegie, November 15.

Collin, S.-O. 1993. The brotherhood of the Swedish sphere. *International Studies of Management and Organization*, (23): 69–86.

Cooke, T. E. 1989. Disclosure in the corporate annual reports of Swedish companies. *Accounting and Business Research*, 19(74): 113–124.

Davidson, S., & J. M. Kohlmeier. 1966. A measure of the impact of some foreign accounting principles. *Journal of Accounting Research*, 4(2): 183–212.

Elmér, H., G. Guibourg, D. Kjellberg, & M. Nessén. 2012. Riksbankens penningpolitiska åtgärder under finanskrisen—utvärdering och lärdomar [in Swedish]. *Penning- och Valutapolitik, Sveriges Riksbank*, (3): 1–23.

Fama, E. 1980. Banking in the theory of finance. *Journal of Monetary Economics*, 6: 39–57.

Fiechter, P. 2011. Reclassification of financial assets under IAS 39: Impact on European banks' financial statements. *Accounting in Europe*, 8(1): 49–67.

Finansinspektionen. 2007. Finansinspektionens beslut 2007–09–27, FI Dnr. 07–6125 [in Swedish]. The Swedish Financial Supervisory Authority's decision regarding Carnegie, September 27.

Gebhardt, G., & Z. Novotny-Farkas. 2011. Mandatory IFRS adoption and accounting quality of European banks. *Journal of Business Finance & Accounting*, 38(3/4): 289–333.

Gersbach, H., H. Haller, & J. Müller. 2015. The macroeconomics of Modigliani—Miller. *Journal of Economic Theory*, 157: 1081–1113.

Hellman, N. 2011a. Soft adoption and reporting incentives: A study of the impact of IFRS on financial statements in Sweden. *Journal of International Accounting Research*, 10(1): 61–83.

Hellman, N. 2011b. Analysis of changing institutional environments, new accounting policies and corporate governance practices in Sweden. In Krivogorsky, V. (Ed.), *Law, Corporate Governance, and Accounting: European Perspectives*, Abingdon, UK: Routledge, ISBN: 978-0-415-87186-0, pp. 210–229.

Henrekson, M., & U. Jacobsson. 2003. The Swedish model of corporate ownership and control in transition. IUI Working Paper Series No. 593, Stockholm, The Research Institute of Industrial Economics.

Leventis, S., P. E. Dimitripoulos, & A. Anandarajan. 2011. Loan loss provisions, earnings management and capital management under IFRS: The case of EU commercial banks. *Journal of Financial Services Research*, 40: 103–122.

Lincoln, E. 1998. Japan's financial problems. *Brookings Papers on Economic Activity*, (2), 347–385.

Monsen, N., & W. A. Wallace. 1995. Evolving financial reporting practices: A comparative study of the Nordic countries' harmonization efforts. *Contemporary Accounting Research*, 11(2): 973–997.

Nobes, C. W. 1983. A judgmental international classification of financial reporting practices. *Journal of Business Finance & Accounting*, 10(1): 1–19.

Novotny-Farkas, Z. 2016. The interaction of the IFRS 9 expected loss approach with supervisory rules and implications for financial stability. *Accounting in Europe*, 13(2): 197–227.

Randøy, T., & J. Nielsen. 2002. Company performance, corporate governance, and CEO compensation in Norway and Sweden. *Journal of Management and Governance*, 6: 57–81.

Riksbanken (the Swedish Central Bank). 2008a. Finansiell stabilitet [in Swedish]. Report 2008:1. Downloaded at: http://archive.riksbank.se/sv/Webbarkiv/Publicerat/Publicerat-fran-Riksbanken/Finansiell-stabilitet/Rapporten-Finansiell-stabilitet/index.html@all=1.html

Riksbanken (the Swedish Central Bank). 2008b. Finansiell stabilitet [in Swedish]. Report 2008:2. Downloaded at: http://archive.riksbank.se/sv/Webbarkiv/Publicerat/Publicerat-fran-Riksbanken/Finansiell-stabilitet/Rapporten-Finansiell-stabilitet/index.html@all=1.html

Riksbanken (the Swedish Central Bank). 2009a. Finansiell stabilitet [in Swedish]. Report 2009:1. Downloaded at: http://archive.riksbank.se/sv/Webbarkiv/Publicerat/Publicerat-fran-Riksbanken/Finansiell-stabilitet/Rapporten-Finansiell-stabilitet/index.html@all=1.html

Riksbanken (the Swedish Central Bank). 2009b. Finansiell stabilitet [in Swedish]. Report 2009:2. Downloaded at: http://archive.riksbank.se/sv/Webbarkiv/Publicerat/Publicerat-fran-Riksbanken/Finansiell-stabilitet/Rapporten-Finansiell-stabilitet/index.html@all=1.html

Stockholms tingsrätt. 2017. Dom i mål nr T 9311–11, T 9306–11, T 17512–11 och T 17809–11 [in Swedish]. Verdict from Stockholm District Court in the HQ law suit trial. December 14.

Van Binsbergen, J., J. Graham, & J. Yang. 2010. The cost of debt. *Journal of Finance*, 65(6): 2089–2136.

Wohlin, L. 1998. Bankkrisens upprinnelse [in Swedish]. *Ekonomisk debatt*, 26(1): 21–30.

Zeff, S. A., & S.-E. Johansson. 1984. The curious accounting treatment of the Swedish government loan to Uddeholm. *The Accounting Review*, 59(2): 342–350.

8 The Financial Crisis Impact on Institutions and Accounting Practices in Spain[1]

José Luis Ucieda[2] and José A. Gonzalo-Angulo

Brief Analyses of the Crisis in Spain

On September 15, 2007, Lehman Brothers fell and one of the most tragic economic and financial crisis spread to the world. The Spanish economy had completed a quite large period of steady growth when it all burst out. However, in the years before the crisis, a rapid growth in the real estate and construction industries, along with other macroeconomic indicators, left the financial system highly leveraged with a rather concentrated loan risk. After the first hit in 2008, the real problems of the crisis in Spain unveiled and the entire financial system required intervention and assistance from European and international institutions. In 2012, the conservative government proved to be a great negotiator by avoiding an European Union (EU) rescue. However, the revamped financial system had fewer entities and no better solvency than before the crisis.

Accounting regulation remained mostly unchanged during the crisis, except for the extraordinary one-hit bad-debt provisions requirement of the government in 2012. This was more a political move to maintain credibility before negotiating with international institutions, rather than a financial or economic measure to tackle the crisis.

The Spanish accounting standard-setting structure, based in four issuers acting simultaneously, is unable to keep up with IASB developments or economic events, and incapable of producing a coherent accounting regulation framework. Thus, financial reporting is perceived to have more of a stewardship role than a decision-usefulness role in Spain.

In this chapter, we address how the international financial crisis impacted Spain in all areas. Even though macroeconomic indicators portray a crisis picture, the two most striking features of the crisis in Spain were the high increase in unemployment and its consequences, especially on young people, and the entire reform of the financial system. The following section describes the evolution and impact of the crisis in terms of macroeconomic indicators, highlighting the "W" shape (or double dip) of the crisis. The following sections explain the impact on capital markets and public debt, including a picture of the pre-crisis Spanish financial system and a description of the impact and the measures taken to tackle the crisis. After this depiction, the paper describes the particular accounting regulation framework with four standard setters and how accounting regulation evolved during the crisis. In the final sections, we conclude that the main outcome of the crisis is a revamped financial industry where savings banks are gone and fewer banks compete for the same clients, resulting in a concentration of deposits and loans in fewer entities. The restructuration was done with public funds using institutions created during the crisis or umbrella-wide agreements to deploy the necessary measures to carry it all out. To date, the net cost of the crisis that Spanish taxpayers will pay is expected to be €62 billion (net financial assistance after expected recoveries).

Economic Impact of the Crisis in Spain

Before the Aftermath

Spain was a member of the European Economy and Monetary Union (EMU) since its inception in mid-1999, accepting the change of old currency (the "peseta") to the euro as a tool to reduce the economic imbalances with the rest of the EU countries. In fact, the Spanish economy is among those that have benefited most from the EMU membership. In the first 10 years of the euro, the Spanish economy enjoyed a period of economic growth where there was real convergence with the core EMU member countries, in terms of low inflation and interest rates, high level of employment, and gross domestic product (GDP) growth. GDP growth was on average 3.7% during the 2000s, while GPD per capita started at 79% of the EU average at the beginning of the decade and reached 95% at the end (see Estrada et al., 2009).

By the end of 2007, Spain had accumulated 14 straight years of economic growth. During this period, in 1999, it became a full member of the EMU and switched to the euro. Since 2000, the GDP grew 3.8% yearly on average (Banco de España, BdE, 2017: p. 29). Employment grew 12.2 percentage points, boosted by women's increasing access to the job market and a significant increase in the population, mostly due to immigration. Inflation grew 3.3% on average during 2000–2007, standing higher than the European average (see Figure 8.1). In 2006 and 2007, the General National Budget (GNB) yielded a surplus. Public debt was brought down to 36% of GDP, the lowest level in more than 20 years (see Figure 8.2).

This positive picture was shadowed by several threats. As a member of the EMU, Spain lost two important macroeconomic and monetary tools: exchange rates and interest rates. Having low interest rates and a stable exchange rate fostered economic imbalances, like an uncontrolled

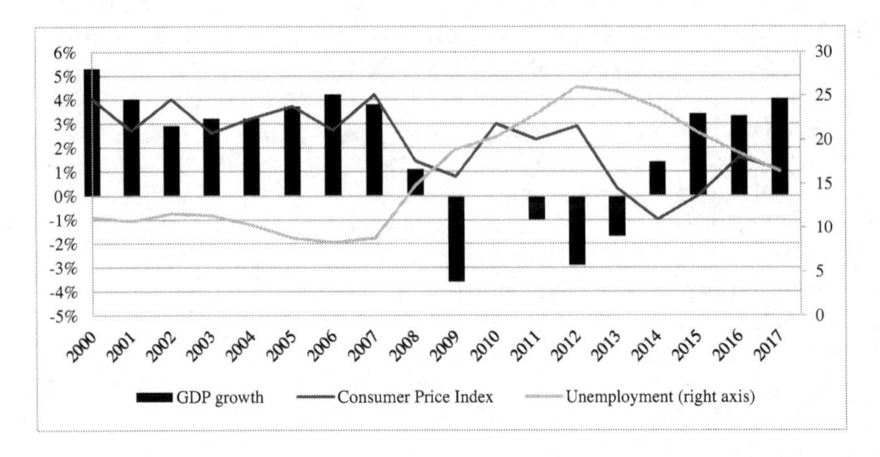

Figure 8.1 GDP growth, Consumer Price Index, and unemployment in Spain during 2000–2017

Source: Data from BdE ("Statistical Bulletin," available at www.bde.es/webbde/en/estadis/infoest/bolest.html); INE ("Economy," available at http://ine.es/dyngs/INEbase/en/categoria.htm?c=EstadisticaP&cid=1254735570541), and Datos Macro, available at www.datosmacro.com/.

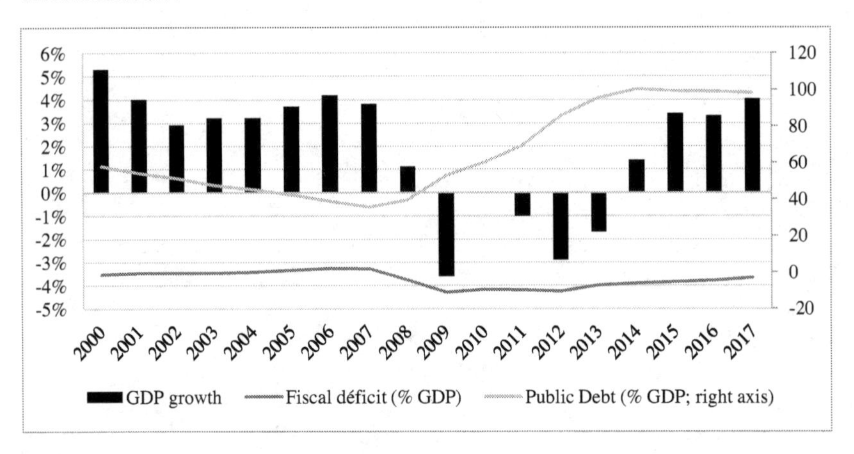

Figure 8.2 GDP growth, fiscal deficit (as % GDP), and public debt (as % GDP) in Spain during 2000–2017

Source: Data from BdE ("Statistical Bulletin," available at www.bde.es/webbde/en/estadis/infoest/bolest.html); INE ("Economy," available at http://ine.es/dyngs/INEbase/en/categoria.htm?c=Estadistica_P&cid=125473557054), and Datos Macro, available at www.datosmacro.com/.

growth of private indebtedness (going from 94% to 191% of GDP), driven by a pushing consumption and investment in real state. Lending concentrated on the real estate industry with an average yearly growth of 20%. Private homes' high construction rates were pushed by higher income expectations, cheaper financing access, population growth due to immigration, and a climbing real estate prices scenario. This promoted a bubble in prices of real estate that leveraged, with a high indebted population, the drastic crisis afterwards.

Another threatening factor was the rising inflation that led to a substantial fall in competitiveness and productivity, in particular, due to increasing wages. Imports grew more than exports and the commercial balance accumulated a 9% deficit in 2007. The strong deficit of the balance of payments (80% of GDP in 2007) was financed by securities issued to international investors backed by loans and other assets, making the country strongly dependent on foreign capital and investments to maintain its growing deficit. Finally, the fiscal surplus in 2006 and 2007 was mostly due to extraordinary income and cyclical effects rather than structural factors, while a significant part of expenditures was becoming structural. The increasing economic and financial risks were highlighted by the International Monetary Fund (IMF), OECD, and the Bank of Spain (Banco de España, BdE), but their future outlook was of a soft recession, quite distinct from the rapid and intense outburst of the crisis.

The Crisis Unleashed: 2008–2011

Forecasts for Spain in 2008 included a slow downturn as the economic cycle showed signs of exhaustion (higher interest rates from the European Central Bank [ECB], and a reduction in demand and prices in the real estate industry). The dramatic crisis hitting the rest of the world hindered access to financing, cut the wealth of families, made financial assets' prices fall, and spread an overall lack of confidence in the system. GDP fell 4.6% from mid-2008 to 2009, in line with other European countries, trading balance became positive due to a substantial cut of imports, and the 2% fiscal surplus in 2007 turned into an 11% deficit in 2009. Public debt was only 36% of GDP in 2007 but it almost doubled in 2011 to 69.5% of GDP (see Figure 8.2).

With a scenario characterized by high default levels, gloomy perspectives, falling official interest rates, and high uncertainty, financial institutions invested their scarce resources and the extra liquidity from the ECB measures in public debt, increasing the volume of public debt by 145% between December 2007 and December 2011 (from €79 billion to €194 billion).

However, one of the most significant features of the impact of the crisis in Spain was the intense job destruction rate. Between 2008 and 2009, 1.5 million jobs (1 million in construction activities) were destroyed and the unemployment rate shifted from 9% at the end of 2007 to 18.7% in 2009. Consequently, consumption dropped and inflation fell to 0.3%. The booming real estate prices before 2007 were now falling 10% in two years, and the number of real estate operations was cut to less than half. Many real estate and construction companies went into bankruptcy during these years, increasing unemployment, and making families lose their homes when they were unable to pay their related mortgage loans.

The financial and economic measures adopted in Spain were able to smooth the rapid deterioration of the Spanish economy. However, while all international organizations forecasted a 0.8% GDP growth, a final 1.1% drop was registered in 2008, making this the largest estimation error ever for IMF, OECD, EU, and BdE. The main reason was the unpredictable impact of the public debt crisis in Europe.

High private indebtedness levels, fears about the impact of real estate prices on the solvency of financial entities, high unemployment rate, weakened public accounts, and the impact of the international financial crisis of public debt (Greece, Ireland, and Portugal) froze down economic activity. For banking credits, the default rate jumped from 1% in 2007 to 8% in 2011. Even though the government highlighted the strength and stability of the Spanish financial system, the overall picture cast a deep shadow of uncertainty over its solvency and capacity to endure the situation.

Overall, when the initial impact of the financial crisis seemed tackled, the lack of credibility on public debt delivered a second economic crisis, called public or sovereign debt crisis, which was deeper than the precedent and hit hard on a rather weakened Spain.

The Crisis Is a "W": 2012–2013

In 2012, financial institutions increased the financial assistance from the Eurosystem (€420 billion, 34% of all invested liquidity). Uncertainty from international volatility on public debt (Greece, Portugal, and Ireland) and tumbling Spanish public deficit pushed the risk premium up more than 700 basis points. (The 10-year bond marginal interest rate was 7.5%.) The new government arisen from the elections in November 2011 carried out several measures[3] to tackle the situation:

- In April 2012, the government passed a law to strengthen the framework for financial stability of public administrations, setting goals in terms of deficit, public debt, and transparency requirements.
- In July 2012, a new law introduced changes in the job market to provide more flexibility in hiring.
- Later, new laws introduced measures to liberalize certain industries, promote competitiveness, and include a Suppliers Payment Plan to provide public administrations liquidity to be able to pay their suppliers in time.

Despite all these measures, uncertainty prevented banks from providing financing to entities and consumers. Unemployment peaked at 26% in 2012 and stayed at 25.5% in 2013. GDP dropped 3.49% and 1.7%

in 2012 and 2013, respectively. Public debt climbed to 95.5% of GDP in 2013. Fiscal deficit increased to 10.5% and 7% of GDP in 2012 and 2013, respectively, even though the European Commission accepted a plan to adjust deficits over a longer period (soft adjustment). The risk premium cooled down from its maximum level in 2012 to 396 basis points by the end of 2012 and 220 by the end of 2013, which provided a foreign investment net positive inflow of €85 billion. The real estate industry shrunk intensively in both number of transactions and price levels (44% drop), representing 4% of GDP in 2013 (compared to 12% in 2006). Lending followed a similar path.

All these metrics provided a rather negative portrait of the Spanish economy. Yet, the high unemployment rate (26%) and the lack of confidence banks and financial institutions had to provide financing to economic agents created a dead-end situation that significantly impaired the wealth and competitiveness of the country.

When the Crisis Gives In: 2014 Onwards

In 2014, all macroeconomic indicators changed their trend into a positive one. GDP grew a positive 2.2%. Competitiveness recovered as labor costs moderated and job losses slowed down (unemployment was cut to 23.6% in 2014 and 16.4% in 2017.) Fiscal deficit stayed at 6% (still high and under close inspection by EU observers). Real estate prices increased for the first time since 2007. General indebtedness decreased 24 basis points since 2010. However, it all came at the cost of public debt breaking 100% of the GDP psychological barrier. Yet, capital markets celebrated the recovery growing 21.4% in 2013 and 3.7% in 2014, with an increase of around 40% of capitalization. From 2015 onwards, GDP has grown steadily around 3% every year.

Impact of the Crisis on Capital Markets

Spanish equity capital markets have followed a similar trend as European capital markets. The main index, IBEX35, reflected the "W" crisis effect in 2008 and 2011–2012, respectively (see Figure 8.3).

In November 2007, it reached the historic maximum of 16,040 points and dropped to 6,702.60 (58% decline) in March 2009. After climbing up to 12,240.50 in January 2010, it plummeted to 5,905.30 in July 2012 and, since then, has not been able to go over 12,000 again (maximum 11,884 in April 2015). Trading volume and capitalization also reflected the crisis. In 2008, capitalization of listed companies dropped 38%. And, between 2009 and 2011, capitalization was reduced by 23% (see Figure 8.4). At the end of 2012, companies in the IBEX35 index had lost almost half of the €832 billion of capitalization they had at the beginning of 2007. Most of that amount has been recovered, as capitalization at the end of 2017 was €701 billion.

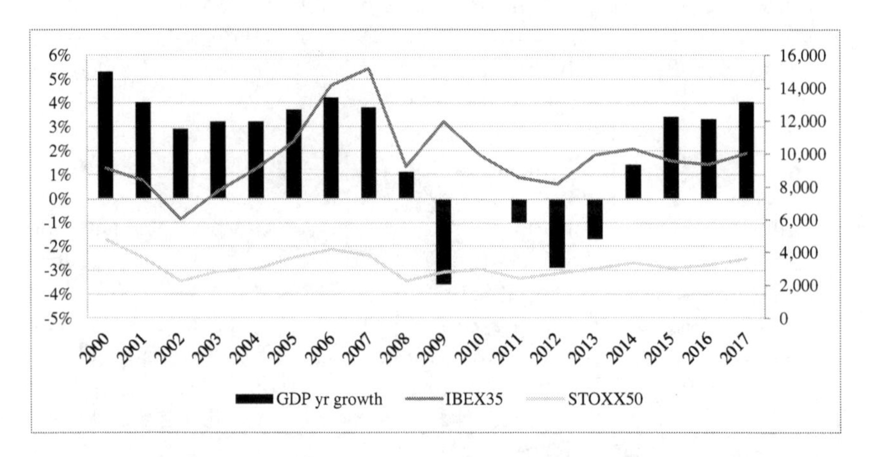

Figure 8.3 IBEX35, STOXX50 yearly closing prices (right axis) compared with Spanish GDP yearly growth during 2000–2017 (left axis)

Source: Data from BdE ("Statistical Bulletin," available at www.bde.es/webbde/en/estadis/infoest/bolest.html); CNMV ("Securities Market Annual Report," available at www.cnmv.es/Portal/Publicaciones/Informes.aspx).

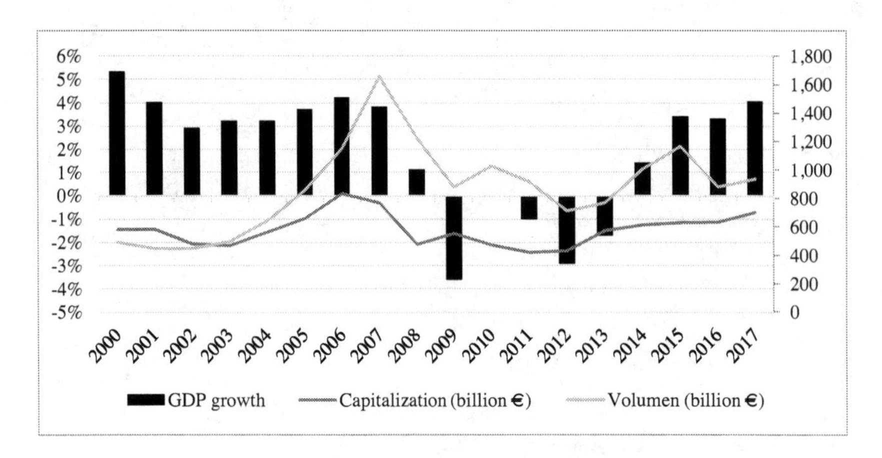

Figure 8.4 IBEX35 trading volume and capitalization (right axis, billion €)

Source: Data from BdE ("Statistical Bulletin," available at www.bde.es/webbde/en/estadis/infoest/bolest.html); CNMV ("Securities Market Annual Report," available at www.cnmv.es/Portal/Publicaciones/Informes.aspx).

The crisis wiped out of the market almost a quarter of all listed companies. In 2007, there were 192 listed entities, but only 150 in 2017. This decline has not been linear in all industries. The number of financial listed entities was reduced from 36 in 2007 to 17 in 2017 (58% reduction, due to mergers and acquisitions), while nonfinancial listed entities went from 156 in 2007 to 133 in 2017 (15% reduction).

Impact of the Crisis on Public and Private Debt

Public debt has played a significant role in the crisis in Spain. Since 2000, the average amount issued every year was €75 billion. However, since 2009, the average rose to €245 billion every year, due to the economic measures taken by the socialist government during the first years of the crisis (2008–2011). During these years, the average yield of the Spanish 10-year bond climbed from around 4% in 2009 to 5.3% during 2010 and 2012 (see Figure 8.5). Increasing public debt was expensive in terms of financial expenses and that played a role in how the crisis unfolded in Spain.

Since 2014, even after some positive indicators that the worst of the crisis was over, the average amount of public debt issued every year stayed around €240 billion (€242 billion in 2017). Therefore, outstanding public debt increased an 11.3% compound rate since the crisis started in 2007, going from €338 billion in 2007 to €989 billion in 2017 (see Figure 8.6).

In terms of percentage of GDP, public debt represented 35.6% of GDP at the end of 2007. In 2008, it started to climb, reaching 100.4% in 2014. In 2017, it stayed at 98.3% of GDP (see Figure 8.7).

A second issue to address in order to understand the impact of public debt in the crisis in Spain is the behavior of the risk premium.[4] Before 2007, the risk premium remained close to zero, or even slightly negative. During the first years of the crisis, mostly due to economic issues, the spread increased to more than 100 basis points. However, after other countries were showing problems dealing with the crisis, the lack of confidence in the government to tackle the situation made the peak spread

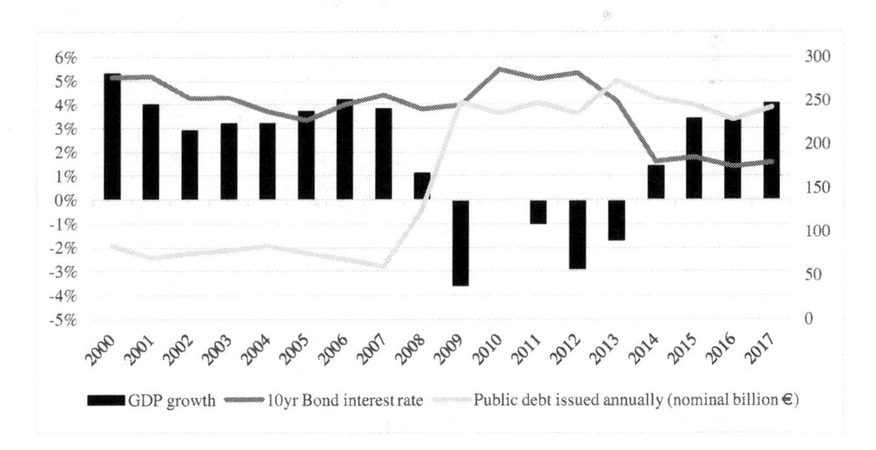

Figure 8.5 Public debt annual issues (right axis) and Spanish 10-year bond yield (left axis) during 2000–2017

Source: Data from BdE ("Statistical Bulletin," available at www.bde.es/webbde/en/estadis/infoest/bolest.html); CNMV ("Securities Market Annual Report," available at www.cnmv.es/Portal/Publicaciones/Informes.aspx), and Datos Macro, available at www.datosmacro.com/.

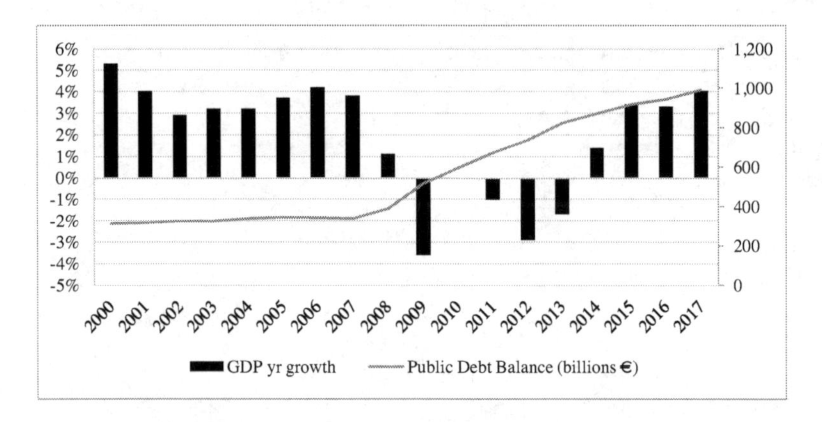

Figure 8.6 Spanish GDP growth and public debt balance during 2000–2017

Source: Data from BdE ("Statistical Bulletin," available at www.bde.es/webbde/en/estadis/infoest/bolest.html); CNMV ("Securities Market Annual Report," available at www.cnmv.es/Portal/Publicaciones/Informes.aspx).

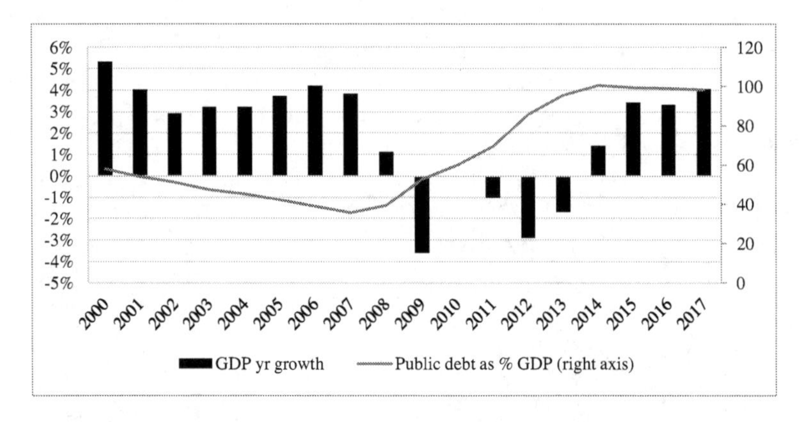

Figure 8.7 Spanish GDP growth and public debt as a percentage of GDP during 2000–2017

Source: Data from BdE ("Statistical Bulletin," available at www.bde.es/webbde/en/estadis/infoest/bolest.html); CNMV ("Securities Market Annual Report," available at www.cnmv.es/Portal/Publicaciones/Informes.aspx).

to a maximum of 650 points in July 2012, after the announcement of the financial rescue of Ireland (Portugal and Greece had been already rescued).[5] This increased restrictions on financing for banks, private entities, and consumers. It also increased the cost of debt for the Spanish government, putting an extra burden on its fiscal deficit (see Figure 8.8).

Private debt increased strongly in the years before the crisis. In 2007, gross issues amounted to €725 billion, and the carrying debt in 2016 was

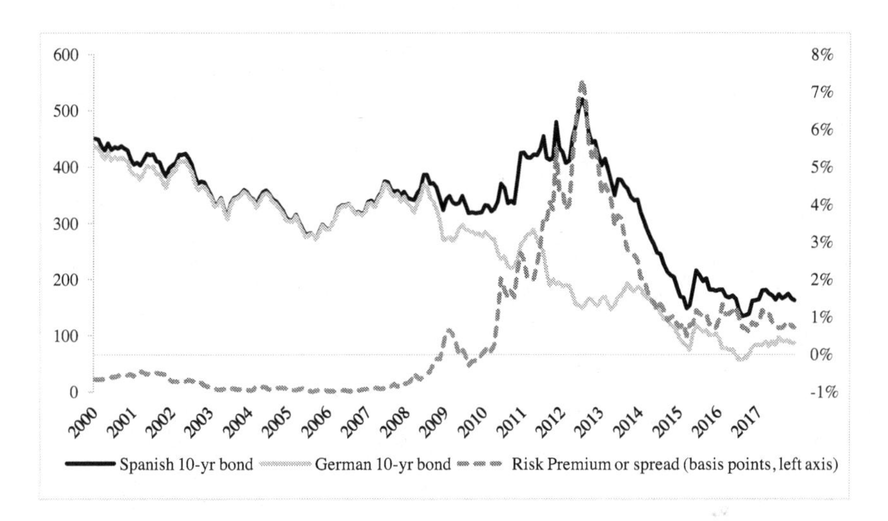

Figure 8.8 Spanish and German 10-year bond yield and the spread (risk premium) during 2000–2017

Source: Data from BdE ("Statistical Bulletin," available at www.bde.es/webbde/en/estadis/infoest/bolest.html); Datos Macro, available at www.datosmacro.com/.

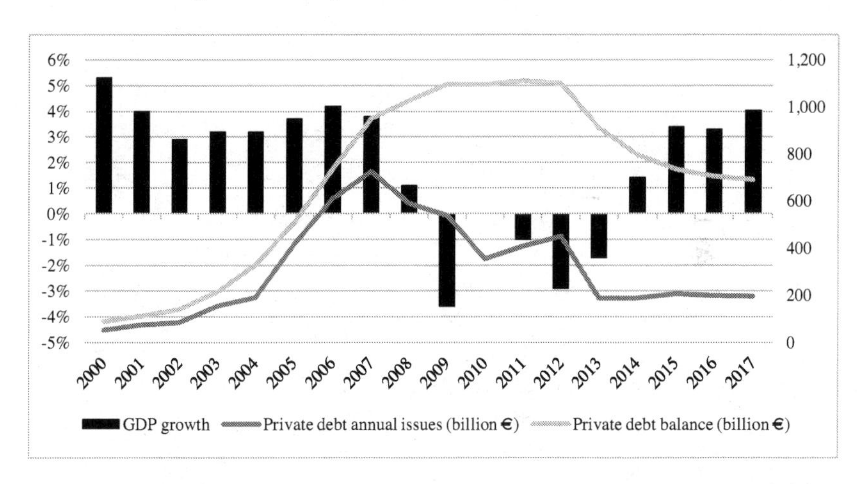

Figure 8.9 Private debt annual issues and accumulated balance (in billions of euros)

Source: Data from BdE ("Statistical Bulletin," available at www.bde.es/webbde/en/estadis/infoest/bolest.html); CNMV ("Securities Market Annual Report," available at www.cnmv.es/Portal/Publicaciones/Informes.aspx).

€722 billion. Gross issues declined in 2008 and have stayed around €200 billion per year since 2013. During the years before 2007, the outstanding balance of private debt doubled to over €1 trillion. Since 2013, private debt started to reduce, ending up at €690 million in 2017 (see Figure 8.9).

From an analytical point of view, during the years before the crisis, companies and consumers increased their leverage under the spell of the great expansion and economic growth. As the crisis burst, the debt became a heavy burden and took a rather high toll on entities and families.

Impact of the Crisis on the Banking Industry

This section addresses the deep changes in the banking industry during the crisis. The next section provides an overview of the main features of the Spanish financial industry before the crisis. The following section details all measures taken by the government and regulators to tackle the crisis that directly affected the banking industry. Finally, we include another section to explain the important role that the dynamic provision, another special feature of the Spanish financial industry, played into how the crisis was (poorly) managed.

Overview of the Spanish Banking System: The Case of Saving Banks

Before 2007, financial institutions in Spain were composed of (1) banks, most of them listed, (2) savings banks, non-profit entities with a governance structure that makes them easy prey for trade unions and political parties (designating power in their boards), and (3) credit unions, a little part of the financial system, with the legal form of credit cooperatives. The Bank of Spain, as a central bank, is an autonomous entity—independent from the government since 1994—that operates the system with total autonomy, in coordination with the Ministry of Economy and the consensus of banks. As a member of the EMU, the Bank of Spain has limited possibilities to manage the credit system. In particular, the Basel Accord sets the regulatory capital requirements, the IASB sets accounting standards (as adopted by the EU), and, since November 2014, the EU Single Supervisory Mechanism (SSM) is in charge of the banking supervisory activity of more relevant entities.

Savings banks have a particular nature that requires further explanation to understand their role in the crisis. The origin of savings banks in Spain dates back to the charitable institutions founded in the nineteenth century by religious orders, intellectuals, or politicians, with the purpose of granting low interest rate loans to less advantaged populations, by using a system of pledging guaranties (Martín-Aceña, 2013). Savings banks are not allowed to issue ordinary shares because they are non-profit entities and thus do not have shareholders. The social dimension of savings banks was developed by foundations attached to the entity through the so-called social and cultural activities budget. Due to the absence of shareholders, a percentage of the savings banks profits was dedicated to financing public libraries, schools, retirement homes, classical music concerts, student grants, and similar disbursements. The operational strategy of such entities has been described as a competitive cooperation (Comín, 2007) made through the Association of Spanish Savings Banks (Confederación Española de Cajas de Ahorro, CECA). From 1989, the Bank of Spain allowed them to grow outside their original geographical area, creating a period of expansion in their fields of activity: customer deposits, consumer loans and mortgages, etc. By the end of the twentieth century, savings banks became financers of the banking system.

Another feature of the Spanish banking system is the high number of bank offices spread throughout the cities and big towns across the country. In the years before the crisis, the rate of offices per 10,000 inhabitants reached almost 10, but this figure was reduced to 6.18 in 2016. Accordingly, bank employees per 1,000 inhabitants was reduced from 6.03 to 4.02 in this same period, a loss of 1 out of 3 jobs between 2007 and 2016.

The Banking System During the Crisis

The Spanish banking crisis has been one of the most prominent in the Eurozone. In short, savings banks, which accumulated roughly half of the loans and deposits of the system before the crisis were converted into banks. The Spanish public sector assumed the restructuring cost with the financial assistance of the EU between 2008 and 2014 (€72.4 billion, approximately 7% of the average annual Spanish GDP for this period). In particular, the number of outstanding banks was reduced from 70 in 2007 to 62 in 2016, and savings banks were reduced from 46 in 2007 to two[6] in 2016.

In the case of Spain, the crisis was not originated due to domestic or international financial markets. The Bank of Spain did not allow entities to operate in credit derivatives markets during the first years of the twenty-first century. However, the lack of liquidity after the Lehman Brothers case reached Spanish banks and corporate credit markets (i.e., securitizations and debt emissions).

As described before, credit by banks, especially savings banks, increased strongly between 2000 and 2007, pushed by a booming construction and real estate industry. Developers acquired rural land and lobbied municipal governments in cities and tourism areas to reclassify it as urban land to allow the construction of buildings (e.g., homes and offices). Constructors and real estate developers were given advantages to increase their activity which, in turn, increased tax collection for local governments whose budgets greatly benefited from the extra taxes (and, in some cases, from bribery). Banks and savings banks supported the operation by granting credits for an unusually large portion of the land price (typically between 50% and 90%). When the reclassification of the rural land into urban was not approved, the lender lost the credit. But when the land was reclassified, the developer succeeded and more land would be purchased to start all over again.

Construction entities increased their activity building and selling houses and offices with the assistance of banks and savings banks who provided mortgages. Figure 8.10 shows annual growth of GDP and credit to companies and individuals (Panel A), and the accumulated growth of GDP and credit (Panel B). From 2000, credit grew faster than GDP. After 2011,

Panel A: GDP and credit to entities and individuals annual growth

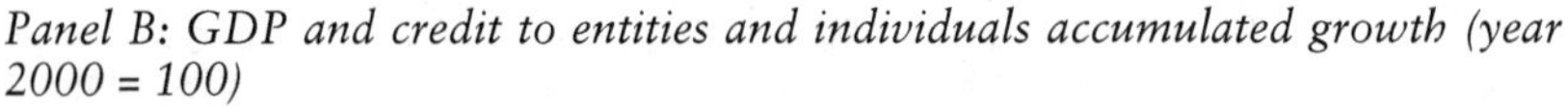

Panel B: GDP and credit to entities and individuals accumulated growth (year 2000 = 100)

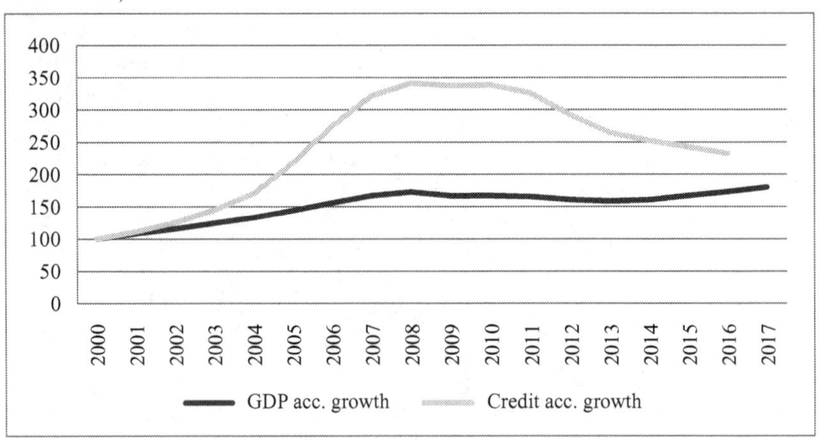

Figure 8.10 GDP and credit to entities and individuals during 2000-2017. Panel A shows annual growth and Panel B shows accumulated growth (year 2000 = 100)

Sources: Data from BdE ("Statistical Bulletin," available at www.bde.es/webbde/en/estadis/infoest/bolest.html); INE ("Economy," available at http://ine.es/dyngs/INEbase/en/categoria.htm?c=Estadistica_P&cid=1254735570541).

credit decreased, even after GDP started to grow in 2014. The explosion of credit from 2000 to 2007, with annual growths between 11% and 27%, was followed by a hard contraction in 2008 and subsequent years until 2016.

This boom in real estate and construction changed the distribution of loans. The portion of loans granted to developers and construction increased from 25% in 2000 to 48% in 2007 (see Figure 8.11). From then on, the portion reduced at a slow pace (27% in 2016).

The great expansion of credit in the two decades before the financial crisis was fostered by two characteristics of the savings banks: (1) savings banks were not subject to markets' capital discipline (IMF, 2012), and (2) savings banks' managers and directors (appointed by local or regional authorities, political parties, and trade unions) concentrated the entity's financial risk in loans to the real estate industry and home mortgages as a way to support and protect the economic development of their geographical area of influence. When the prices of these assets collapsed after the summer of 2007, sales decreased, reducing the capacity of lenders to repay their debts, and savings banks suffered big losses. Developers, like Martinsa-Fadesa or Astroc, that were financially supported by savings banks went into bankruptcy or significantly cut most of their operations.

Based on EU banking regulations, in 2010, the Bank of Spain concentrated savings banks in so-called institutional protection schemes (known as SIPs in the Spanish acronym), a sort of mutual union among entities to share profits and avoid losses, consolidated for capital

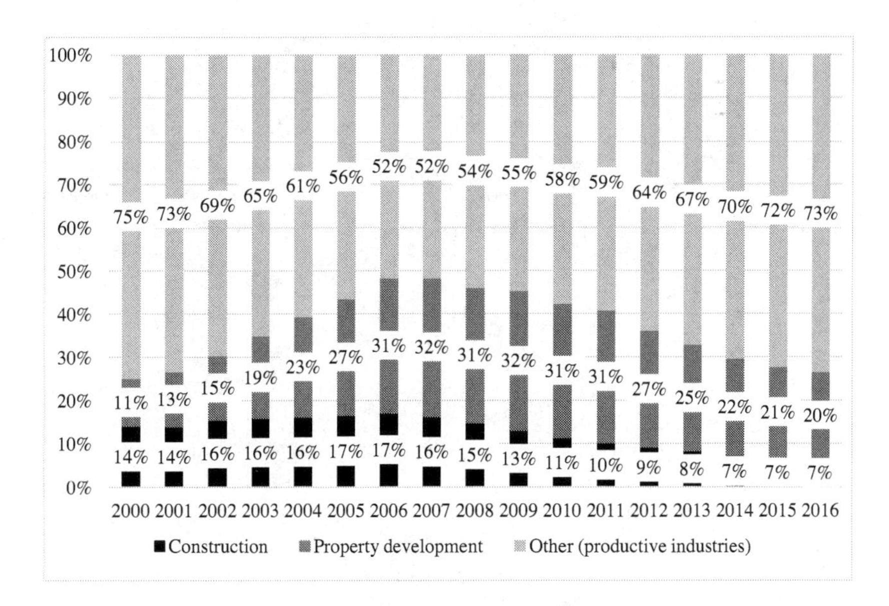

Figure 8.11 Concentration of loan risk by industry during 2000–2016

Source: Data from BdE ("Statistical Bulletin," available at www.bde.es/webbde/en/estadis/infoest/bolest.html).

requirements, supervisory, and financial reporting purposes. Even though the supervisor required a common business strategy, as well as mutual support between the participants in terms of solvency and liquidity, individual entities could keep their image, offices, and directors. Hence, SIPs failed and, in 2011, savings banks were merged or transformed into new banks that assumed the cultural and social side of the savings banks. The most relevant case was Bankia, which was created in May 2011 by a cold merger of seven savings banks and was bailed out in 2012.[7]

As a further note, savings banks faced an important loss of reputation after issuing subordinated securities named "preferred shares," a widespread practice from the 1990s. During the crisis, in 2009 and 2010, the issuance of preferred shares was rejected by financial intermediaries after most savings banks had already placed some €30 billion among small companies and families. After the bailout, preferred shares were converted to equity (mandated by the supervisor or the resolution authority), and investors lost most of their money when share prices collapsed. The placement of these securities as retail bank products, similar to term deposits with high yields, has been deemed as mis-selling by the Spanish courts and savings banks and banks to which they have been converted have refunded to clients most of the amounts collected (Zunzunegui, 2014).

Impairment of Credit: The Dynamic Provision of the Bank of Spain

The rapid growth of credit before 2007 pushed financial institutions into a rather competitive race where loan granting requirement policies became looser due to expectations of raising housing prices and, little by little, the quality of credit portfolios suffered a dramatic impairment. However, the impact of the mortgage credit losses was much less important than those derived from loans to constructors and real estate developers. While in 2000 the share of non-performing loans in real estate and construction industries was 25% of the total, it abruptly climbed to 72% in 2008 and reached its maximum (74%) in 2011 (see Figure 8.12). Even in 2016, more than a half of non-performing loans (54%) belonged to real estate and construction entities.

From an accounting point of view, impairment represented on average around 1.4% of the previous year's balance of financial assets or 4.3% of the previous year's equity (see Figure 8.13). The peak in 2012 was due to a set of dramatic measures taken by the government when it negotiated the EU assistance for failed banks.

To interpret this situation, one must understand the so-called dynamic provision, one of the most controversial tools of prudential regulation in Spain, in force from 2000 to 2016 (Saurina Salas, 2009, and Saurina Salas and Trucharte, 2017). Basically, banks are allowed to build up buffer

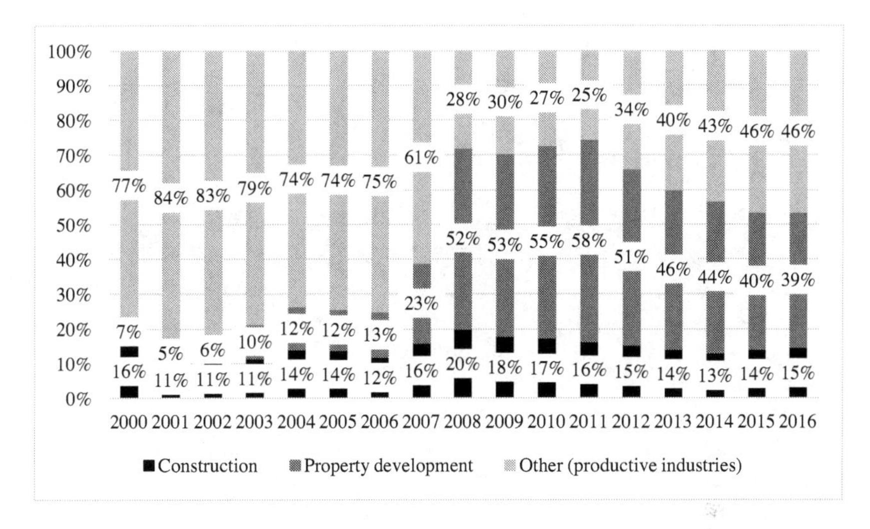

Figure 8.12 Non-performing loans in construction, real estate, and other industries during 2000–2016

Source: Data from BdE ("Statistical Bulletin," available at www.bde.es/webbde/en/estadis/infoest/bolest.html).

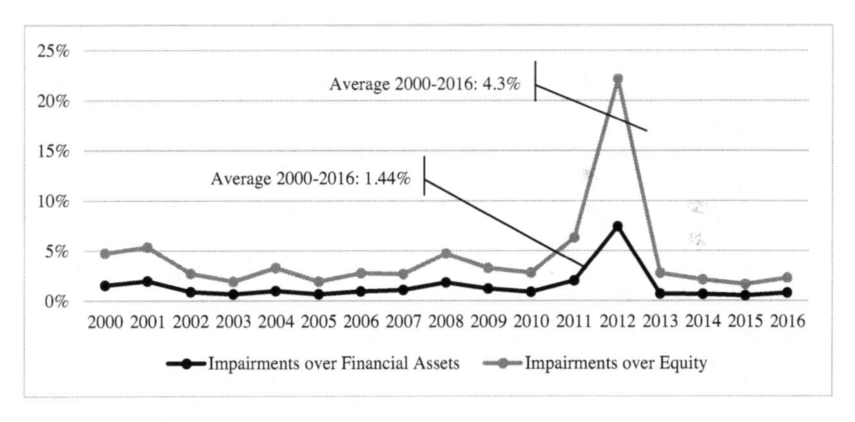

Figure 8.13 Financial impairments as a percentage of previous year financial assets and equity

Source: Data from BdE ("Statistical Bulletin," available at www.bde.es/webbde/en/estadis/infoest/bolest.html).

provisions for loan credit impairments in good times to be used in bad times. Thus, additional charges to net income when credit increases in the expansion economic phase of the cycle are followed by credits to net income in the recession phase of the cycle. This buffer was fed until 2007, proportionally to the credit risk profile assumed by each financial institution. From 2008 onwards, the accumulated balance of the provision

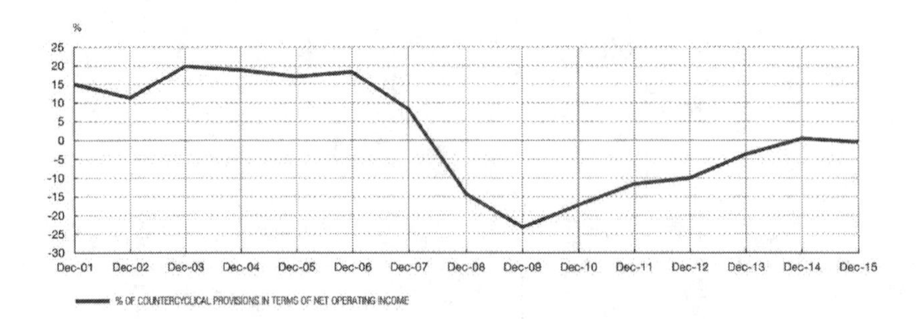

Figure 8.14 Weight of the dynamic provisions in the income statement of the Spanish banking system

Source: Saurina Salas and Trucharte (2017, p. 65).

was released to the income statement, allowing banks to report profits even though the actual operating results were negative. Figure 8.14 shows how the dynamic provision was used by financial entities between 2000 and 2015.

Proponents of the dynamic provision at the Bank of Spain state that it fulfilled its anticyclical purpose between 2007 and 2012, the years of the financial crisis. However, opponents argue that it was merely an artificial device, incompatible with generally accepted accounting principles, allowing banks to smooth earnings, failing to properly signal the impairment of performance measures and, therefore, prevent taking timely measures in the early years of the crisis. Another collateral effect was the generation of fiscal savings that reduce the amount of public aid received by some institutions during this difficult period, for an amount close to 1% of the Spanish GDP (Trucharte and Saurina Salas, 2013).

The Bank of Spain officially declared that the dynamic provision met the requirements of measurement settled in IAS 39, even when it reflected non-incurred losses. At the time, the IASB was discussing the new principle for measuring loan impairments in 2010, and the Spanish regulator supported the adoption of such a countercyclical provision in the new international standard (IFRS 9). After considering its significance and effects, the IASB rejected the proposal of a countercyclical buffer, arguing that this practice would mask the effect of changes in credit loss expectations when a lifetime expected impairment loss model was used (IFRS 9, Basis for Conclusions, BC5.284, in IASB, 2014).

From a technical point of view, charges in the income statement due to the dynamic provision recognize non-incurred losses and, therefore, are not expenses of the year but retained earnings. However, the Bank of Spain's accounting rules required, from 2000 to 2016, the recognition of these additional charges in the income statement and among the liabilities, thus avoiding their distributions as dividends. In addition to the technical discussion, banks claimed that those charges were tax-deductible, and, eventually, they were allowed to be. The literature shows that banks smooth the volatility of their earnings with loan loss provisions (Norden and Stoian, 2013), so the use of dynamic provisions could be interpreted as a kind of explicit legitimation to manipulate earnings via accounting standards.

Overall, the worst effect of the dynamic provisions was the artificial increase in profits (or losses avoidance) during 2008–2010, which allowed the Bank of Spain to speak proudly of the healthy situation of the Spanish financial system because of the prudential measures taken during the previous years, and thus take no action.

Financial Support Measures Implemented to Combat the Crisis

The two most relevant financial support measures taken to combat the crisis were the creation of the FROB in 2009 and the signature of the Memorandum of Understanding in 2012. Other measures taken were temporal or were insufficient.

In 2008, Spain adopted several measures to tackle the crisis in the banking industry to maintain stability and protect deposits. One of the first measures was to increase the amount of deposits guaranteed by the Deposit Guarantee Scheme (Fondo de Garantía de Depósitos, FGD), €20,000 to €100,000, even before EU directive 2009/14/CE required it.[8] Other measures included the creation of the Fund for the Acquisition of Financial Assets (Fondo de Adquisición de Activos Financieros, FAAF), with the goal of endorsing financial entities by acquiring their financial assets issued by financial entities up to a limit of €50 billion.[9] However, the FAAF was meant to be a temporal measure,[10] and as the crisis deepened, in July 2009, the government created the Funds for the Orderly Restructuring of the Banking Sector (Fondo de Reestructuración Ordenada Bancaria, FROB)[11] to manage the restructuring process of financial entities and to contribute to strengthening the capital and resources of these entities.

FROB is an independent legal entity with the authority to operate to achieve its goals (FROB, 2009) and serves, among other things, as a bank resolution authority. The initial contribution was €9 billion provided by the General National Budget (GNB) and Deposit Guarantee Scheme (Fondo de Garantía de Depósitos, FGD), and it added €6 billion more in 2012, but is able to raise capital or borrow in financial markets. As of December 31, 2017, funds contributed to the FROB are €45 billion, most of them from the GNB (FROB, 2017). However, equity is negative due to negative retained earnings.

FROB was not just another institution but a change in the strategy to deal with financial entities in trouble. Liquidating an entity in financial distress (1) drains much value, in particular for clients (deposit owners), whose deposits are not fully guaranteed through the Deposit Guarantee Scheme, and (2) increases the risk of contagion of uncertainty and lack of confidence in the entire financial system. FROB was a strategy to assist and support financial entities and protect clients with the minimum cost for public finances and maintain financial stability. The choice to provide funds to these entities would not address the problem that caused the situation, for instance, a bad corporate governance structure in saving banks.

FROB has played a key role in the restructuration of the Spanish banking system. Its actions are divided into two stages. The former one, called FROB I, extends from its creation until 2011. In this stage, FROB acquired preferred stock of financial entities to support mergers among them for a total of €9.7 billion, mostly in savings banks (BdE, 2017, p. 119). In the next stage, FROB II, since RD 2/2011, acquired ordinary shares and became a shareholder of financial entities (for a maximum period of five years) to assist them in complying with new regulatory capital requirements (later known as Basel III and CRR/CRD IV). Total assistance was €4.8 billion.[12] These amounts are included in the computation of total cost of the Spanish financial system restructuring.

In the middle of the process of restructuring financial entities, the FROB was allowed[13] to require entities receiving assistance to transfer their problematic assets (mostly impaired loans to real estate and foreclosed assets) to the Company for the Management of Assets proceeding from Restructuring of the Banking System (Sociedad de Gestión de Activos Procedentes de la Reestructuración Bancaria, SAREB). The SAREB, created in November 2012 by Law 9/2012 and RD 1559/2012, is a public limited liability company owned by private investors (55%) and FROB (45%) with the goal to acquire, manage, and sell assets transferred from entities receiving financial assistance (mostly real estate assets). Total contributed resources amounted to €4.8 billion (€1.2 billion capital). The entity will extinguish in 2027.

On average, financial entities impaired their assets 53% before transferring the assets to SAREB for a final valuation (based on expert valuers' assessments) of €50 billion (BdE, 2017, p. 183). In exchange, financial entities received SAREB's estate-backed senior bonds. SAREB is supervised by the Bank of Spain and is subject to specific accounting rules.

From an accounting point of view, SAREB has had losses since its creation (in 2017, €565 million). The European Commission demands more action on the administration side to tackle the stream of losses.[14] Equity turned negative in 2014 (€1.7 billion negative; €3.7 billion in 2017), due to the changes in the fair value of derivatives designated as hedging of cash flows.[15] In 2017, equity is even more negative (€3.7 billion) due to the same issue and charges to equity of the impairment of financial assets and real estate assets received as debt repayments.[16]

However, the subtotal of contributed capital plus retained earnings have remained positive (€2 billion in 2017).

According to the FROB (2017), only €37 billion transferred assets remain in the SAREB balance sheet (74%), out of which 68% are financial assets, and 32% real estate.[17] It is unclear what the final outcome of SAREB will be. In five years, SAREB was able to sell 26% (€13 billion) of transferred assets. Given the 2027 deadline, there are only nine years left to dispose of the remaining €37 billion of assets. Only a healthy and strong economy might be able to absorb all those "toxic" assets. As a final note, FROB 2017 financial statements show that the 45.9% investment in SAREB, with a cost of €996 million, has been totally impaired with a charge of €841 million to earnings. Moreover, subordinated debt of SAREB owned by FROB (€656 million) has been impaired for €106 million. The 2017 financial statement notes explain that the estimation has considered the business plan of SAREB and its main hypotheses: (1) sales according to estimation of transactions and curve of real estate market prices of independent experts, considering internal analyses of pace to absorption capacity of the market, and (2) the adaptation and verification of the market reality and experience (FROB, 2017).

In November 2011, the conservative political party won the general elections and had to face a rather critical situation. In June 2012, the government requested financial assistance for restructuring and recapitalization of the Spanish banking sector, and on July 20, they signed the Memorandum of Understanding (MoU).[18] The assistance had a €100 billion limit and the main goal was to "increase the long term flexibility of the entire banking sector to reestablish the access to the [capital] market" (par. 8). Secondary goals included (1) segregating impaired assets (which would end up in the creation of SAREB), (2) reducing risk concentration in the real estate industry, resetting market-based financing, and reducing dependence on the ECB liquidity support measures, and (3) improving the mechanisms to identify risks and manage the crisis. The MoU included a road map with several measures including the classification of banks into four groups according to the results of a stress test, discussed next, and recapitalization plans. Overall, the MoU allowed the Spanish government to retain certain control over managing the crisis.

Spain was no exception to the stress test of the financial system. The results in 2010, 2011, 2012, 2014, and 2016 failed to detect problems for some individual participants, and to signal the severe risk of the entire system in 2010 and 2011.[19] In the 2010 test, five Spanish savings banks did not pass the test of 6% Tier 1 capital in an adverse scenario. All of them are today gone or merged with other entities. The same happened with six other entities with a tier ratio between 6% and 8%. BdE, in a public release, defended the endeavors of these entities and their ability to reinforce their capital and increase revenues in the future. Surprisingly, two savings banks among those identified as entities with "minor problems," Caja Madrid (now merged in Bankia) and Caixa Catalunya (acquired by BBVA), drew most of the financial assistance from the FROB between 2012 and 2014.

Oliver Wyman (2012) carried out the 2012 stress test for the Bank of Spain. The report identified three banks and four savings banks failing in an adverse scenario. Only one of them currently exists (Liberbank) and the others have been intervened and bailed out by the FROB. Moreover, the forecast for capital recovery has also failed. The methodology and results of the test have been criticized in scientific literature (Climent-Serrano, 2016).

The EBA and ECB carried out the 2014 stress test where none of the 15 entities analyzed needed more capital. At this point, the Spanish banking system was in a recovering phase. However, results failed to identify a couple of troubled entities that were bailed out and sold to other banks in 2017: BMN (a new bank resulting from the merger of four savings banks in 2010 and later merged with Bankia) and Banco Popular (a traditional and well-established bank that was resolved by the Single Resolution Mechanism of the EU and sold for €1 to Banco Santander in June 2017). The stress test carried out by European authorities in 2016 was applied only to six Spanish big banks. All of them passed the adverse scenario with an acceptable fully loaded CET1, including Banco Popular.

The evidence shows that the effectiveness of stress tests in identifying problems in the Spanish banking system was limited at best. Data quality collected, models used, and results do not seem to care much for micro-prudential supervisory goals in Spain.

Accounting Regulation Before and After the Crisis

Accounting regulation in Spain has usually been quite passive (reactive) in nature, taking a secondary role to serve other purposes. The crisis is no exception to the rule and, while some changes and additions were added to accounting regulation, they can still be considered reactive. Furthermore, accounting was (ab)used by the government to address the critical situation of the banking industry during the crisis. The next section includes a review of accounting regulation before the crisis,[20] including the particular standard-setting bodies and their relationships, and the following section walks through the changes that took place during the crisis.

Overview of Accounting Regulation in Spain Before the Crisis

The financial reporting regulation in Spain comes from government specialized agencies. The conceptual framework is settled by the Commercial Code, whose last amendment was passed by Parliament in 2007. It contains the general obligation to keep accounting records and prepare financial statements by partnerships, companies, and entrepreneurs, and a list of generally accepted accounting principles, including definitions of the main elements (assets, liabilities, equity, revenues, and expenses).

The main instrument of standardization, dated from 1973, is the General Accounting Plan (Plan General de Contabilidad, PGC) issued by the Spanish government through the Ministry of Economy and developed by the Spanish Institute of Accounting and Auditing (Instituto de Contabilidad y Auditoría de Cuentas, ICAC), which has also the power to make interpretations of the PGC. The PGC was updated by the Spanish government in 1990, after the country became a member of the EU, to adopt the EU accounting directives. Later, in 2007, it was again updated to adopt the IFRS issued by that time (impairment, intangibles, financial instruments, hedging, and business combinations) and to introduce a complete set of financial statements (financial situation, profit and losses, changes in equity, and cash flows), with standardized and detailed formats for each one of them, plus the notes to the financial statements. This evolution reflects the shift of focus from a tax complying system to a system that produces relevant financial information to interested parties (owners, investors, banks, public sector, and other stakeholders).

Notwithstanding the standardization power of PGC, accounting standard setting in Spain is different for financial and nonfinancial entities. While nonfinancial accounting standards were developed following tax needs in the 1970s, financial accounting regulation was issued to answer financial agencies and banking and insurance authorities in need of information for regulatory and supervisory purposes in the 1980s.
Accounting regulation for nonfinancial companies is based on the PGC. Following the EU directives, there is an abridged version for SMEs and a special regime for micro entities, including more simplified formats and disclosures for preparing financial statements. According to EU regulations, since 2005, listed companies must prepare their consolidated financial statements using IFRS as adopted by the EU. Non-listed groups may choose to apply local consolidation standards or IFRSs, although choosing IFRS is irreversible. Table 8.1 contains a summary of the structure of accounting regulation for nonfinancial entities.

Table 8.1 Nonfinancial entities accounting regulation framework

<table>
<tr><td></td><td colspan="3">Nonfinancial</td></tr>
<tr><td></td><td>Parent-only</td><td colspan="2">Consolidated</td></tr>
<tr><td>Listed</td><td rowspan="3">PGC
(with adaptations for SMEs and micro entities)</td><td colspan="2">IFRSs</td></tr>
<tr><td rowspan="2">Non-listed</td><td rowspan="2">OPTIONAL</td><td>IFRS (irreversible)</td></tr>
<tr><td>Local standards (based on the PGC)</td></tr>
</table>

Source: Created by authors.

Table 8.2 Listed and financial entities financial reporting framework

<table>
<tr><th rowspan="2"></th><th colspan="3">Individual Financial Statements</th><th colspan="2" rowspan="2">Consolidated Financial Statements</th></tr>
<tr><th>Banks</th><th>Insurance Companies</th><th>Investment Firms and Services</th></tr>
<tr><td>Listed</td><td rowspan="3">BdE Circulars</td><td rowspan="3">Insurances Accounting Plan</td><td rowspan="3">CNMV Circulars</td><td colspan="2">IFRSs</td></tr>
<tr><td rowspan="2">Non-listed</td><td rowspan="2">OPTION</td><td>IFRSs (irreversible)</td></tr>
<tr><td>Local standards (BdE, DGSFP, CNMV)</td></tr>
</table>

Source: Created by authors.

The accounting regulation framework for financial entities is regulated by three supervisory agencies. Table 8.2 summarizes the Spanish accounting regulation for listed and financial entities:

1. BdE issues accounting circulars containing the requirements and standards for banks and other credit entities (leasing, factoring, etc.), to prepare both public and reserved or regulatory financial statements.
2. The Directorate-General of Insurances and Pension Plans (Dirección General de Seguros y Fondos de Pensiones, DGSFP) elaborates an accounting plan for insurance companies that is promulgated by the government.
3. The Spanish Stock Exchange Commission (Comisión Nacional del Mercado de Valores, CNMV) supervises public investment and financial services entities, and has the power to issue accounting rules and financial statements models for these entities.

These agencies play a double role as accounting standard setters and supervisors. Over time, financial reporting standards have evolved from rules to comply with regulatory and supervisory needs, to rules that make the information from banks, insurance companies, and other financial institutions comparable, avoiding the differences between the application of local standards and IFRS. The purpose of the accounting standards declared by regulators is to closely align with IFRS.

Even though the ICAC, BdE, DGSFP, and CNMV have means to participate in the discussion and approval of accounting standards settled by each other, the goals of the agencies, the working style, and the speed in adapting new standards are so different that the consistency of the final standards may not be guaranteed. These problems became more evident during the crisis. For instance, the ICAC has rejected, in some cases, adopting complex standards (i.e., fair value for agriculture, due to the inexistence of market measurement tradition, or government grants as liabilities or less value of assets, because the companies' leverage levels impact). In others, it has delayed the adoption for years.[21] As the PGC is targeted at all nonfinancial entities (the simplifications for SMEs or micro entities are adopted on a voluntarily basis), a frequent change policy following new IASB developments is costly for companies and practically impossible to assume. A possible solution is to adopt IFRS-rules for SMEs, more stable in time, but broadly consistent with those used in consolidated statements.[22]

Finally, when the main purpose of financial reporting (for financial entities) is collecting information for supervisory and regulatory purposes, both at the individual and system level, accounting standards may not always provide relevant information for making decisions. For instance, capital, leverage, and liquidity information requirements are reported following the prudential supervision methodology as promulgated by the European Banking Authority and, thus, accounting measurement and disclosure rules are designed to help with prudential regulation, rather than to satisfy owners' or lenders' needs. As a consequence, there is conflict in achieving the goals of the Basel pillars 2 (supervision) and 3 (market discipline). This is the case in dynamic provisions, that could be good instruments for maintaining resources within financial entities (solvency), but fails as an accounting treatment when included as an expense (or income in the case of reversion) giving rise to a misstatements of banking profits.

This is the case of the dynamic provision of the BdE. The instrument was designed by the BdE to create a reserve in good years by increasing the amount of the loan loss provision and thus, reducing earnings. It was a prudential measure to strengthen the solvency and stability of the Spanish financial system. However, during the years of the crisis, banks and savings banks reversed this provision and provided a picture of a strong financial system when in reality, the reverse of the provision was lessening the impact of the crisis in their earnings. International regulators have claimed that the dynamic provision, contracyclical provision, is a good prudential instrument but should not be used for accounting reporting as it does not faithfully provide a fair view of the financial situation, income, and cash flows of the entity.

Evolution of Accounting Standards in Spain: 2007–2017

One could describe the Spanish accounting regulation style as reactive and imitative. Reactive (i.e., non-proactive) because the accounting setters react by changing financial reporting rules only when they are obliged by international institutions, agreements, EU directives, or regulations, or as a reaction to adverse circumstances. Maybe the only exception to this feature is the implementation of the dynamic provisions for banks. It is imitative (i.e., non-original) because the main inspiration source of local standards issued are the IFRSs; standards are usually a good Spanish translated summary of the relevant IFRS, with fewer options and, for banks, more detailed disclosure requirements.

The first adoption of IFRS into local standards was made in 2004 with the BdE Circular 4/2004 for banks, and in 2007 for nonfinancial companies, through the new General Accounting Plan. No further reaction was observed in the first years of the financial crisis, from 2007 to 2009. A relevant and original characteristic of the Spanish accounting standards is the treatment of intergroup transactions, measured at fair value, treating any difference with the transaction price according to the economic substance thereof. This includes, in the case of banks, credits and services. For instance, a zero-interest loan (below market interest rate) granted by the parent entity to a subsidiary could be considered as a component of the investment in the subsidiary measured as the present value of interests using market interest rate. Likewise, an above-the-market interest loan could be considered as a distribution of equity by the subsidiary for the difference of rates. On the other hand, intragroup mergers and acquisitions are accounted for at their book values, without recognizing any goodwill or remeasurement of assets, as there are no third parties involved in the transaction. In regard to credit risk, the model adopted by the Circular of 2004 was the incurred loss approach of IAS 39, with impairment computed as the difference between the present value of expected cash flows considering credit events already occurred, and the book value of the debt financial instrument. Nevertheless, the Circular allowed the automatic computation of impairments in proportion to the payment delay above 90 days from the due date. The procedure of dynamic provisions, computing an additional percentage of credits granted, was deemed incompatible with IAS 39, but was maintained until 2016 for individual financial statements of banks as well as for consolidated statements of non-listed banks.

In 2010, consolidation accounting standards were issued for nonfinancial entities, adopting most of the criteria contained in the drafts of the IFRS 10 (issued in 2011). At the same time, the PGC was modified to include the approach adopted by the IFRS 3 revised in 2008.

The banking crisis in Spain had no response in terms of financial reporting and disclosure regulation until 2012. The new conservative government promulgated two Royal Decrees-Laws, then endorsed by the Parliament as formal laws, which contain measures: (1) to restructure the governance of the banking system, (2) to require additional provisions for real estate assets and credits (non-performing loans and foreclosed assets resulting from the property guaranties in a range of 25%–60% of their book values), and (3) to require an additional 7% provision charge for performing loans to cover future losses.

Consistent with the political cost hypothesis, this measure may be considered as a "big-bath theory" tool (Giner and Mora, 2018, pp. 4–5). In short, the government overstated the need to recognize impairment as a means for achieving other political goals, and to gain credibility in the international financial community (and as a result, avoiding the EU rescue mechanisms).

The Royal Decrees-Law weakened the financial position of some banks and virtually all savings banks. The government retained control of the financial system but had to reinforce the FROB, settle SAREB to sell the property assets accumulated by the banks and savings banks, and accept financial assistance from the EU for some €41 billion.

In 2015, the Bank of Spain adopted the FINREP, the reporting system required by the European Banking Authority (EBA), a set of definitions, terminology, preparation criteria, and formats that are a prerequisite for the implementation of the statistical and supervisory requirements of the EU authorities, in order to provide inputs needed for the Single Supervisory Mechanism (SSM).

The Circular 4/2004, on financial statements of banks, was modified in 2016 and 2017 to adopt IFRS 9, in force from 2018 onwards. The main problem was the adoption of the new "expected credit losses" approach of the IFRS 9, and the classification of financial assets in three stages, depending on the evolution of the credit risk since the inception of the credit. The change means a significant additional charge to earnings.

The adoption was made in two steps to distribute additional charges. The first one came with Circular 4/2016, which is an amendment of Circular 4/2004, where banks were asked to develop internal risk models or to use models developed for capital requirement purposes when calculating credit impairments. They were permitted to use old methods based on the length of time from the due date of the payments, but with higher percentages for automatic depletion. The second step was the entire rewording of the Accounting Circular, giving rise to the new Circular 4/2017 in force in 2018, which incorporated IFRS 9 in terms of classification and accounting treatment of financial assets, credit impairment according to the expected credit losses approach, and the new regulation of hedging.

The impact of the change of approach in the recognition of credit impairments is relevant for the Spanish banking system as a whole, but it can be worse for some entities depending on their risk profile. An assessment of this impact has been made by Rocamora et al. (2017), not only for new provisions but in terms of regulatory additional requirements:

> We have estimated what would be the impact of IFRS 9 for the Spanish banking system in the changeover phase and in a subsequent downturn. Although the impact of IFRS 9 seems limited for the system as a whole (a 21% increase in provisions equivalent to 67 bps of erosion of CET1 in the changeover), it is very heterogeneous across individual banks.

In 2018, the bank accounting regulator faces the adoption of IFRS 16, on leases, for non-listed banks and separate financial statements of listed banks, which will be effective in 2019. Although the Spanish banking system has an extensive list of abusing clauses designed to avoid the financial lease classification in own properties (headquarters, offices, etc.), no significant impact is expected in their balance sheets. Because of the uniformity required by the regulator, an early adoption of this standard is not probable, even for listed banks whose financial reporting is not covered by the BdE accounting circulars. The same is true for the insurance industry that is regulated by the DGSFP. The current Insurance Companies Accounting Plan dates back to 2008 and had a main amendment in 2015, when the Spanish regulator and supervisor adopted Solvency II. After the approval of IFRS 17, which implies a major revision of the measurement and reporting standards for insurance companies, the regulator is working on a draft to have a local accounting and financial standard compatible with IFRS by 2021, the initial effective date of IFRS 17.

Conclusions

According to the IMF (2018), Spain is the thirteenth largest economy by GDP in the world, and the fifth in the EU. Interconnected markets and commerce spread the international financial crisis worldwide and Spain could not avoid either. However, the crisis hit at the weakest point in the Spanish economic situation especially in the case of the real estate industry. The rapid growth in previous years had left a huge amount of credit granted to real estate and construction entities and to house-owning families. Most of the credit was granted by savings banks, whose particular governance and operating features made them easy prey for the crisis effects. Even though there were some warnings of the situation, no one did anything to stop it. Thus, we argue that the real problem in the crisis was the lack of action by regulators to control the growth of loan risk concentration in the real estate and construction industry.

The Bank of Spain publicly defended the solvency of the Spanish financial system as banks reported profits using the dynamic provisions mechanism. It was not until 2009 that the government created the FROB to tackle the first problems in a rather paternalistic way. Things got worse after the EU rescued Greece, Ireland, and Portugal. Spain was next in line and, in 2012, when the conservative party won the elections, it made a frantic move to avoid the rescue (a "big bath" move) and signed an MoU to provide financial assistance to the financial system, and thus maintain financial stability and political credibility. The government required all financial entities to recognize extraordinary bad debt provisions that probably exceeded the losses incurred to date. A great proportion of savings banks failed in terms of regulatory capital and equity. The entire financial system was revamped using cold mergers where nearly all savings banks disappeared (usually by converting into banks). Overall, the financial system coming out of the crisis has fewer financial entities and it is unclear that the solvency of the system improved. With all savings banks gone and fewer banks, pictures a banking sector where deposits and loans are far more concentrated than before. Although one may argue that current banks are larger and may compete better in international markets, most of Spanish financial entities compete fiercely for domestic clients, whose needs are best answered by domestic solutions (deposits and loans).

The deemed cost of this financial assistance, from 2008 to 2018, has been estimated by the Bank of Spain to be €76.9 billion, 7% of the current Spanish GDP. The MoU provided access to a €100 billion credit to assist and support financial entities by the FROB and the DGSFP. In summary, savings banks received €71.2 billion and banks (only two) received €5.7 billion. To date,[23] €4.5 billion has already been recovered and another €10.4 billion is expected to be recovered (see Figure 8.15). Overall, the net financial assistance—considering only the recovered amount—is €72.4 billion, roughly 6.7% of the 2007 Spanish GDP (BdE, 2017, p. 246). This amount will very likely be assumed by Spanish taxpayers in the future. FROB assistance comes from the General National Budget, and FGD assistance comes from private banks, as they contribute to the FGD as a self-insurance (and ultimately are charged to bank customers via interests and fees).

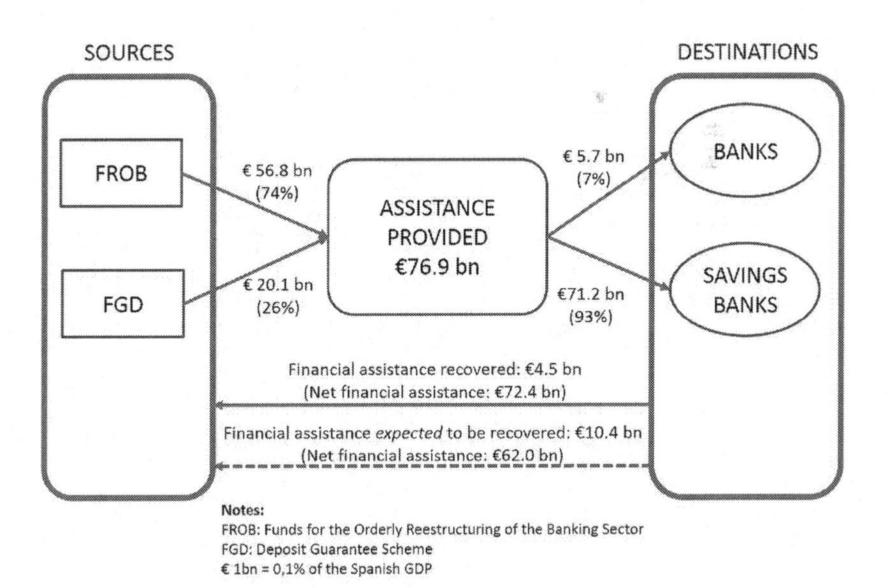

Figure 8.15 Cost of the Spanish banking crisis 2008–2017

Source: Authors' design from data in BdE (2017, p. 246).

Accounting regulation has been passive (i.e., non-existent) and slow during the crisis. Leaving aside the extraordinary provisions required by the government (a one-time hit), in a clear move to maintain international credibility, accounting standards have not changed as a response to the crisis, but rather as a response to international requirements and interventions (or to avoid them). The Spanish standard-setting structure, split into four bodies with different regulatory goals, makes it difficult to provide a coherent accounting regulation framework, despite their intention to closely follow IFRSs. Moreover, it is unable to cope with the speed of new standard issuances of the IASB or with economic events like the crisis requiring intervention. Even though accounting standards have gained merit as a source of relevant information for economic decisions, it is not yet a tool of (proactive) economic and business regulation.

Notes

1. The authors wish to thank Professor Anne Garvey for her helpful comments and insight of the chapter. All remaining errors are our own.
2. To our families, with love.
3. Later we address other measures taken by financial and international institutions.
4. We use the expression "risk premium" as the spread between the Spanish 10-year bond and the German 10-year bond, or "Bund." When the spread is positive, Spanish public debt is perceived as riskier than German public debt, and vice versa.
5. El Economista (July 25, 2012), "Nuevo récord de la prima de riesgo: toca los 650 puntos, con el bono al 7, 6%" retrieved from www.eleconomista.es/mercados-cotizaciones/noticias/4142462/07/12/Nuevo-record-de-la-prima-de-riesgo-sube-a-646-puntos-con-el-bono-al-76-.html, last accessed on June 4, 2018.
6. That are actually small in size and very local in their operations.
7. For further detail on Bankia creation and bailout, see Giner and Mora (2018).
8. Royal Decree 1642/2008.
9. Royal Decree 6/2008 and Royal Decree 7/2008, see BdE (2017, p. 115).
10. It was liquidated in July 2012 with a global profit of €650 million (loc. cit.)
11. Royal Decree 9/2009.
12. This amount is distributed among three savings banks where FROB acquired more than 90% ownership.
13. Law 9/2012 also limited the compensation of directors of financial entities to €500,000 or €300,000, if the entity had received assistance from the FROB.
14. El Pais (April 16, 2018), "La Comisión Europea critica que el 'banco malo' siga en pérdidas desde 2012," retrieved from https://elpais.com/economia/2018/04/16/actualidad/1523904732_388055.html.
15. SAREB Annual Report 2014.
16. According to article 2, RD 4/2016, any impairment of these assets must be charged, net of taxes, to equity, and is reclassified to profit and loss when the entity makes profits (before taxes). These adjustments are not considered equity regarding certain transactions. See SAREB 2017 Annual Report.
17. This amount is for accounting purposes, before applying estimated impairment in SAREB financial statements (FROB, 2017).

18. Ministry of Economy, retrieved from: www.mineco.gob.es/stfls/mineco/prensa/ficheros/noticias/2012/120720_MOU_espanyol_2_rubrica_MECC_VVV.pdf.
19. In most cases, there were important problems in the quality of data collected and the presentation of results by the Bank of Spain. In most cases of entities with bad results, the regulator issued a message of calm and confidence in the reaction capacity of banks or savings banks concerned.
20. See Cañibano and Ucieda (2005) for an earlier picture of financial reporting regulation in Spain.
21. Several examples of this are (1) the ICAC rejected adoption of some parts of the standard for financial instruments, alleging the unduly cost or effort of implementation; (2) the accounting treatment for goodwill according to IFRS 3 was abandoned in 2016, not only because of the mandatory requirement to amortize it according the EU Accounting Directive of 2013, but because of the failure of the impairment-only model, which was costly and difficult to apply for most non-listed groups; and (3) the new treatment for lease transactions in IFRS 16, which is in process of adoption by financial entities, will be difficult to assume because the mentality of companies and, ultimately, it could damage the financial sector.
22. See Cañibano and Herranz (2018) for a discussion of alternatives.
23. The online version of BdE (2017), includes data as of July 2017, after FROB annual accounts have been approved. Printed version includes data as of 2015.

References

Banco de España, BdE (2017). *Report on the financial and banking crisis in Spain, 2008–2014*. May. Retrieved from [www.bde.es/f/webbde/Secciones/Publicaciones/OtrasPublicaciones/Fich/InformeCrisis_Completo_web_en.pdf].

Cañibano, L. and Herranz, F. (2018). La contabilidad en la encrucijada. *Consejeros: la revista del buen gobierno y la responsabilidad corporativa* 134(January): 59–62.

Cañibano, L. and Ucieda, J. L. (2005). Accounting and financial reporting in Spain, ed. Mora, A. and Cañibano, L. *Readings on European Accounting*, Madrid: AECA.

Climent-Serrano, S. (2016). Stress test based on Oliver Wyman in Bank of Spain: An evaluation. *Banks and Bank Systems* 11(3): 66–74. Retrieved from [http://dx.doi.org/10.21511/bbs.11(3).2016.07].

Comín, F. (2007). Spanish savings banks and the competitive cooperation model (1928–2002). *Revista de Historia Económica/Journal of Iberian and Latin American Economic History* 25(2), 201–232. doi:10.1017/S0212610900000011.

Estrada, A., Jimeno, J. F. and Malo de Molina. J. L. (2009). The Spanish economy in EMU: The first ten years. *Documentos Ocasionales N° 0901, Banco de España*. Retrieved from [www.bde.es/f/webbde/SES/Secciones/Publicaciones/PublicacionesSeriadas/DocumentosOcasionales/09/Fic/do0901e.pdf].

FROB (2009). *2009 Annual report*. Retrieved from [www.frob.es/en/Lists/Contenidos/Attachments/304/Cuentas2009protIngles.pdf].

FROB (2017). *2017 Annual report*. Retrieved from [www.frob.es/en/Lists/Contenidos/Attachments/553/FROBCCAA2017ENG.pdf].

Giner, B. and Mora, A. (2018). *Political interference in financial reporting in financial industry: Evidence from Spain*. March. Retrieved from [https://papers.ssrn.com/sol3/papers.cfm?abstract_id=3138620].

International Monetary Fund, IMF (2012). Spain: The reform of Spanish savings banks technical notes. *IMF Country Report No. 12/141*, Washington, DC, June. Retrieved from [www.imf.org/external/pubs/ft/scr/2012/cr12141.pdf].

International Monetary Fund, IMF (2018). World economic outlook database. *International Monetary Fund*, 7 June. Retrieved from: [www.imf.org/external/pubs/ft/weo/2018/01/weodata/index.aspx].

Martín-Aceña, P. (2013). The savings-banks crisis in Spain. When and how? *The World Savings Banks Institute*, March. Retrieved from [www.wsbi-esbg.org/press/Documents/Martin-AcenaWeb.pdf].

Norden, L. and Stoian, A. (2013). Bank earnings management through loan loss provisions: A double-edged sword. De Neederlanden Bank (DNB) *Working Paper 404*, December. Retrieved from [www.dnb.nl/binaries/working Paper 404_tcm46-301517.pdf].

Rocamora, M., Plata Garcia, C. T., Villar Burke, J. and Rubio González, A. (2017). *IFRS 9: Pro-cyclicality of provisions*. Spanish Banks as an Illustration (October 8). Retrieved from SSRN: [https://ssrn.com/abstract=3120445].

Saurina Salas, J. (2009). Dynamic Provisioning. The Experience of Spain. The World Bank *Note number 7*, July. Retrieved from [http://siteresources.worldbank.org/EXTFINANCIALSECTOR/Resources/282884-1303327122200/Note7.pdf].

Saurina Salas, J. and Trucharte Artigas, C. (2017). Presentation of the book '*The countercyclical provisions of the Banco de España, 2000–2016*'. *Estabilidad Financiera* 33(May): 61–68. Retrieved from [www.bde.es/f/webbde/GAP/Secciones/Publicaciones/InformesBoletinesRevistas/RevistaEstabilidadFinanciera/17/NOV17/Articulo-Saurina-Trucharte.pdf].

Trucharte Artigas, C. and Saurina Salas, J. (2013). Spanish dynamic provisions: Main numerical features. *Estabilidad Financiera* 25(November): 11–47. Retrieved from [www.bde.es/f/webbde/GAP/Secciones/Publicaciones/InformesBoletinesRevistas/RevistaEstabilidadFinanciera/13/Noviembre/Fic/ref2013251.pdf].

Wyman, O. (2012). *Asset quality review and bottom-up stress test exercise, Bank of Spain*. Retrieved from [www.bde.es/f/webbde/SSICOM/20120928/informe_ow280912e.pdf. 51].

Zunzunegui, F. (2014). Mis-selling of preferred shares to Spanish retail clients. *Journal of International Law Banking and Regulation* 3, 174–186. Retrieved from [www.rdmf.es/wp-content/uploads/2014/01/Copia-Articulo-en-JIBLR.pdf].

9 The Impact of the Economic Crisis on the Financial System and Accounting in Brazil

Marcelo Botelho C. Moraes

Introduction

In this first section, we will focus on three major financial markets in Brazil: the banking industry, which is the largest intermediation market and highly concentrated in only six financial institutions; the equity market on the B3 (São Paulo) stock exchange; and the bond markets for corporate and government bonds, also on the B3 after the merger of BM&FBovespa (stock exchange, future, and commodities markets) and Cetip (over the counter [OTC] markets) in 2017. Following this description of Brazilian markets, we will discuss the accounting regulations and financial instruments since the full adoption of International Financial Reporting Standards (IFRS) in 2010.

To understand the Brazilian market, we must know its institutional structure. Brazil is one of the largest countries in the world; in 2016 Brazil had a population over 206 million people and a gross domestic product (GDP) of USD 1,796.2 billion (OECD, 2018) with a projection of GDP USD 2,138.9 billion for 2018 (IMF, 2018), which makes it the ninth largest economy in the world and the largest in Latin America. Despite its great potential, the Brazilian market is not an easy place to do business, especially because of bureaucracy; it ranks in the 125th position on the World Bank's Doing Business Index (World Bank, 2018), as we can see in Figure 9.1.

There are two systems in the Brazilian financial system: normative and intermediate. Normative institutions regulate financial institutions and are responsible for controlling the financial market to avoid abuses and implementing federal policies. The National Monetary Council (CMN, Conselho Montetário Nacional) mainly controls this system for currency, credit (and debt), equity, and foreign exchange, and the Central Bank of Brazil (BCB, Banco Central do Brasil) and the Securities and Exchange Commission (CVM, Comissão de Valores Mobiliários) serve a supervisory function. In other words, CMN controls the financial markets examined in this chapter.

CMN's main function is to establish the defining guidelines for government monetary policy regarding Brazilian bonds and interest rates,

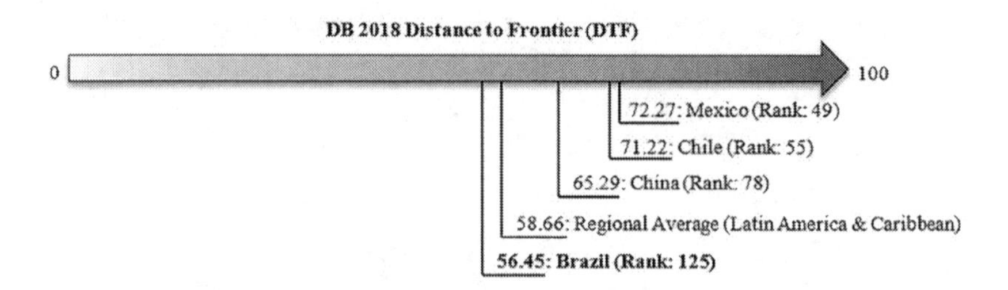

Figure 9.1 Brazilian position in the World Bank's Doing Business Index

Source: World Bank (2018).

Note: The distance to frontier (DTF) measure shows the distance of each economy to the "frontier," which represents the best performance observed on each of the indicators across all economies in the Doing Business Index since 2005. An economy's distance to frontier is reflected on a scale from 0 to 100, where 0 represents the lowest performance and 100 represents the frontier. The ease of doing business ranking ranges from 1 to 190.

monetary policies, credit supply, inflation targets, and the exchange rate of the real, Brazil's currency (BRL). CMN is the highest entity in the Brazilian financial system, and it is only normative as it works as an economic policy council. The actual council is composed of the minister of finance (the president of CMN), the minister of planning, and the president of the Central Bank of Brazil.

Since we have introduced the main regulation for the Brazilian National Financial System (SFN, Sistema Financeiro Nacional), let us learn more about each of these markets (the banking industry, equity markets, and bond markets).

The State of the Banking Industry

The Central Bank of Brazil (BCB) is the main executive of the banking industry and acts as a Federal Reserve Bank. BCB's function is to apply CMN policies. Through the BCB, the Brazilian federal government controls the financial system. The independence of BCB has been discussed, but the choice of the president of BCB remains the prerogative of the President of the Republic.

The banking market provides credit through intermediation, and its volume was 47.1% of GDP in 2017 (BCB, 2017); this volume was over 50% in 2015 and declined because of the Brazilian economic crisis. Total assets were over USD 2,114 billion in 2017 (BCB, 2018). BCB works with compulsory deposits and rediscount operations for banks and provides operations permits and supervision. BCB also executes monetary policy, including selling Brazilian federal bonds and defining the interest rate, controlling payment and compensation, issuing Brazilian currency, and concentrating foreign exchange intermediation. The intermediation system, also known as operators, are banking institutions (banks, savings banks, and credit unions), and nonbanking institutions (investment banks, development banks, credit societies, and leasing companies, among others) which only trade securities and foreign currencies.

Here, we can see the segments of Brazilian banks and savings banks according to BCB (2018) (we chose not to detail other types of financial institutions such as credit unions and other nonbanking institutions because they are beyond the scope of this chapter):

- Multiple banks: multiple banks are private/public or governmental financial institutions that carry out assets, liabilities, and accessory operations for the various types of financial institutions through the following portfolios: commercial, investment and/or development, real estate credit, leasing and credit, financing, and investment. These transactions are subject to the same legal and regulatory rules applicable to the singular institutions corresponding to their portfolios. The multiple bank must have at least two portfolios and one must be commercial or investment.
- Commercial banks: commercial banks are private/public or governmental financial institutions with the main objective of providing the resources to finance general industries with bank deposits.
- Savings bank: Caixa Econômica Federal (CEF, or Federal Savings Bank) is the major savings bank in Brazil and is a government bank controlled by the Ministry of Finance. Like commercial banks, Caixa has a big role in granting loans and financing social programs, health, education, work, urban transport, and sports. Savings banks can provide consumer credit, durable goods to consumers, credit with guarantees, the monopoly of a loan under pledge, and lottery. Caixa also controls funds from the FGTS (Fundo de Garantia por Tempo de Serviço), a compulsory discount on workers' payroll to save that is used to finance housing loans on federal credit lines.
- Foreign exchange banks: exchange banks are financial institutions authorized to perform foreign exchange operations and credit operations linked to foreign exchange.
- National Bank for Economic and Social Development (BNDES): BNDES (Banco Nacional de Desenvolvimento Econômico e Social) is one of the largest development banks in the world and is controlled by the federal government for long-term financing and investment in all segments of the Brazilian economy through financial investment and underwriting securities.
- Development banks: development banks are controlled by state governments, and their primary objective is to provide funds to state economic and social development programs. Liabilities include long-term deposits, external loans, issuance or endorsement of mortgage bonds, and issuance of bonds.

- Investment banks: investment banks are financial institutions that specialize in equity funds, funding capital expenditures and money.

Multiple banks were responsible for 82% of the assets and 77% of the income in the banking industry with an average return on equity (ROE) of 17% in 2017. Table 9.1 summarizes some information about the six largest institutions in this industry in Brazil.

Brazil has highly concentrated banking as compared to the major economies in the world. As we can see in Table 9.2, asset concentration in five major banks is approximately 82% in Brazilian banks (excluding BNDES). Table 9.2 shows the data for the top 10 economies.

Table 9.1 Industry banks in Brazil in 2017

Banks	*Capital*	*Assets*	*Liabilities*	*Equity*	*Income*	*ROE (%)*
Itaú	Public	418,330,784	375,858,653	42,472,131	6,382,552	15.0
Banco do Brasil	Mixed*	413,740,442	387,020,660	26,719,782	3,375,407	12.6
CEF	Government	381,411,017	371,007,724	10,403,293	3,767,751	36.2
Bradesco	Public	318,948,698	285,274,716	33,673,982	4,443,186	13.2
BNDES	Government	260,463,218	241,464,516	18,998,702	1,869,572	9.8
Santander Brasil	Public**	203,991,006	185,341,004	18,650,002	2,709,053	14.5

Source: Data from BCB (2018), in thousands of USD.

Note: *Public with federal government control.
** Santander Spain control.

Table 9.2 Concentration ration of the five largest banks by total assets (%)

Countries	*2006*	*2008*	*2010*	*2012*	*2014*	*2016*
United States	35	38	44	45	44	43
China	55	51	49	45	41	37
Japan	45	46	46	47	51	51
Germany	29	27	40	38	37	35
United Kingdom	50	45	53	54	51	48
France	–	77	81	81	81	82
India	40	37	35	35	35	36
Italy	26	31	40	40	41	43
Brazil	**60**	**73**	**76**	**77**	**78**	**82**
Canada	82	81	81	83	81	81

Source: Adapted from BCB (2017).

It should be noted that the supply of bank credit is highly dependent on the governmental banks, especially Banco do Brasil and Caixa. In 2017, together these banks represented 50.8% of the total credit supply for personal credit, and together with BNDES (development bank), these three banks represented 52.4% of the credit supply to firms.

BCB calculated the Herfindahl-Hirschman Normalized Index[1] (HHI) and found that the concentration ratio for the top five banks in Brazil in 2017 was HHI 0.1404 for total assets, 0.1571 for total deposits, and 0.1618 for credit operations. The HH index is a value between 0 and 1; BCB considers a value between 0.1000 and 0.1800 a moderate concentration (BCB, 2017).

Equity Markets Development

B3 (the São Paulo Stock Exchange, formerly BM&FBovespa) was created in 1890 and is the tenth largest stock exchange in the world, with a market capitalization over USD 1 trillion at the end of 2017. This was distributed between 344 public firms, where only 305 firms had at least one trade in 2017 (B3, 2018). This number of public companies has decayed in the last three years because of the Brazilian economic crisis, returning the equity market capitalization to the level of 2005.

The main index of the B3 is the Ibovespa index, which measures the average yield of the main shares traded on the stock exchange; this is usually approximately 60 different shares. To be part of the Ibovespa index, the asset must meet the following criteria cumulatively:

1. Negotiability: highly negotiated shares measured by negotiation level, which together represent 85% of the total sum of these indicators.
2. Attendance: having 95% presence on the trading floor during the period of validity of the previous three portfolios.
3. Financial volume: representation equal to or greater than 0.1% in the spot market for the period of validity of the previous three portfolios.

The actual composition of the Ibovespa index is 67 shares from 64 different companies because three of companies have more than one type of share in the index (Bradesco, Eletrobras, and Petrobras). The five major components of the Ibovespa index correspond to 46.2% of the index, as we can see in Table 9.3. The B3 stock exchange accepts two types of shares: ON (ordinary, with voting rights) and PN (preferred, with preference on dividend receipt and no voting rights [non-voting shares]).

Table 9.3 Ibovespa composition

Company	*Industry*	*Type*	*%*
Vale	Mining	ON	12.9
Itaú	Financial	PN	10.2
Bradesco	Financial	PN	7.2
Ambev (ABInbev)	Beverage	ON	6.7
Petrobras	Oil	PN	5.6
		ON	3.6

Source: Data from B3 (2018).

Notes: ON—ordinary with voting rights; PN—preferred with preference in dividends receipt.

Another characteristic of the Brazilian stock market is the existence of premium listings for companies with corporate governance practices. B3 was the first stock exchange to allow listed companies to voluntarily commit themselves to standards of corporate governance practices (Carvalho & Pennacchi, 2012). Level 1 of this standard has requirements such as improvement in accounting disclosure, disclosure of quarterly information, obligation to report consolidated numbers, and special audit review; Level 2 of this standard has some additional requirements, for example, changing the entire board of directors within a maximum of two years, providing tag-along rights to noncontrolling shareholders, and using market arbitration for conflict resolution. The highest level is called Novo Mercado (New Market) and includes all the other requirements plus the exclusive issue of voting rights shares (ON).

Despite the benefits of premium listing in reducing the cost of capital (Carvalho & Pennacchi, 2012), approximately only half of the firms on the B3 (189) are listed in one of the levels: 27 in Level 1, 21 in Level 2, and 141 in Novo Mercado (B3, 2018); most firms additionally have highly concentrated ownership and control (García-Teruel, Martínez-Solano & Sánchez-Ballesta, 2009). The Brazilian equity market depends on foreign capital, as we can see in Table 9.4. Therefore, the Ibovespa index is highly affected by international investment flows.

As shown in Figure 9.2, foreign investors increased their share of the equity market negotiation from 32.8% in 2005 to 52.28% in 2017. Additionally, in 2017, individuals owned only 14% of Brazil's equity, institutional investors held approximately 29%, and financial institutions held 4%. We can see that investment in the equity market does not come from the Brazilian population. Historically, Brazil has a lower savings ratio, which is associated with a banking culture of investment that can explain part of this foreign dependence. The gross savings ratio as a percentage of GDP is approximately 14%, while the 2016 world average

Table 9.4 Participation by investor type

Types of Investors	*Buy*		*Sell*		*Total*
	BRL	*Part. (%)*	*BRL*	*Part. (%)*	*Part. (%)*
Individuals	30,046,276	7.07%	28,609,081	6.73%	13.80%
Institutional	62,587,195	14.73%	62,157,983	14.63%	29.36%
Foreign	103,893,313	24.45%	109,741,831	25.83%	50.28%
Public/private firms	7,102,705	1.67%	3,525,960	0.83%	2.50%
Financial institutions	8,824,687	2.08%	8,419,142	1.98%	4.06%
Others	0	0.00%	180	0.00%	0.00%
Total in thousands of BRL (buy + sell): 428,908,353					**100%**

Source: Data from B3 (2018).

Note: All values in BRL thousand.

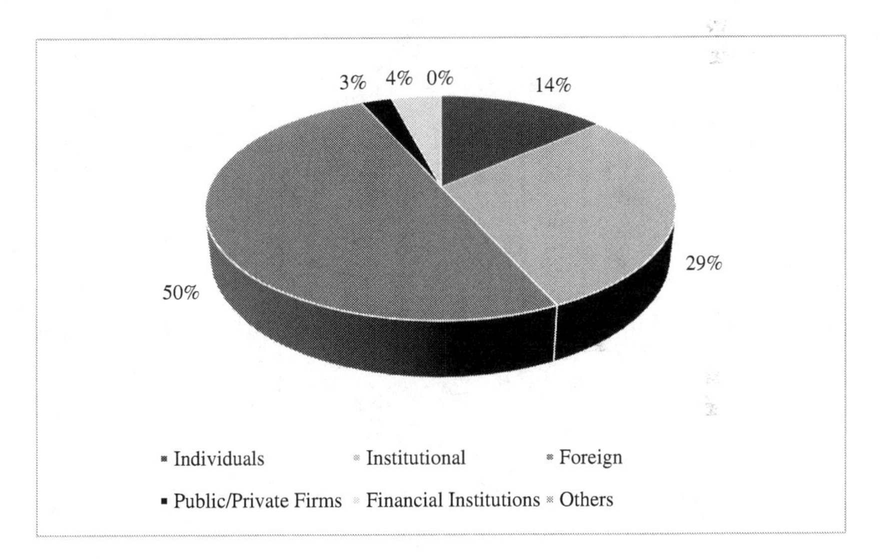

Figure 9.2 Participation by investor type
Source: Data from B3 (2018).

was 24.5% and the average for Latin America and the Caribbean was approximately 17.5% (World Bank, 2018).

The Bond Market's Development

We segregate the Brazilian bond market in two markets for this chapter: government bonds and corporate bonds. However, there are other markets not covered here.

Government Bonds

The Brazilian government bond market was BRL 48.5 billion (about USD 14.7 billion) in 2017 according to National Treasury data (Tesouro Nacional, 2018). This market's objective is to efficiently manage federal public debt to meet federal government borrowing requirements at the lowest possible long-term financing cost, while maintaining prudent risk levels and the smooth operation of the Brazilian government bond market (Tesouro Nacional, 2018). There are six types of federal bonds, with the following main characteristics (Tesouro Nacional, 2018):

- Letra do Tesouro Nacional (LTN): yields are defined at purchase with a fixed rate and payment at maturity.
- Letra Financeira do Tesouro (LFT): floating rate bond whose daily yields are linked to the economy's basic interest rate (average rate of repo operations with public bonds registered in the SELIC system, or simply called the SELIC rate) and payment at maturity.
- Nota do Tesouro Nacional—B Series (NTN-B): yields are linked to variations in the Consumer Price Index (IPCA), the interest is defined at purchase, and a payment is made every six months (interest) and at maturity (principal).
- Nota do Tesouro Nacional—B Series Principal (NTN-B Principal): yields are linked to variations in the Consumer Price Index (IPCA), the interest is defined at purchase, and payment is made only at maturity (principal + interest).
- Nota do Tesouro Nacional—C Series (NTN-C): yields are linked to variations in the General Market Price Index (IGPM), the interest is defined at purchase, and payment is made every six months (interest) and at maturity (principal); this type is no longer issued.
- Nota do Tesouro Nacional—F Series (NTN-F): bond with fixed-rate yields, the interest is defined at purchase, and payment is made every six months (interest) and at maturity (principal).

Figure 9.3 shows the composition of the government bonds in January of 2018. We can see the prevalence of Tesouro IPCA+ in the market for government bonds; it stands at 49% of the market. Figure 9.4 shows the evolution of Brazilian public debt composition in the last 10 years.

Corporate Bonds

An option for firms wishing to raise funds is the issuance of corporate bonds, such as debentures or commercial papers, according to the company's own capital structure policy (debt vs. equity funding) or as an alternative to bank credit with lower cost and longer maturities. Commercial papers and debentures also have their trade and custody on the B3.

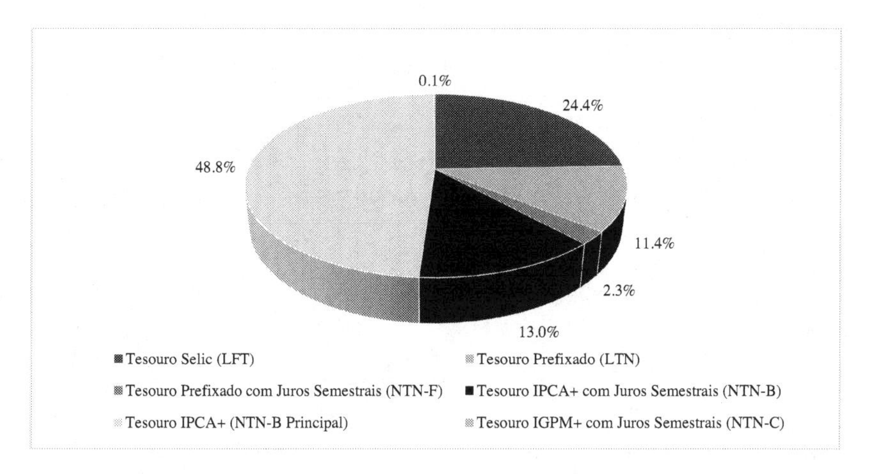

Figure 9.3 Brazilian government bond market
Source: Data from Tesouro Nacional (2018).

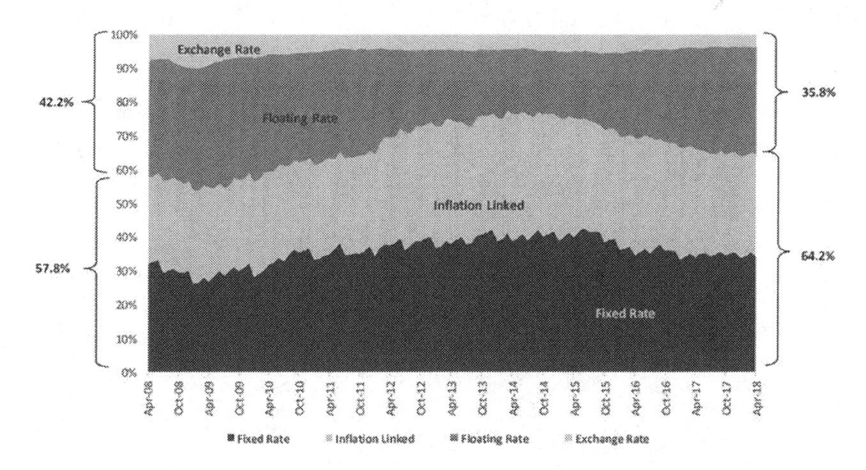

Figure 9.4 Brazilian government bond composition evolution, 2010–2018
Source: Tesouro Nacional (2018).

Debentures are fixed-income debt bonds with medium to long-term maturity and a guarantee of credit issued by public or private firms. The issuance itself can also be public, but only if the issuer is a public company and in local or foreign markets (BM&FBovespa, 2015). In 2017, more than BRL 566 million was issued in public trade debentures (B3, 2018). There are different types and conditions of issuing debentures, and this kind of detail exceeds this chapter's scope.

Commercial paper is a short-term bond with a fixed interest rate and a unique maturity under 360 days; it is usually used to fund working capital with public or private trade. This bond has a credit risk from the issuer and no guarantee of liquidity in the secondary market.

Accounting Regimes

In Brazil, as in many other countries, there are accounting standards that define which accounting reports are required and how they should be presented. In Brazil, this set of mandatory reports is defined by corporate law 6,404/1976 and amended by laws 11,638/2007 and 11,941/2009 for corporations (S.A.—*Sociedade Anônima*), which serves as guidance for other types of companies.

Until 2007, Brazil's generally accepted accounting principles (BR GAAP) were totally based on code law (or civil law) tradition, in this case corporate law 6,404/1976. However, in 2007, law 11,638 made major changes to BR GAAP to more closely adhere to international financial reporting standards (IFRS) by the International Accounting Standards Board (IASB) and the associated local Comitê de Pronunciamentos Contábeis (CPC, the Brazilian Accounting Pronouncements Committee). CPC is the Brazilian standard-setting body responsible for the development and issuance of accounting standards, and the provider of interpretations and guidance for Brazilian companies. Its standards are enforced by CVM for public entities and by the Conselho Federal de Contabilidade (CFC, Accounting Professional Federal Council) for nonpublic entities, with the support of regulatory agencies for specific industries, such as BCB for the banking industry (IFRS Foundation, 2017).

The Brazilian convergence plan is unique; it began in 2008 and reached full adoption in 2010 with the local CPC version of IFRS. In most cases, CPC standards are only translations with a few variations or additions to adapt the IFRS to Brazilian corporate law. IFRS has been mandatory for consolidated and unconsolidated (separate company) financial statements of companies whose debt or equity securities are traded in a public market since the financial year ending December 31, 2010 (IFRS Foundation, 2017).

Nonpublicly traded companies are obliged to prepare their financial statements in accordance with BR GAAP but are permitted to adopt IFRS standards for their consolidated financial statements (in Brazil both consolidated and separate statements are disclosed). Small and medium-sized firms are required to apply the Brazilian equivalent of the IFRS for SMEs Standard (small and medium-sized entities) and they may opt to apply full BR GAAP/IFRS standards. Large entities are defined by corporate law (11,638/07) as a company or group of companies under common control whose total assets, in the previous year, amounted to over BRL 240 million or whose total annual gross revenues exceed BRL 300 million.

There are some minor differences between BR GAPP and IFRS standards. These differences are caused by Brazilian corporate law.

Differences include the disallowance of the revaluation of assets under corporate law, the presentation of the income statement separately from comprehensive income (IFRS allows a choice between one statement and two statements), the effective date of businesses combinations must be revalued only back to January 1, 2009 when IFRS allows companies to go back further, and the requirement of a Value Added Statement (DVA, Demonstração do Valor Adicionado) by CPC and corporate law but not IFRS, among other differences.

In the banking industry, BCB has required the presentation of consolidated financial statements prepared in accordance with IFRS as supplemental information since 2010 (IFRS Foundation, 2017). However, there are statutory accounts required to follow accounting practices adopted by the Central Bank of Brazil called COSIF (Plano Contábil das Instituições do Sistema Financeiro Nacional, or Accounting Plan for Financial Institutions). COSIF standards do not adopt full IFRS standards, but there is a convergence process that has occurred since 2007 and most of the standards are currently classified as partially divergent (BCB, 2018). Banks listed on the B3 must present both IFRS and COSIF financial statements for B3 and BCB respectively.

Market-Based Capital Adequacy Requirements

Law 4,595/1964 is the main regulation and supervision for banks and other financial institutions in Brazil. This law sets out the legal framework for the financial system and establishes the National Monetary Council (CMN) as the authority responsible for money and credit policy and the Central Bank of Brazil (BCB) as the authority responsible for the functioning and supervising of financial institutions, issuing currency, controlling banks and other financial institutions, regulating capital requirements, producing accounting procedures, and supervising managers' liabilities (Bonamin et al., 2017). Brazil follows the recommendations of the Basel Committee on Banking Supervision[2] (BCBS) including Basel III and received the highest grade from the Basel Committee in 2017 (BIS, 2017). The CMN and BCB are continuously working on capital adequacy requirements to maintain alignment with international standards and to ensure an efficient ongoing process of adaptation by financial institutions; this includes for instance Statement 20615/2015 issued by BCB with the schedule for Basel III compliance for Brazilian financial institutions (Bonamin et al., 2017). CMN and BCB are both responsible for implementing the Basel LCR standards (liquidity coverage ratio, LCR) in Brazilian regulations. The LCR minimum is being phased in from 2015 to 2019, starting at 60% as of October 1, 2015 and increasing by 10 percentage points annually to reach 100% on January 1, 2019 (BIS, 2017). The requirements apply to all multiple banks, commercial banks, investment banks, foreign exchange banks, and savings banks that (1) have total assets of more

Table 9.5 Summary of assessment grades

Key Component of the Basel LCR Framework	*Grade*
Overall grade	C
• Definition of high-quality liquid assets (numerator)	C
• Definition of net outflows (denominator)	C
• Definition of net inflows (denominator)	C
• LCR disclosure requirements	C

Source: BIS (2017).

Note: Compliance assessment scale (see also Section 1.3): C (compliant), LC (largely compliant), MNC (materially non-compliant), and NC (non-compliant).

than BRL 100 billion; or (2) are part of a prudential conglomerate with total assets of more than BRL 100 billion. Currently, eight banks must meet the LCR requirements, six of which are internationally active (BIS, 2017). The Basel Committee on Banking Supervision judged the Brazilian LCR requirements to be compliant with the Basel standard (Table 9.5). We can see that Basel LCR are compliant in all dimensions.

The regulations set out different bases of capital for minimum capital requirements:

- Reference capital (patrimônio de referência, PR).
- Main capital (capital principal).
- Minimum required net worth (patrimônio líquido exigido, PLE).

PR is the minimum capital that financial institutions must have to be authorized to operate in Brazil, main capital comprises the bank's equity and accrued profits, and PLE measures the capital of the financial institution, adjusted based on the risk-weighted assets and its off-balance exposure (Bonamin et al., 2017).

The BCB monitors the capital adequacy of banks and other financial institutions daily and can impose administrative sanctions on banks which do not comply with the regulations (Bonamin et al., 2017). Brazilian banks follow BCBS rules, and only one financial institution (Caixa Econômica Federal, or Federal Savings Bank) must manage a higher capital requirement to fit Basel III in 2019, when it will reach 100% of the LCR minimum.

Mark-to-Market Accounting

Brazilian accounting standards (CPC 46, Mensuração do Valor Justo), following IFRS 13—Fair Value Measurement, use the concept of mark-to-market accounting for assets and liabilities as a way to estimate the "the price at which an orderly transaction to sell the asset or to transfer the liability would take place between market participants at the measurement date under current market conditions" (IASB, 2011).

This IFRS standard considers the principal market for the asset/liability or, in its absence, the most advantageous market with participants seeking their own economic best interests (IASB, 2011). To apply the fair value measurement of an asset, the entity should consider the following characteristics, for example:

- The condition and location of the asset.
- Restrictions, if any, on the sale or use of the asset.

Financial (e.g., financial instruments) or nonfinancial assets and liabilities can be measured using fair value. This process must consider three components: transaction, price, and market participants.

The fair value measurement requires a valuation to estimate the transaction price for the asset or liability among market participants under current market conditions. Three valuation techniques are widely used: (a) market approach; (b) cost approach; and (c) income approach. To apply the market approach, we use price and other relevant information from market transactions involving assets, liabilities, or a group of assets and liabilities (e.g., business), with similar or comparable characteristics. In the cost approach, the value is based on what would be required to replace the asset's service capacity, usually the current replacement cost. The income approach converts future amounts such as cash flows or income and expenses to a single current (discounted) amount, reflecting current market expectations about those future amounts.

The fair value measurement standard also requires disclosure according to fair value hierarchy on three different levels (IASB, 2011):

- Level 1: prices in active markets (unadjusted) for the same assets or liabilities as the entity may have access to at the measurement date, usually financial assets and liabilities.
- Level 2: observable information for the assets/liabilities, directly or indirectly, other than quoted prices included in Level 1, such as prices for similar assets or liabilities or in non-active markets.
- Level 3: based on unobservable data (on assets or liabilities) to measure fair value, for situations in which there is no market activity (or little activity) for the asset or liability on the measurement date.

Mark-to-market accounting is applied through fair value measurement of Level 1 information. We use the fair value from active markets for subsequent recognition of the asset/liability and the gain or loss of the difference is on the income statement for the period.

For financial institutions, COSIF also adopts mark-to-market accounting for financial instruments in a similar way to IFRS 9 recognition/ derecognition and measurement, beside the fact that there is no specific mention of fair value hierarchy in COSIF standards. The fair value concept of COSIF is comparable to IFRS 13 and its application follows the market value, similar to IFRS 9 Level 1.

The best case of Level 1 information is securities traded on the stock exchange, such as stocks, debentures, and derivatives traded on the financial markets as future contracts. All these securities are financial instruments, as we will see in next section.

Financial Instruments

Brazil has an extensive financial market for financial instruments, especially derivatives. The traditional trade derivatives, such as stock options and future contracts, are traded on the B3 futures market for commodities (crystal sugar, anhydrous fuel ethanol, hydrous ethanol, arabica coffee, corn, gold, live cattle, oil, and soybeans), exchange rates futures and options (the US dollar and currencies from another 12 countries), and equities futures and indexes (inflation, Ibovespa futures). The B3 OTC market also trades derivatives: flexible options (based on rules and nonstandard features), forward contracts and swap contracts, and financial securities in agribusiness and bank certificates of deposit.

Financial instrument accounting regulations in Brazil follow IFRS 9—Financial Instruments (local BR GAAP CPC 48, Instrumentos Financeiros) which has been mandatory since January 1, 2018. IFRS 9 presents the standards for financial instrument recognition (and derecognition), classification, measurement, and hedge accounting. For financial institutions, COSIF accounting standards have a similar treatment to financial instruments.

The Effects of Economic Crisis in Brazil

The Brazilian market has been facing an economic crisis since 2014, but the origins of this crisis come from the 2008 international financial crisis, which began with the subprime lending crisis in the US. In this section, we will study the economic crisis in Brazil, its impact on banks and equity markets, and the changes in the institutional environment.

The Economic Crisis

The Brazilian economy experienced expansive growth in the early 2000s, propelled by international commodities prices (e.g., food and minerals). However, with the beginning of global financial crisis in 2008, Brazil's GDP had its first negative growth in 2009 (Figure 9.5). Former President

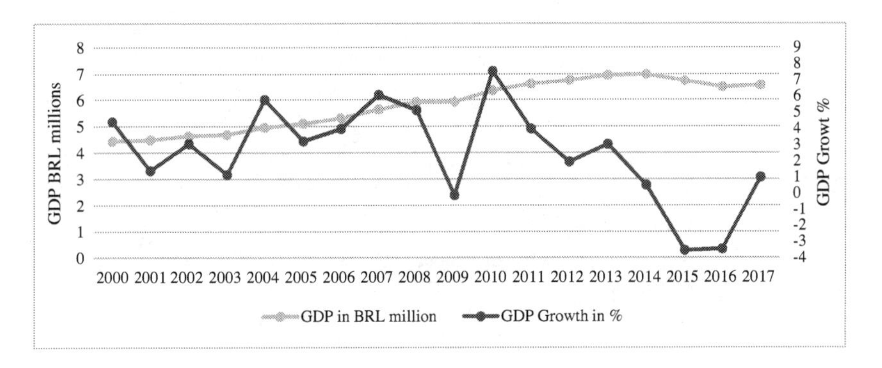

Figure 9.5 Brazilian GDP evolution
Source: Data from BCB (2018).

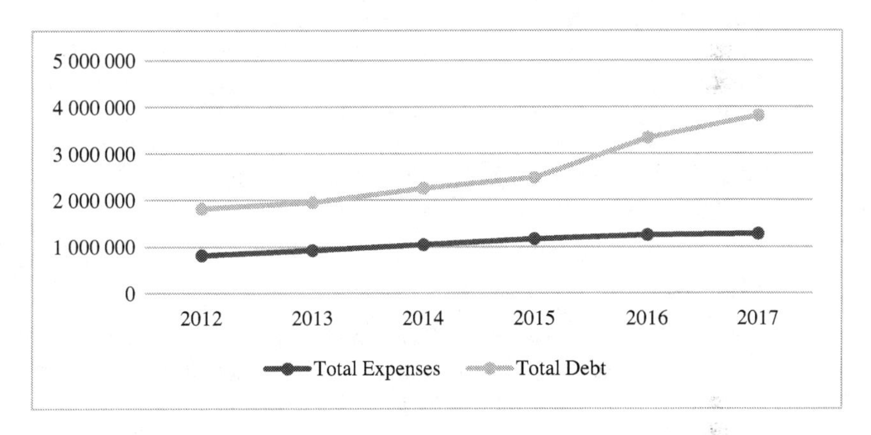

Figure 9.6 Brazilian federal government expenses and debt
Source: Data from BCB (2018).

Luiz Inácio Lula da Silva, known as President Lula, implemented a series of counter measurements to stimulate the economy based on government investments over USD 878 billion between 2010 and 2014 (Reuters, 2010) and credit expansion through national banks Banco do Brasil, Caixa Econômica Federal, and BNDES development bank (Rapoza, 2013).

In the short-term, this economic strategy was successful in mitigating the effects of the international financial crises and made it possible for former president Lula's successor Dilma Rousseff to be elected president in 2010. However, after 2010, government expenses and public debt grew expansively (Figure 9.6) because of social security, federal employees, and government grants for specific industries.

Even though former president Dilma Rousseff succeed in her re-election bid in 2013, scandals about Lula's administration endured, including corruption and bribes from Petrobras, the largest Brazilian firm at that time, the poor performance of the economy, the loss of value for commodities in international markets, and the prosecution of Dilma's administration for illegal creative accounting; former president Dilma Rousseff was impeached in 2016.

Following this, Vice President Michel Temer became president of Brazil, though he had few successes in approving reforms in Congress. President Temer approved an important labor reform which made labor contracts more flexible (Adghirni & Lima, 2017). However, Temer's administration also faces allegations of corruption and bribery and Brazil has been in a political crisis since 2017 due to uncertainty about the 2018 elections for president, governors, and congress.

The economic crisis is still a reality in Brazil; real investment fell by approximately 30% between the beginning of 2014 and the beginning of 2017 with deterioration in Brazil's medium-term growth prospects, falling terms of trade, rising uncertainty related to economic policy, rising levels of corporate leverage, and lower cash flow, but with some impetus for a recovery (Krznar & Matheson, 2018). However, the rise of US dollar and oil in the international markets are a concern in 2018. Nevertheless, SELIC effective annual interest rate fell from 13.65% in December 2016 to 6.40% in May 2018 (BCB, 2018) and inflation is at one of the lowest levels in the last few years.

The Bank's Business Model Crisis

The global financial crisis had an impact on Brazilian banks; we highlight the increase in banking concentration in the largest banks due to their gain in market share and the merger and acquisition processes by the publicly traded banks Itaú and Bradesco, as well as the reduction in the return on assets (ROA). However, this also led to a higher level of leverage, which made it possible to maintain return on equity (ROE) after the 2008 crisis.

Figure 9.7 shows the evolution of ROA from 2000 to 2017 for the largest banks. We can see the effect of the 2008 financial crisis, especially on Itaú and Bradesco, the two major nongovernmental banks, with a ROA average of approximately 1.2% after 2008 for these six banks.

If we consider the ROE, the increment of leverage sustained the profitability (Figure 9.8). In fact, the nominal income increased more than 1,000% for these banks in the period from 2000 to 2018, except for Santander Brasil, which had an initial public offering (IPO) in 2008. Remember that these six banks represent approximately 82% of the total banking industry assets. Caixa Econômica Federal had a major loss in 2001 but recovered in the next years.

The increase in leverage raised concern because of the government's policy of expanding credit, especially in government banks (Banco do Brasil and Caixa), which were responsible for 49.2% of credit operations

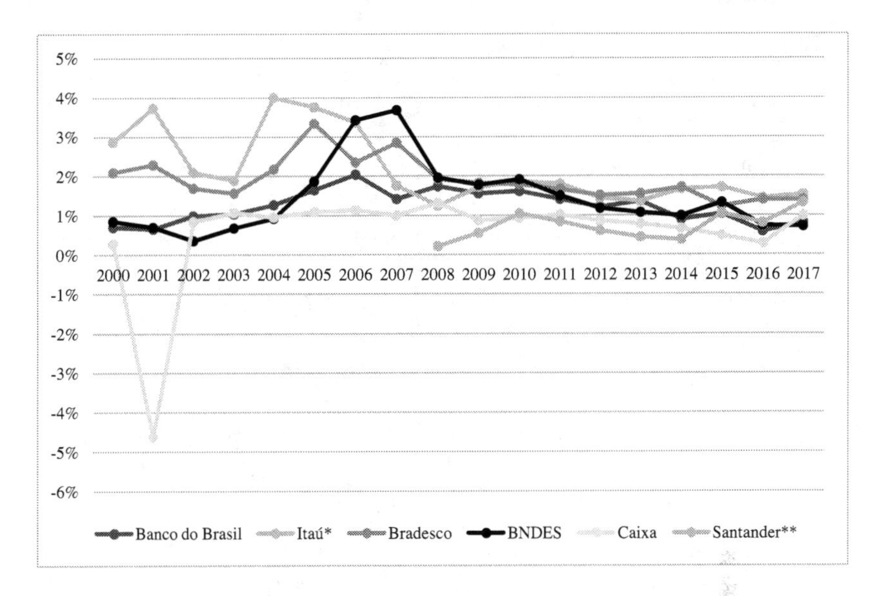

Figure 9.7 ROA evolution in major six banks, 2000–2017

Source: Data from BCB (2018).

Notes: * Itaú merged a large bank (Unibanco) in 2010;
** Santander IPO in Brazil was in 2008.

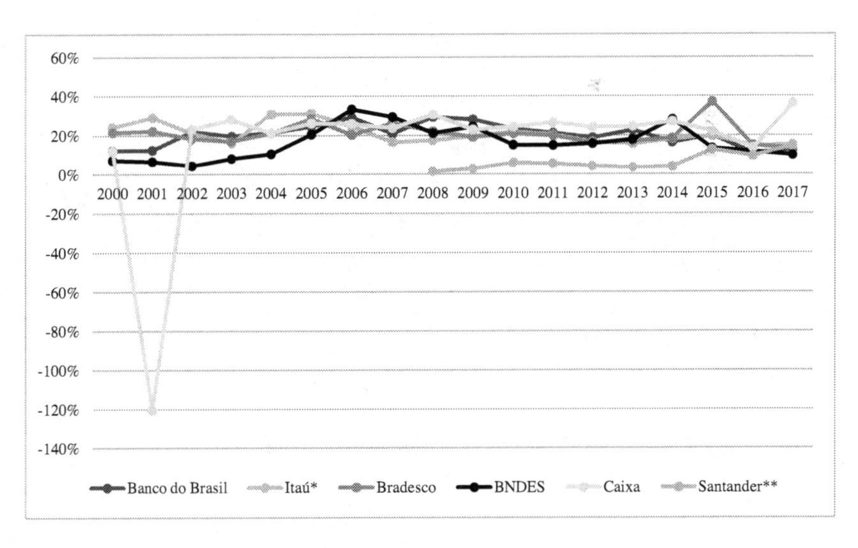

Figure 9.8 ROE evolution in major six banks, 2000–2018

Source: Data from BCB (2018).

Notes: *Itaú merged a large bank (Unibanco) in 2010;
**Santander IPO in Brazil was in 2008.

in 2013 (Rapoza, 2013) and the increase in default rates. This raised concerns about the possibility of a banking crisis beginning in 2017, which included the Bank of International Settlements (BIS) in 2014, what with economic deterioration and poor credit quality indicators (Rapoza, 2014). Nevertheless, the control of the BCB associated with the restructuring of the banks' credit portfolios, the increase in interest rates, and a better credit selection reversed this trend. The strength of the Brazilian financial system was proven out by the BIS in 2017.

The control system of the Central Bank of Brazil (BCB) has a high level of integration with the banks, and is able to obtain the daily consolidation of financial positions, which contributed much to this control. The liquidity risk is low, and credit aggregates returned to good levels with lower credit expansion rates in last three years (BCB, 2018).

The Impact of the Crisis on Equity Markets

The international financial crisis had a large effect in 2008 with a bear market and a good recovery in 2009 with a governmental increase in credit, as in the banking industry. However, after 2013, the Brazilian equity market experienced another decline with the Brazilian economy crisis.

Figure 9.9 shows the evolution of Ibovespa from 2000 to 2018. We can see the effect of the 2008 financial crisis, which affected the major markets in the world, starting with the subprime crisis in the US. We can also see the Brazilian economic crisis starting in 2014, with a recovery in local currency (Brazilian real, BRL) starting in 2016; however, the economic

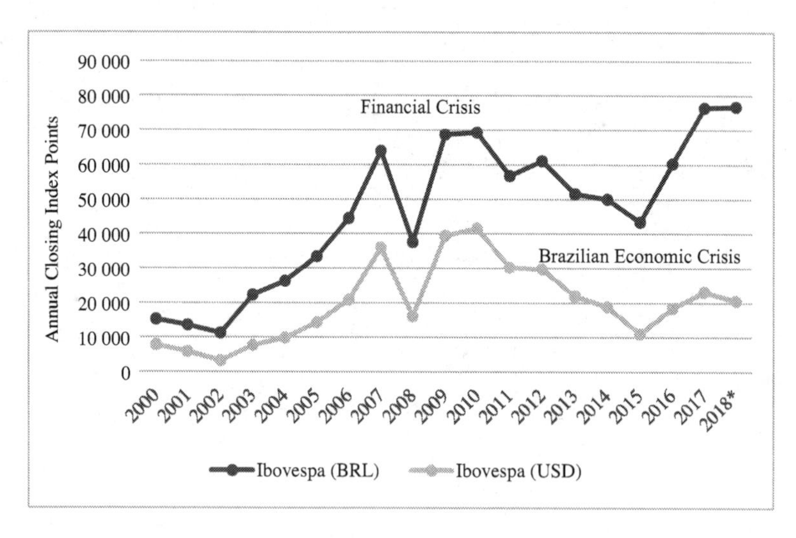

Figure 9.9 Ibovespa annual evolution, 2000–2018

Source: Data from B3 (2018).

Notes: *until May 2018.

crisis changed the foreign exchange rate level and the Ibovespa in USD remains at a lower level than in 2012.

Regulatory Regimes and Financial Stability

Although Brazil continues to be in an economic crisis due to political decisions to expand credit and increase public spending, which began in part to control the effects of the 2008 international financial crisis, it has not seen major changes to the regulation of the financial system and has had no incidences of bankruptcy or insolvency by financial institutions. The regulatory structure of the Brazilian financial industry is still comprised of four specific regulators: CVM (securities), the Central Bank (prudential and financial institution supervision), SUSEP (insurance), and PREVIC (pension); the last two are outside the scope of this chapter.

All four regulators function under the National Monetary Council (CMN), but CMN does not have supervisory powers—it issues general guidelines that apply to the entire financial services sector in Brazil. Coordination among the regulators was enhanced in 2006, when a presidential decree created a committee called COREMEC (Comitê de Regulação e Fiscalização dos Mercados Financeiro, de Capitais, de Seguros, de Previdência e Capitalização, or the Committee for the Regulation and Supervision of Financial, Securities, Insurance, and Complementary Pension) within the Ministry of Finance. It has an advisory role and aims at promoting coordination among the four regulators which all are COREMEC members (CVM, 2018). Figure 9.10 illustrates the regulatory

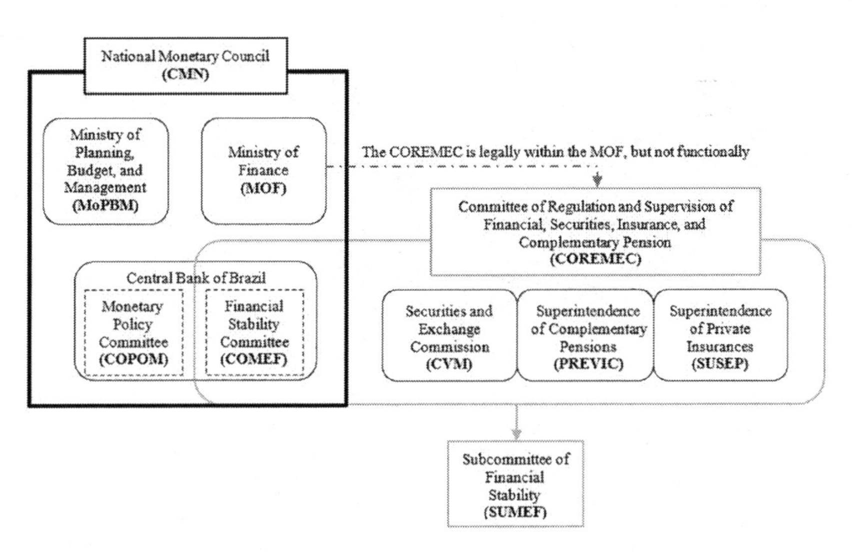

Figure 9.10 Regulatory structure in Brazil

Source: CVM (2018).

structure. In accounting regulation, CPC continues to issue accounting standards following IFRS, with the full adoption of amended IFRS which adhere to corporate law.

Financial stability increased after 2016; however, Brazil still faces uncertainty about the 2018 presidential elections and the subsequent consequences for fiscal policy and the current poor performance of the economy. The risk of deepening the economic crisis continues, and Brazil needs deep reforms, especially in social security (which has a high deficit) and politics to improve the functioning of the country's institutional environment.

Notes

1. For more information about the Herfindahl-Hirschman Normalized Index see Akio Matsumoto, Ugo Merlone & Ferenc Szidarovszky (2011). Some notes on applying the Herfindahl-Hirschman Index, *Applied Economics Letters*, 19:2, 181–184, DOI: 10.1080/13504851.2011.570705.
2. For more information about Basel Committee on Banking Supervision and Basel I, II, and III requirements visit www.bis.org/bcbs.

References

Adghirni, S., and Lima, M. S. "Brazil labor reform approved despite rising political crisis." *Bloomberg*, (2017). Accessed June 20, 2018. www.bloomberg.com

B3. "Brasil Bolsa Balcão." (2018). Accessed June 20, 2018. www.bmfbovespa.com.br

BCB. "Relatório de Economia Bancária." *Banco Central do Brasil (BCB)* 1, no. 1 (2017). Accessed June 20, 2018. www.bcb.gov.br

BCB. "Banco Central do Brasil (BCB)." (2018). Accessed June 20, 2018. www.bcb.gov.br

BIS. "Regulatory Consistency Assessment Programme (RCAP) assessment of Basel III LCR regulations—Brazil." *Bank for International Settlements—Basel Committee on Banking Supervision*, (2017). Accessed June 20, 2018. www.bis.org/

BM&FBovespa. "Guia de Debêntures." *BM&FBovespa*, (2015). Accessed June 20, 2018. www.bmfbovespa.com.br

Bonamin, A., Cintra, A. F. A., Cavalcanti, F., Ferreira, K., and Vieira, R. "Bank regulation in Brazil: Overview." *Thomson Reuters, Practical Law*, (2017). Accessed June 20, 2018. https://uk.practicallaw.thomsonreuters.com/w-006-8837

Carvalho, A. G. De, and Pennacchi, G. G. "Can a stock exchange improve corporate behavior? Evidence from firms migration to premium listings in Brazil." *Journal of Corporate Finance* 18, no. 4 (2012): 883–903. doi:10.1016/j.jcorpfin.2011.01.003.

CVM. "Comissão de Valores Mobiliários (CVM)." (2018). Accessed June 20, 2018. www.cvm.gov.br/

García-Teruel, P. J., Martínez-Solano, P., and Sánchez-Ballesta, J. P. "Accruals quality and corporate cash holdings." *Accounting and Finance* 49, no. 1 (2009): 95–115.

IASB. "IFRS 13—Fair Value Measurement." International Accounting Standard Board (IASB), (2011).

IFRS Foundation. "IFRS application around the world—Jurisdictional profile: Brazil." International Financial Reporting Standards Foundation (IFRS Foundation), (2017).

IMF. "International Monetary Fund (IMF)." (2018). Accessed June 20, 2018. www.imf.org/

Krznar, I., and Matheson, T. "Investments in Brazil: From Crisis to Recovery." *IMF Working Paper—International Monetary Fund*, (2018).

OECD. "The Organisation for Economic Co-operation and Development (OECD)." (2018). Accessed June 20, 2018. www.oecd.org/

Rapoza, K. "Brazil credit expansion shrinks." *Forbes*, (2013). Accessed June 20, 2018. www.forbes.com

Rapoza, K. "Brazil bank crisis likely in three years." *Forbes*, (2014). Accessed June 20, 2018. www.forbes.com

Reuters. "Brazil's Lula unveils $878 billion investment plan." *Reuters*, (2010). Accessed June 20, 2018. www.reuters.com

Tesouro Nacional. "Tesouro Nacional—Ministério da Fazenda." (2018). Accessed June 20, 2018. www.tesouro.fazenda.gov.br/

World Bank. "The World Bank." (2018). Accessed June 20, 2018. www.worldbank.org/Table 2.4b (Continued)

Index

Note: Page numbers in italics indicate figures and in bold indicate tables on the corresponding pages.